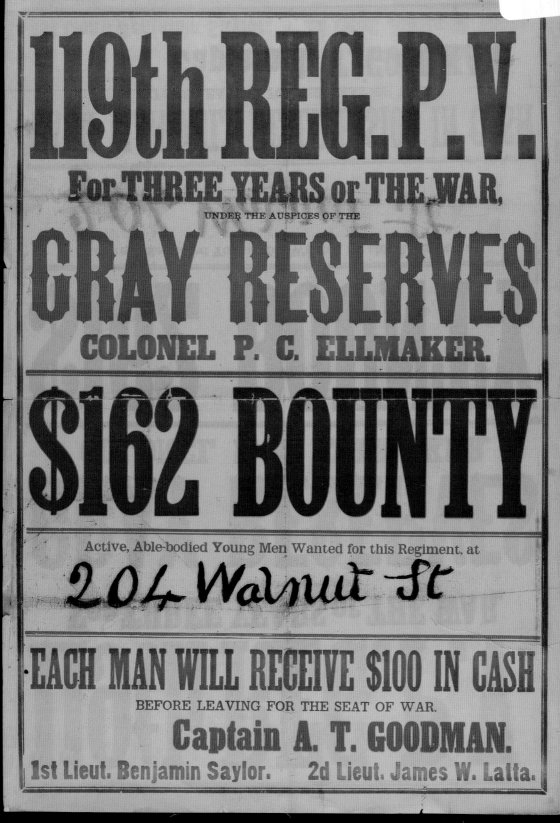

119th REG. P. V.

For THREE YEARS or THE WAR,

UNDER THE AUSPICES OF THE

GRAY RESERVES

COLONEL P. C. ELLMAKER.

$162 BOUNTY

Active, Able-bodied Young Men Wanted for this Regiment, at

204 Walnut St

EACH MAN WILL RECEIVE $100 IN CASH

BEFORE LEAVING FOR THE SEAT OF WAR.

Captain A. T. GOODMAN.

1st Lieut. Benjamin Saylor.   2d Lieut. James W. Latta.

SMITHSONIAN
CIVIL WAR
～ INSIDE *the* NATIONAL COLLECTION ～

Foreword by
Jon Meacham

Introduction by
Michelle Delaney

*Principal
photography by*
Hugh Talman

Edited by
Neil Kagan and Stephen G. Hyslop

Smithsonian Editorial Committee James G. Barber, Tom Crouch, Michelle Delaney,
Rex M. Ellis, Paul Gardullo, Frank H. Goodyear III, Eleanor Jones Harvey,
Pamela M. Henson, Jennifer L. Jones, William S. Pretzer, Harry R. Rubenstein

Smithsonian Books, Washington, D.C.

SMITHSONIAN CONTRIBUTORS

Anacostia Community Museum
Alcione M. Amos, Researcher and Curator AMA

Consortium for Understanding the American Experience
Michelle Delaney, Director MD

Cooper-Hewitt National Design Museum
Sarah D. Coffin, Curator and Head, Product Design and
  Decorative Arts SDC
Gail S. Davidson, Curator and Head, Drawings, Prints,
  and Graphic Design GSD

National Air and Space Museum
Tom Crouch, Senior Curator of Aeronautics TC

National Museum of African American History and Culture
Nancy Bercaw, Curator of Community Life NB
Rex M. Ellis, Associate Director for Curatorial Affairs RME
Paul Gardullo, Museum Curator PG
Michèle Gates Moresi, Curator of Collections MGM
Elaine Nichols, Senior Curator of Culture EN
William S. Pretzer, Senior Curator of History WSP
Jacquelyn Days Serwer, Chief Curator JDS

National Museum of American History
David K. Allison, Associate Director for Curatorial Affairs DKA
Joan Boudreau, Curator, Graphic Arts Collection JB
Judy M. Chelnick, Associate Curator, Medicine and Science JMC
Dick Doty, Curator, National Numismatic Collection RD
Natalie G. Elder, Collections Manager, Armed Forces History NGE
Kathy Golden, Associate Curator, Armed Forces History KG
Lisa Kathleen Graddy, Deputy Chair and Curator, Political History LKG
Barton C. Hacker, Curator, Armed Forces History BCH
Connie Holland, Records Assistant, Work and Industry CH
Debbie Schaefer-Jacobs, Associate Curator, Home and
  Community Life DSJ
Jennifer L. Jones, Chair and Curator, Armed Forces History JLJ
Stacey L. Kluck, Chair and Curator, Culture and the Arts SLK
Ryan Lintelman, Project Assistant, Armed Forces History RL
David D. Miller III, Associate Curator, Armed Forces History DDM
Mary Noxon, Research Assistant, National Numismatic Collection MN
Craig A. Orr, Associate Curator, Archives Center CAO
Shannon Thomas Perich, Curator, Photographic History STP
Harry R. Rubenstein, Chair and Curator, Political History HRR
Margaret Vining, Curator, Armed Forces History MV
Hal Wallace, Associate Curator, Electricity HW

National Museum of American History (cont.)
Deborah Jean Warner, Curator, Physical Sciences DJW
Diane Wendt, Associate Curator, Medicine and Science DW

National Portrait Gallery
James G. Barber, Historian JGB
Sarah M. Campbell, Research Assistant, Department of
  Photographs SMC
Anne Collins Goodyear, Curator of Prints and Drawings ACG
Frank H. Goodyear III, Curator of Photographs FHG
Dorothy Moss, Assistant Curator of Painting and Sculpture DM
E. Warren Perry Jr., Writer and Researcher for the Catalog
  of American Portraits EWP
Ann M. Shumard, Senior Curator of Photographs AMS
David C. Ward, Historian DCW

National Postal Museum
Cheryl R. Ganz, Chief Curator of Philately CRG
Lynn Heidelbaugh, Curator of Postal Operations LH
Thomas Lera, Winton M. Blount Research Chair TL
Nancy Pope, Curator of Postal Operations NP

Smithsonian American Art Museum
Eleanor Jones Harvey, Senior Curator EJH

Smithsonian Institution Archives
Pamela M. Henson, Director of the Institutional History Division PMH

Smithsonian Libraries
Lilla Vekerdy, Head of Special Collections LV

Thanks to Smithsonian staff and volunteers for their support:
Ernest Amoroso, Renee S. Anderson, Mildred Baldwin, Mary
Ballard, Amy Baskette, Courtney G. Bellizzi, Susan Brown,
Kira Cherrix, Caitlin Condell, Laura Coyle, Brian I. Daniels,
Kathleen Dorman, Mary Elliott, Petrina Foti, Amy Giarmo, Joshua
Gorman, Carol Grissom, Mark Gulezian, Debra Hashim, Emily
Houf, Donald Hurlbert, Melissa Keiser, Doug Litts, Nora Lockshin,
William Lommel, Eric Long, Pat Mansfield, Ann McMullen,
T. Logan Metesh, Christopher Milensky, Adam Minakowski,
Jennifer Morris, Sara Murphy, Jaclyn Nash, NPM Collections and
Conservation Departments, Daisy Njoku, Thomas Paone, Felicia
Pickering, Gina Rappaport, Lizanne Reger, Jessica Rotella, Erin
Rushing, Krewasky Salter, Heather Shannon, Richard Sorensen,
Hugh Talman, Kirsten Tyree, Ruthann R. Uithol, Gene Young.

Author initials appear at the end of each entry.

A NOTE FROM THE SECRETARY

CICERO DESCRIBED HISTORY AS "THE WITNESS that testifies to the passing of time," and the photograph of the Smithsonian Castle above testifies to the progress of the past century and a half. When the picture was taken in 1863 during the height of the Civil War, the Castle *was* the Smithsonian Institution. The Arts and Industries Building, the first building created solely to house the U.S. National Museum, was still eighteen years away. East of the Castle, the U.S. Capitol was undergoing the construction of a new dome made of cast iron to replace the original made of wood and copper. The Smithsonian has remained constant in its mission to increase and diffuse knowledge, even as it expanded beyond the Castle to encompass nineteen museums and galleries, numerous research centers, and the National Zoo. Its vast collections contain objects that help define us as a people and give insights to our history. Here in this book the compelling story of the Civil War is told through objects, artifacts, photographs, and paintings culled exclusively from the Smithsonian collections.

The work draws on the resources of thirteen Smithsonian museums and archives, and includes forty-nine contributing authors who had a hand in bringing this book to life. A cursory look at the list of contributors (opposite) will give readers a glimpse into the wide range of disciplines in which Smithsonian experts work. Uniting these disparate fields of study to complete this project aligns with one of our core missions: to understand the American experience. The Civil War was arguably the nation's defining moment, and the Castle was there through it all. Thanks to the efforts of our curators, educators, researchers, and scientists, this volume allows Smithsonian objects to tell the stories of the people who gave their lives during that tragic time in our history, but also reminds us of the resilience of this nation conceived in liberty.

G. WAYNE CLOUGH
TWELFTH SECRETARY OF THE SMITHSONIAN

CONTENTS

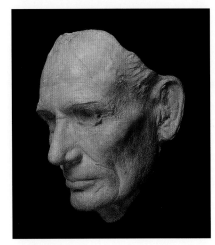

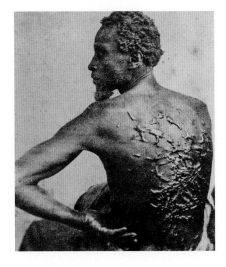

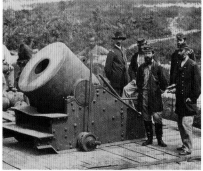

Images from left to right: Lincoln's life mask (entry 15), red kepi (entry 61), scarred back of an escaped slave (entry 76), Union cavalry jacket (entry 94), a massive mortar (entry 103), and C.S.A. belt plate (entry 54).

FOREWORD

THE WEATHER HAD BEEN MISERABLE FOR DAYS. Yet on Saturday, March 4, 1865, when Abraham Lincoln rose to deliver his second inaugural address on the East Front of the Capitol, the gloom gave way; writing for the *New York Times*, Walt Whitman noted the "flooding splendor from heaven's most excellent sun."

It was fitting that Lincoln gave his speech at an hour of shifting light, for his message to the nation was subtle. Reflecting on North and South, the president took a broad view: "Both read the same Bible and pray to the same God, and each invokes His aid against the other," Lincoln said. "It may seem strange that any men should dare to ask a just God's assistance in wringing their bread from the sweat of other men's faces, but let us judge not, that we be not judged. The prayers of both could not be answered. That of neither has been answered fully. The Almighty has His own purposes." Classic Lincoln: he was

> *It may seem strange that any men should dare to ask a just God's assistance in wringing their bread from the sweat of other men's faces.*
>
> **ABRAHAM LINCOLN, MARCH 4, 1865**

casting the war as a fundamentally mysterious inevitability in the Jeffersonian course of human events. The war was like the Fall of Man: it was the tragic lot of the American Union to exorcise the nation's original sin of African American slavery by enduring a regrettable conflict for four painful years. For Lincoln, the fact of the matter was straightforward—not simple, but straightforward: that the war came.

And the war came. In his time, Lincoln spoke of history and theology. Now, a century and a half later, it is our good fortune to experience the past not only intellectually and imaginatively but tangibly. Our myths can be told and touched.

Such is the genius and the gift of the book you hold in your hands. *Smithsonian Civil War: Inside the National Collection* is a dazzling and moving historical record of the war whose cause and course are our *Aeneid*. From an ivory cane presented to John Quincy Adams in honor of his opposition to the Gag Rule that foreclosed debates over slavery to the hoods worn by the jailed conspirators in Lincoln's assassination, the curators of the Smithsonian's invaluable collections have brought the seemingly distant events of the Civil War to vivid, tactile life.

Americans of the twenty-first century need books like this and institutions like the Smithsonian, for without photographic images of the brutally scarred back of a slave or of the dead on battlefields and in trenches that we tend to associate more with the Somme than with our own land, the Civil War risks receding into fable rather than urgent fact. And make no mistake: when you gaze on a primitive medical kit with its "Stronger Ether," or on John Brown's pike, or on Jeb Stuart's pistol, you will be brought face to face with the seemingly mundane elements that, taken together, liberated a people and saved the soul of a nation.

Overstated? Hardly. It is impossible, I think, to assign too much importance to the Civil War. History is not a fairy tale; nothing is inevitable. The fates of empires and of armies depend as much on ordinary mortal men as they do on the grand impersonal forces of economics and even of geography. Look at the chairs in which Ulysses S. Grant and Robert E. Lee sat at Appomattox, and the single handwritten page of the terms of surrender, and all the high strategy and diplomatic maneuvering comes down to what history is truly made of, and by: individual human beings doing the best they can in a complicated and conflicted world.

If we fail to understand this or to remember always that history is not clinical but human, shaped for better and for worse by individual hearts and minds, then we risk limiting

the roles we ourselves can play in the unfolding drama of the nation and of the world. The soldier who wrote the terms of surrender in that long-ago April had been considered a failure before the war, reduced to selling firewood on the streets of St. Louis. The hour gave him another chance, and his armies fulfilled a promise articulated at Philadelphia four score and nine years before. Look again at his chair—it's not Olympian, it's human, and of a scale you and I should do more to reach.

"Fondly do we hope, fervently do we pray, that this scourge of war may speedily pass away," Lincoln said on that March day in Washington, D.C. His hope and his prayer were soon to be answered. Our own hope and prayer—that we may always

remember the sacrifices and fruits of that war—should find fresh force when we read this fine book, a book not only about who we were, but who we are, and who we could yet become: Americans who keep faith with the promise of equality, and seek a more perfect Union. ✝ JON MEACHAM

One of twenty-nine distinct photographic likenesses of Abraham Lincoln in the National Portrait Gallery's collection, this ambrotype was made on October 11, 1858, two days before the sixth Lincoln-Douglas debate. Other rare photographs of Lincoln can be found throughout this volume including the famous "cracked negative" print (pages 310–11) made shortly before Lincoln's assassination.

INTRODUCTION/CIVIL WAR 150

THIS EXTRAORDINARY BOOK COMMEMORATES the 150th anniversary of the Civil War by exhibiting treasured relics and images of that conflict, drawn from the Smithsonian's vast collection and interpreted by its curators and historians in 150 thematic essays, organized chronologically from the war's prelude to its aftermath. The Civil War ushered in sweeping changes that transformed America, including the abolition of slavery, advances in science and technology, and the expansion of the federal government. The Smithsonian itself was transformed by the conflict, which set the stage for its evolution from a single building to a monumental complex of nineteen museums and nine research centers whose holdings now embrace almost every aspect of the nation's history and culture. Significant Civil War artifacts have been collected by Smithsonian curators for more than a century, including Abraham Lincoln's office suit and the hat he wore to Ford's Theatre on the night he was assassinated (opposite). The war that Lincoln waged and won looms large in America's vision of its past and in the Smithsonian's own history. That victory preserved the Union and allowed Americans to meet the challenge of developing a great nation with a fast-growing national institution to preserve its heritage.

Established in 1846, the Smithsonian had no headquarters until the structure known affectionately as "the Castle," which stands today on the National Mall roughly midway between the Washington Monument and the U.S. Capitol, was completed in 1855, just six years before the war's first shots were fired at Fort Sumter. Smithsonian Secretary Joseph Henry, a distinguished scientist who oversaw the Institution from its inception until his death in 1878, moved into an apartment on the second floor of the new building with his wife, Harriet, three daughters, Caroline, Mary Anna, and Helen, and son, William. The secretary aimed to maintain the neutrality of the Smithsonian, vowing to continue daily operations of scientific research and collecting. He succeeded in preventing the building from being used for military purposes. From the Castle, the Henrys witnessed firsthand the onset of war. "We went up into the high tower to see the troops pass over into Virginia," wrote Mary Henry on July 16, 1861, in the detailed diary she kept throughout the conflict. Three years later, after Confederates advanced to the outskirts of Washington, D.C., and were beaten back, she went on an outing with her father, who encountered a Union soldier and spoke to him of the "severe battle" in which three hundred men reportedly lost their lives repelling the invaders. "Oh, that is nothing," the soldier replied, "we don't consider that anything of a battle these days." As Mary commented in her diary: "Life has grown sadly cheap within the last few years."

COLLECTING AMERICA'S PAST

At the time Mary Henry composed her revealing record of wartime Washington, preserved today in the Smithsonian Institution Archives, her father had no idea that documenting the Civil War and other events in American history would become a vital function of the institution he headed. Joseph

TOKENS OF SLAVERY *Thomas H. Porter, a slave trader from Barbados, had these buttons bearing his name sewn onto clothing worn by those he held in bondage and whom he sold or hired out along the coast of the American South in the 1820s. These tokens of slavery are held by the Smithsonian's new National Museum of African American History and Culture.*

Henry wanted the Smithsonian to serve primarily as a research center for scientists. He tolerated the presence of a museum in the Castle displaying to the public objects of scientific, historical, and cultural significance. But he considered the museum a distraction and left its direction to Assistant Secretary Spencer Fullerton Baird, an avid naturalist. Some of the items Baird displayed there were collected during far-ranging expeditions sponsored by the Smithsonian during and after the Civil War. Members of the Megatherium Club (named for an extinct giant sloth), including marine biologist William Stimpson, naturalist Robert Kennicott, painter and photographer Henry Ulke, and ornithologist Henry Bryant, lived in the Castle for several years in the 1860s, venturing out on collecting trips and returning for the winter with specimens to be catalogued.

In 1876 Baird organized government exhibits for the nation's Centennial Exposition in Philadelphia. He then persuaded other exhibitors there to donate their collections to the Smithsonian. Shortly after Baird succeeded Henry as secretary of the Smithsonian in 1878, work began on a new home for the fast-expanding U.S. National Museum. Completed in 1881, what is now known as the Arts and Industries Building drew more than 165,000 visitors in its first year. With the impetus provided by Baird, the Smithsonian won renown for its natural history collection, but it also acquired a remarkable assortment of Civil War–era relics and artifacts, some transferred from other federal institutions after the conflict ended. From the U.S. Quartermaster Corps came a superb collection of Union uniforms, made at the Schuylkill Arsenal in Philadelphia and exhibited at the Centennial Exposition before it was entrusted to the Smithsonian (pages 232–36). From the War Department came the hat Lincoln wore the night he was shot, and the shackles and hoods worn in jail by those convicted of conspiring against him (pages 320–23). Numerous gifts from private donors, including descendants of leading Civil War figures, supplemented those public accessions.

Beginning in the twentieth century, the Smithsonian expanded rapidly, and as a result, its voluminous Civil War holdings now spread out across more than a dozen museums

ACTION SHOT *This intriguing ambrotype from the Smithsonian collection (LEFT) shows what appears to be a soldier in a Zouave uniform advancing with weapon in hand. The man shown here—whether he was a soldier or a civilian portraying one is unknown—was actually posing for photographer and abolitionist T. P. Collins, likely as a study for a painting.*

MOSBY'S COAT *Among the many Civil War artifacts donated to the Smithsonian by the original owners or their heirs is the frock coat of Confederate colonel John Singleton Mosby, shown in two views (OPPOSITE). Donations to the Smithsonian from Confederates were rare, but Mosby was an exception: after the war, he worked to reunite the nation and as a resident of Washington, D.C., was familiar with the Smithsonian's mission.*

and archives. Featured in this book are ornithological specimens from the National Museum of Natural History (created in 1858), contributed by a Civil War officer who was killed while collecting for the Smithsonian; the original "Old Glory" flag, flown when Union troops occupied Nashville, Tennessee, in 1862, one of thousands of Civil War artifacts held by the National Museum of American History (1957); compelling portraits of Frederick Douglass, Harriet Beecher Stowe, Sojourner Truth, and other abolitionists and reformers by photographers and painters whose works reside at the National Portrait Gallery (1962); seminal paintings that convey a human narrative of the Civil War belonging to the Smithsonian American Art Museum (1906); futuristic Civil War–era aircraft designs from the National Air and Space Museum (1946); an engraved copper printing plate for Confederate five-cent Jefferson Davis stamps from the National Postal Museum (1997); and tags worn by slaves who were hired out by their owners to work in Charleston, South Carolina, contributed by the Smithsonian's newest branch, the National Museum of African American History and Culture, founded in 2003 and scheduled for completion in late 2015. Other artifacts displayed in this book come from the Smithsonian's Anacostia Community Museum (1967), the Cooper-Hewitt National Design Museum (1968), the Hirshhorn Museum and Sculpture Garden (1966), and the National Museum of the

PATRIOTIC GIFT *Mary Rockhold Teter of Indiana made this "Stars and Stripes" quilt for her son George after he enlisted in the Union Army in 1861. She based the design on a pattern published in Peterson's Magazine in July of that year. The thirty-four stars at center and along the border of the quilt represent all the states at that time, including Southern states that seceded but were still claimed by the Union. George Teter later gave this quilt to his grandson's wife to honor her service as an army nurse during World War I. She and her husband donated it to the Smithsonian in 1940.*

American Indian (1989), as well as the Smithsonian Institution Archives and Libraries. Never before have Civil War treasures from throughout the Smithsonian been assembled and interpreted in one place as they are here.

AN EXHIBIT BETWEEN HARD COVERS

Producing this book involved a collaborative effort of unprecedented scope at the Smithsonian, including more than one hundred staff members from thirteen museums and archives. Curators, archivists, historians, interns, and volunteers spent hours in locked vaults, storage rooms, and cabinets, researching and evaluating items, documenting the causes and consequences of the conflict as well as its battles and campaigns. Selecting for inclusion the most significant and revealing Civil War artifacts from among tens of thousands held by the Smithsonian fell to the Civil War 150 Editorial Committee, and was no small task. They debated at length which objects had the greatest historical value or the most compelling stories attached to them. Eventually, a consensus emerged that the selection process should be guided not just by the individual merits of a particular object or image but by how the object or image fit within the scope of the book, designed by editor Neil Kagan as an exhibit between hard covers. Like a museum exhibition, this volume is accessible to those wishing to browse selectively among its treasures but is meant to be viewed as a whole, from beginning to end. It follows the course of a nation haunted and divided by slavery through a tragic and transformative war to the ultimate challenge facing Americans when the shooting stopped—reconstructing the Union and redefining its core principles.

Many of the 150 entries that follow interpret objects and images brought together from various Smithsonian museums and archives for the first time. For example, an early portrait of John Brown, taken by an African American photographer in Connecticut in the mid-1840s and held by the National Portrait Gallery, appears alongside weapons that Brown and his men carried later in Kansas and at Harpers Ferry, held by the National Museum of American History (pages 44–47). For Smithsonian authors and curators, selecting and interpreting historical artifacts for this book has meant exploring anew the

nation's own unrivaled collection of Civil War treasures. One of the truly wonderful things about working at the Smithsonian is the opportunity to pull open a drawer and encounter an object that was instrumental in shaping the nation, reveals an untold story, or simply makes the often-mythic past more real. The Civil War collection shown on these pages sparks so many questions, offers so many new discoveries, and allows us to enter those turbulent years as no other material can. This book shares not only the collection but also our knowledge of and enthusiasm for these national treasures that continue to inspire and to challenge our conceptions of the American experience. ✢ MICHELLE DELANEY

CIVIL WAR HAND GRENADES *Patented by William F. Ketchum of Buffalo, New York, in August 1861, these hand grenades were filled with gunpowder and detonated by a percussion cap. Union forces found them to be unreliable in battle. These examples are held by the Armed Forces History division of the National Museum of American History.*

1

WARTIME SMITHSONIAN

TENSIONS BETWEEN NORTH AND SOUTH AFFECTED the Smithsonian from its inception. In 1835 President Andrew Jackson announced that British scientist James Smithson (ca. 1765–1829) had bequeathed his fortune to the United States to found "an establishment for the increase and diffusion of knowledge." Southern advocates of states' rights argued that there was no constitutional basis for such a national institution, but former president John Quincy Adams of Massachusetts and others in Congress overcame those objections and passed an act founding the Smithsonian in 1846. Several Southerners, including Jefferson Davis, served on its board of regents.

As storm clouds of war gathered over Washington, D.C., in 1861, the Smithsonian—which consisted then of a single building, the Castle, housing Smithsonian Secretary Joseph Henry and his family along with a museum, library, and other facilities—experienced the tumult of a divided nation. A noted physicist, Henry faced questions about his loyalty to the Union. He had close friends who favored secession, including Smithsonian regents who were expelled from the board for Confederate sympathies. A "scientific racist," Henry believed that people of African descent were biologically inferior. He opposed the abolition of slavery and was criticized for halting a lecture series on that subject and refusing to allow Frederick Douglass to speak. Washington was only lightly defended when the Civil War began, and Henry would not fly the Union flag atop the Castle for fear of provoking Confederates across the Potomac River. On April 20, 1861, Secretary of War Simon Cameron supplied Henry with twelve muskets and ammunition to defend the Castle against "lawless attacks."

Other wartime challenges included suspension of the Smithsonian's national network of weather observers and a sharp decline in funding. The U.S. Treasury paid interest on Smithson's bequest in devalued paper currency, and federal appropriations for the museum were halted. Henry, never a fan of the museum, warned that he might have to close the doors or charge admission. Yet Washington was teeming with troops and war workers, and he had to admit that the free museum was "continually thronged with visitors."

Budgetary restrictions did not stop Henry from contributing to the Union war effort. He backed Thaddeus Lowe, an aeronaut who conducted military reconnaissance in balloons. Henry also served on a scientific commission that evaluated proposed inventions and designs for the U.S. Navy.

During those trying war years, Henry lost his son to typhoid fever. He nearly lost the Smithsonian when fire engulfed the Castle on January 24, 1865, destroying part of the building, collections, and documents. The Union soon emerged from the conflict victorious, however, and its national institutions grew stronger—including the Smithsonian, which represented a reunited America and its collective heritage. ✣ PMH

SOUTHERN OVERSEER *Jefferson Davis (1808–1889), pictured around 1855, served as a Smithsonian regent from 1847 to 1851. He was among the prominent Southerners whose friendship with Joseph Henry caused controversy as war enveloped the Castle, shown at left about 1860.*

Hon. Jefferson Davis
Regent of Smithsonian Inst'n

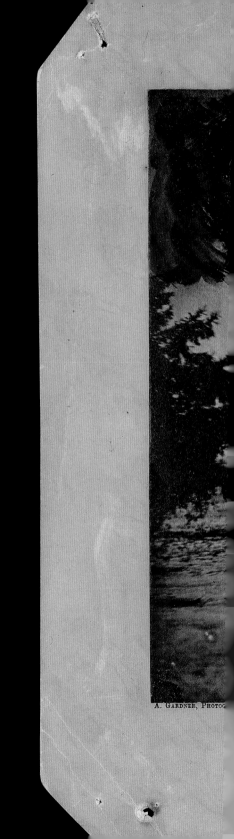

A. GARDNER, PHOTOG

FIRST SECRETARY *Pictured above in the 1850s, Joseph Henry (1797–1878) was one of America's foremost scientists when he took charge of the newly founded Smithsonian, which he thought should focus on scientific research. Although he touted the popularity of the Castle's museum, he called the fire there in 1865, shown in this retouched photograph by Alexander Gardner, an "act of divine Providence" and used it as an excuse to reduce the museum's collections. His successor, Spencer Fullerton Baird, enhanced the museum and its holdings*

WASHINGTON, D. C.

Burning of the Smithsonian Institution,

January 24, 1865.

2

"AM I NOT A MAN AND A BROTHER?"

THE FUTURE OF SLAVERY IN A NATION DEDICATED to liberty was fiercely debated by Americans in the years leading up to the Civil War. The organized struggle against slavery went back to the 1700s, however, and involved quiet symbolic gestures as well as forceful acts of resistance, rebellion, and protest by people both free and enslaved on both sides of the Atlantic. Two small objects in Smithsonian collections shed light on that emerging international antislavery movement.

A jasperware cameo of a kneeling slave, inscribed with the motto, "Am I not a man and a brother?" was produced in 1787 by Josiah Wedgwood, a British ceramic manufacturer and committed abolitionist. It soon became an icon in Great Britain and the United States, where Benjamin Franklin received a shipment of the cameos to be worn as medallions by those who thought slavery had no rightful place in America. It portrayed the enslaved African as a fellow human being, entitled to freedom, and evoked biblical lessons such as the words of Joseph to his brethren: "I am your brother . . . whom you sold into Egypt." (Genesis 45:4)

Another biblical passage (Galatians 3:28) inspired the opening line of a sampler stitched in silk thread in 1803 by Mary Emiston, a student at New York City's African Free School: "In Christ Jesus there is neither bond nor free." A rare early example of needlework by an African American schoolgirl, this sampler was similar to a diploma and would have been displayed in the student's home to demonstrate her dexterity, literacy, and moral fiber. Like Wedgwood's cameo, her work shows how the campaign against slavery was waged not just in the political arena but in the homes and hearts of people who expressed their convictions through everyday objects they made or purchased. ⊹ PG

A STELLAR CAMEO *Josiah Wedgwood turned out thousands of these compelling cameos (OPPOSITE) for abolitionists in Britain and America. The image became so popular that it was mass-produced in print and in many other formats—as tokens to raise money for the cause; in women's needlework; and on teapots, jugs, snuffboxes, and broaches.*

ODE TO FREEDOM *Mary Emiston made this sampler (RIGHT) at the African Free School, where some students were free and others remained slaves until they were adults under New York's gradual process of emancipation. By 1835, when the school became public, it had educated thousands of black children.*

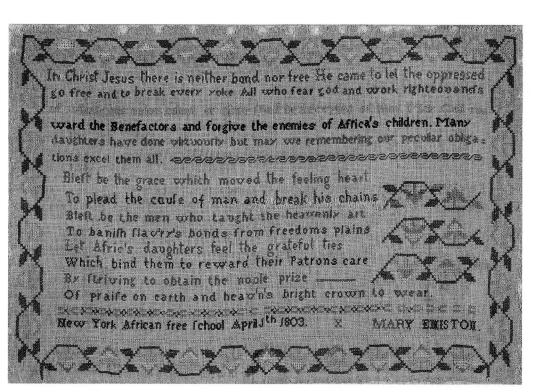

3

ENDING THE GAG RULE

IN MARCH 1844 HENRY ELLSWORTH, COMMISSIONER of the U.S. Patent Office, presented John Quincy Adams (1767–1848) with this elegant three-foot-long ivory cane, carved from a single elephant tusk. The cane was decorated on top with a gold-inlaid American eagle (inset), grasping in its talons a petition. On a band below the knob, Adams's name was inscribed along with the Latin words *"Justum et tenacem propositi virum"* (A man just and firm of purpose).

This was a gift from Julius Pratt and Company of Meriden, Connecticut, one of the country's leading importers of ivory. Pratt was an active abolitionist and asked Ellsworth to present the cane to Adams to honor him for his long campaign against the Gag Rule: measures adopted by the U.S. House of Representatives to prevent antislavery petitions from being considered there. Pratt requested that when Adams successfully defeated the rule, he add the date of his victory to the inscription. Adams wrote in his diary, "I accepted the cane as a trust to be returned when the date of the extinction of the gag-rule shall be accomplished," and asked Ellsworth to keep the cane until that time.

The campaign to defeat the Gag Rule had become a major symbolic focus of the revitalized antislavery movement. In an effort to promote a national debate on slavery, abolitionists had organized petitioning drives in the 1830s, calling on Congress to prohibit slavery in the nation's capital, the one undisputed area the legislature controlled. Traditionally, petitions to the House of Representatives were presented individually and then assigned to the appropriate committee, which would recommend action.

Southern representatives and their Northern allies argued that giving this attention to the subject would serve to heighten regional tensions and to promote violent slave rebellions. To cut off the abolitionists' efforts, the House of Representatives adopted on May 25, 1836, a resolution that all petitions, resolutions, and memorials regarding slavery or abolition would be tabled without being read, referred, or printed. The Gag Rule, which was enacted by the House each year, was denounced as an infringement of the First Amendment right to petition the government. Rather than discouraging petitioners, it energized the movement. Petitions from antislavery societies, often organized by women, flooded the Capitol.

The petitioners found a champion for their cause in the former president, John Quincy Adams, who returned to Congress in 1831 to represent his Massachusetts district. Year after year, Adams introduced antislavery petitions and called for defeat of the Gag Rule. Each time the House voted against his resolutions. But mounting political pressure finally won out. On December 3, 1844, in a vote of 108 to 80, Congress abolished the Gag Rule. The vote was a seen as a major defeat for the supporters of slavery, who recognized that their power in Congress was beginning to wane.

Following Adams's victory, Ellsworth had engraved on the scroll above the eagle "Right of Petition Triumphant" and sent it on to Adams for him to add the date. On the tips of the eagle's wings a jeweler added "3 December" and "1844." Adams, who normally refused gifts from political supporters, returned the cane to the Patent Office. In his will Adams bequeathed it to the United States, and the Patent Office later transferred it to the Smithsonian's National Museum. ☩ HRR

OLD MAN ELOQUENT *This portrait of John Quincy Adams was made in the 1840s, around the time he overturned the Gag Rule and received the ivory cane shown at left. Known as "Old Man Eloquent" for his persuasive powers, he suffered a stroke on February 21, 1848, collapsed on the floor of the House, and died two days later at the age of eighty.*

4

INVENTIONS FOR PLANTERS

SLAVERY BECAME MORE PROFITABLE AND WIDE-spread in the South as inventors found more efficient ways of processing cash crops produced by slaves. In 1792, New Englander Eli Whitney, a recent Yale graduate, traveled to Georgia where he devised a machine that helped give rise to the Cotton Kingdom. Before cotton could be spun into thread and woven, seeds had to be removed from the fiber. Existing devices could remove seeds from long-staple cotton, which grew only in coastal areas. Whitney's innovative cotton gin used coarse wire teeth to extract seeds from short-staple cotton, which could be grown inland.

Despite Whitney's patent, others soon copied his design and developed improved cotton gins, which contributed to the rapid expansion of short-staple cotton production from Georgia and the Carolinas westward to Texas. With that came the rapid expansion of slavery. In Mississippi alone, the number of slaves increased from 32,000 in 1820 to 436,000 in 1860, or more than half the state's population. "Cotton is king," declared Senator James Hammond of South Carolina in 1858, and that kingdom was dependent on slavery.

Sugarcane was another product of slave labor that became more profitable as a result of innovations. A major advance was made by inventor Norbert Rillieux, who was born in New Orleans in 1806 to a free woman of color and a wealthy white entrepreneur of French descent. Rillieux was educated in France and returned in 1830 to Louisiana, where he devised his multiple-effect evaporator. This apparatus greatly improved on the traditional method of processing sugarcane that involved ladling hot juice from one boiling kettle to another until the sugar granulated. That method was dangerous for slaves who performed the task and costly for planters because it consumed large amounts of fuel. Rillieux's energy-efficient evaporator contained vacuum pans, which lowered the boiling point of the juice, and used the steam from one pan to heat another.

After arranging with a Philadelphia firm to manufacture his apparatus, Rillieux faced the problem of selling the expensive device to planters. The financial depression of the late 1830s set sugar production back for a while, but recovery was rapid, aided by the protective sugar tariff of 1842. Enterprising planters who invested in Rillieux's apparatus were soon producing high-quality sugar and reaping soaring profits. Judah P. Benjamin, a future Confederate secretary of war, hired Rillieux to install an evaporator at his Louisiana plantation in 1843 and stated that its output rivaled "the best double refined sugar of our northern refineries."

Rillieux's technique was safer than the traditional method of processing sugarcane, but like Whitney's cotton gin, his invention profited slave owners. The multiple-effect evaporator did nothing to improve conditions for the slaves who raised the crops and whose tasks were particularly brutal on sugar plantations. The increasing dependence of white Southerners on slavery also made life difficult for free men of color like Rillieux who faced mounting hostility and discrimination as the Civil War loomed. He returned to France in the late 1850s and later went on to obtain several French patents. Rillieux was recognized posthumously as a pioneering African American inventor. ✛ DJW

MODELS OF EFFICIENCY *Eli Whitney's model of his cotton gin (INSET), equipped with a hand crank to remove seeds, was given to the Smithsonian by his son in 1884. Norbert Rilleux submitted the model opposite for his improved sugar-processing method, patented in 1843.*

5

PREWAR PORTRAITS

THE DISPUTE BETWEEN NORTH AND SOUTH that boiled over in 1861 had been simmering ever since Americans won independence from Britain and began quarreling over slavery and states' rights. Tensions escalated significantly, however, with passage of the Fugitive Slave Act of 1850 and the Kansas-Nebraska Act in 1854, which led to clashes between antislavery and proslavery forces in Kansas. John Brown's raid at Harpers Ferry in 1859 and Abraham Lincoln's election the following year provided the sparks that kindled the Civil War.

Some who took center stage during the conflict were well known beforehand. Jefferson Davis had served as secretary of war, and Robert E. Lee had been superintendent at West Point.

Others, however, were relative unknowns, including a soldier turned farmer named Ulysses S. Grant and the best man at his wedding, James Longstreet. A military officer stationed in the remote Southwest when the war began, Longstreet would become Lee's second-in-command.

The portraits presented here and on the following pages were all taken before the war. Most are daguerreotypes, an early photographic process that produced an image on a silver-plated copper sheet. Such photographs were unique objects that functioned most often as private keepsakes. By 1861 photographers were venturing out from their studios with portable equipment, and the Civil War became the first major conflict extensively documented on camera. ✛ FHG

You do not know how forsaken I feel here. I do nothing but sit in my room and read and occasionally take a short ride on one of the public horses.

ULYSSES S. GRANT, BEFORE LEAVING THE ARMY IN 1854

ULYSSES S. GRANT *An undated tintype made from a daguerreotype (LEFT), this photograph of Ulysses S. Grant (1822–1885) shows the future Union Army commander and eighteenth president after he was promoted to brevet captain in 1847 for his bravery at the storming of Chapultepec during the Mexican War. Grant married in 1848 soon after that conflict ended and eventually grew weary of army life, retiring in 1854 to take up farming. The Civil War's outbreak led him to return to the military, where he emerged as Lincoln's most successful general.*

THOMAS J. JACKSON *The man who became known during the Civil War as Stonewall Jackson (1824–1863) sat for this likeness in 1855 (OPPOSITE), six years before he emerged as one of the South's most brilliant military tacticians. Jackson had earned more citations for valor in the Mexican War than any other American officer, but few cadets who knew him as an awkward professor at Virginia Military Institute thought he was destined for greatness.*

HORACE GREELEY

As founder and longtime editor of the influential New York Tribune, *Horace Greeley (1811–1872), pictured here around 1850, was a powerful advocate for reform. In editorials and lectures, he championed a host of progressive movements, from women's rights to organized labor; he railed against slavery and encouraged western settlement. A supporter of free homesteading as an anecdote to the evils of industrialization, Greeley popularized the saying "Go west, young man." In 1860 he backed Lincoln for president and later encouraged him to issue the Emancipation Proclamation.*

LUCRETIA MOTT

A devout Quaker whose activism proved unsettling to some members of her faith, Lucretia Mott (1793–1880), portrayed here in 1851, assumed a highly visible role in the abolitionist movement. After joining William Lloyd Garrison to launch the American Anti-Slavery Society, she helped found the Philadelphia Female Anti-Slavery Society in 1833. Her concern for women's rights grew out of her abolitionist efforts. In 1848, Mott and Elizabeth Cady Stanton organized the convention at Seneca Falls, New York, that gave birth to the women's suffrage movement. A pacifist, she was torn by the Civil War, which horrified her but brought an end to the slave system she abhorred.

PHINEAS T. BARNUM

New York showman P. T. Barnum (1810–1891) was as skilled in promoting legitimate entertainment as he was in marketing outlandish frauds such as the Feejee Mermaid. In 1842 he scored one of his greatest triumphs when he discovered the diminutive Charles S. Stratton and introduced him to the public as "Tom Thumb." Photographed here with Barnum about 1850, Stratton became a phenomenally popular entertainer who sang, danced, and performed a variety of costumed roles. Stratton's marriage in February 1863 to little Lavinia Warren, a fellow performer, drew international headlines and briefly diverted public attention from the bloody war.

GEORGE HENRY THOMAS

A former instructor at West Point with a fine record as an artillery officer in the Mexican War, George Thomas (1816–1870) won fame as "the rock of Chickamauga" for tenaciously holding his ground on that Georgia battlefield in September 1863. A Virginian who remained with the Union during the Civil War, Thomas was considered by foes like fellow Virginian J.E.B. Stuart as a traitor who deserved to be hanged. But Unionists hailed him for his stand at Chickamauga and his decisive victory in late 1864 at Nashville, where he shattered John Bell Hood's Army of Tennessee.

DOROTHEA DIX

Social reformer Dorothea Dix (1802–1887), pictured with pen and paper at hand, launched a vigorous campaign in 1841 to secure humane treatment for those afflicted with mental illness at a time when they were more often imprisoned and abused than cared for. She became a tireless advocate for their welfare, giving speeches, publishing articles, and submitting petitions to lawmakers. Thanks to her efforts, facilities for the mentally ill were improved and expanded. Soon after the Civil War began, she became superintendent of the Union Army's female nurses and instructed them to care for wounded men on both sides of the conflict.

SAMUEL COOPER

Like George Thomas, Samuel Cooper (1798–1876), pictured in the mid-1850s as adjutant general of the U.S. Army, went against the loyalties of his home state during the Civil War. Born in New York, he married a Virginian and worked closely with Secretary of War Jefferson Davis in Washington, D.C., before resigning his commission in March 1861 to serve the South and its new president. Prized for his administrative abilities, he became the highest-ranking Confederate Army officer. In 1864 Cooper had the unenviable task of carrying out an ill-fated order from Davis: fire Joseph Johnston as commander of the Army of Tennessee and replace him with John Bell Hood.

PETER COOPER

Inventor and industrialist Peter Cooper (1791–1883), who built America's first successful steam locomotive in 1830, sat for this family portrait two decades later with his wife Sarah, his daughter Sarah Amelia, and his son Edward, who later became mayor of New York City. A philanthropist who viewed wealth as a trust to be used "for the education and uplifting of the common people," he founded New York City's Cooper Union in 1859—an innovative institution offering free vocational courses to adults. In February 1860 Abraham Lincoln gave a celebrated speech there that helped propel him to the Republican nomination and the presidency.

W. P. PHIPPS, ARTIST, LEX.

JOHN C. BRECKINRIDGE

Elected to Congress from Kentucky in 1851, John Breckinridge (1821–1875) was influential in debates regarding the future of slavery. He played a key role in securing passage of the ill-fated Kansas-Nebraska Act before becoming vice president under James Buchanan in 1856, around the time he posed for this daguerreotype. In 1860, he ran unsuccessfully against Lincoln as presidential nominee of defiant Southern Democrats while insisting that he remained true to the Union and its Constitution. When secession ensued, Breckinridge was unable to preserve Kentucky's neutrality and sided with the Confederacy as a general and later as secretary of war.

HENRY DAVID THOREAU

Described as "the apostle of individuality in an age of association and compromise," author Henry David Thoreau (1817–1862) followed his own moral compass and urged readers to do the same in works such as Walden *and "Resistance to Civil Government." When an admirer asked for his portrait in 1856 and offered to defray its cost, he reluctantly obliged by sitting for this daguerreotype. A fervent abolitionist, he protested the Fugitive Slave Act by refusing to pay taxes to Massachusetts—whose officials were required to apprehend fugitive slaves and return them to their owners—and later praised John Brown for raiding Harpers Ferry to obtain weapons for a slave revolt*

MATHEW BRADY

Although scarcely more than twenty years old when he opened his first studio in New York City in 1844, photographer Mathew Brady (ca.1823–1896) soon won accolades for his work. By the early 1850s when he made this self-portrait—the earliest known photo of him, alongside his wife, Julia (left), and a woman believed to be his sister—many prominent figures were seeking him out to have their pictures taken. America's best-known photographer when the Civil War began, Brady documented the conflict with the help of gifted assistants such as Alexander Gardner and Timothy O'Sullivan who followed troops on campaigns and portrayed the horrific aftermath of battles

6

SOLD DOWN THE RIVER

THE SLAVE TRADE IN AMERICA—AND REVULSION against it—altered the nation's conception of freedom, which, until slavery was abolished in 1865, included the right to hold people as property and sell them to the highest bidder. That internal traffic in humans flourished long after January 1, 1808, when a constitutional provision allowing slaves to be imported to the United States expired. Thereafter, Americans were prohibited from taking part in the transatlantic slave trade—a deadly business that began in the 1500s and forcibly shipped as many as fourteen million Africans to the Caribbean and the Americas. Their harrowing ordeal, known as the Middle Passage, is better known today than the traumatic "Second Middle Passage" that took place within the nation's borders in the 1800s. During that time, many African Americans whose ancestors had been packed into slave ships were uprooted in similar fashion and "sold down the river" to distant masters.

Prohibition of the transatlantic slave trade made the domestic slave trade more profitable by limiting the supply of captive laborers as demand for them increased. Spurring that demand was cotton cultivation, which spread westward across the lower South to Mississippi, Louisiana, and Texas, where new plantations thrived while older plantations in the upper South and Southeast were growing less productive. Planters there compensated by selling slaves to owners living in the Southwest or resettling there. The result was the forced migration of around one million African Americans between the early 1800s and the Civil War.

Many were literally sold down the river—shipped to new owners down the Ohio and Mississippi Rivers or down coastal

waterways to the Atlantic and the Gulf of Mexico. One witness aboard an American slave ship in 1834 saw men and women crammed into holds "about five or six feet deep . . . as close as they can be stowed." Those destined for places inaccessible by ship were driven overland in shackles to massive cotton plantations or sweltering sugar plantations, where their lives were often miserable and short. Their high death rate increased the need for slave labor and the prices paid by slave owners. By 1860, the nearly four million slaves in the South were worth some $3.5 billion, making them the largest financial asset in the entire U.S. economy, worth more than all the nation's factories and railroads combined and crucial to the livelihood of planters, traders, bankers, manufacturers, and others.

The nation's domestic slave trade shattered slave families and communities on plantations in states such as Virginia, where an estimated 300,000 African Americans were packed off to the Deep South. Free blacks also increasingly ran the risk of being kidnapped or sold illegally. One victim of the slave trade recalled the dismal scene when he and others were put up for sale in Kentucky: "Men and women down on their knees begging to be purchased to go with their wives or husbands . . . children crying and imploring not to have their parents sent away from them; but all their beseeching and tears were of no avail. They were ruthlessly separated, most of them forever." ⊹ PG

SLAVE SHIP *Captive Africans crowd the Portuguese ship* Diligente, *seized by the British in 1837 for slave trading. Similar ships were built in the United States, where the brutal domestic slave trade continued long after the importation of slaves was banned in 1808.*

Report and Manifest of the Cargo of Slaves on board the Schooner Lafayett of norfolk whereof Benjamin Bissell is master burthen 120 45/95 Tons bound from the port of alexandria in the D.C. for the port of natchez State of Mississippi Via new orleans

Number	Names of Slaves	Height Feet	Height Inches	Age	Complexion	By whom Shipped	Residence of Shipper	To whom Consigned	Residence of Consignee
1	Richard Gains	5	11½	25	Black	Franklin and Armfield	Alexandria	Isaac Franklin & Co	
2	James Parker	5	7½	21	Do				
3	John Harris	5	3	16	Do				
4	Sam Murry	4	83/4	14	Do				
5	George Eaton	5	3	21	Do				
6	John Carroll	5	3	28	Do				
7	Dorthy Jackson	5	4 3/4	28	Do				
8	Ahnis Robinson	5	5½	23	Do				
9	David Moore	5	9½	25	Do				
10	Henry Hall	5	6	21	Yellow				
11	Nancy Fantleroy	5	2 3/4	15	Black				
12	Milly Harris	5	1 3/4	[illegible]	[illegible]				
13	Ephe Hall	4	11	15	Do				
14	Kitty Jackson	5	1/4	14	Do				
15	Suy Bill	5	3	17	Black				
16	Altrey Millard	5	1½	16	Do				
17	Kitty Williams	5		17	Yellow				
18	Cathine Mason	5	2½	17	Black				
19	Child Eliza Mason			3 month	Do				
20	Sayan Nicholson	4	11	18	Do				
21	Child Mariah			18 months	Do				
22	Jane Lomax	5	3	16	Do				
23	Mary Brent	5	0	16	Do				
24	Sharlat Marshall	5	3½	19 ~~3 month~~	Do				
25	Child			3 months	Do				
26	Maryan Hoskins	4	9½	17	Do				
27	Ann Eaglin	4	8½	11	Do				
28	Loueiser Carter	4	11½	14	Do				
29	John Counter	5	9	21	Do				
30	Lewis Tompkins	4	4½	11	Yellow				
31	Aaron Hammonds	5	0	17	Black				
32	July Wilmore	5	2	17	Do				
33	Sophia Satt	4	7½	12	Do				
34	Carter Bone	5	3 1/4	18	Do				
35	Lery Chew	5	0 3/4	18	Do				
36	Ralph Bone	4	6 1/4	12	Do				
37	Lucy Willis	5	2	18	Do				
38	Lary Smith	4	8 3/4	12	Do				
39	Louis Henderson	5	4½	28	Do				
40	Henry Green	5	3	17	Do				
41	Lewis Henson Simmes	5	3 3/4	13	Do				
42	James Shrugs	5	6	22	Yellow				
43	James Scott	5		25	Bk				
44	Nelson Scott	5	3	27	Do				
45	Samuel Lewis	5	6	22	Do				

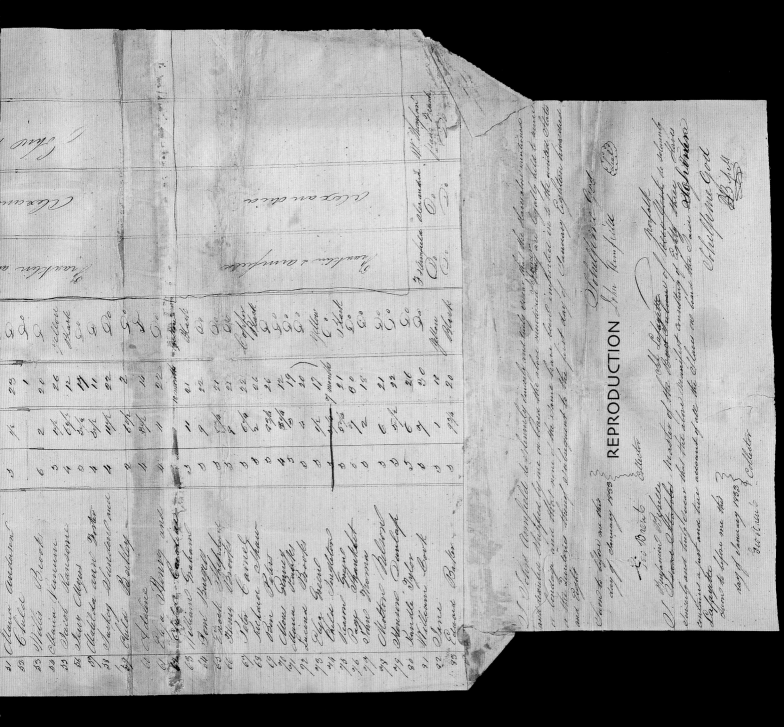

HUMAN CARGO *A vital document of the nation's internal slave traffic, this ship's manifest lists by name, height, age, and complexion eighty-three African Americans who were conveyed in 1833 aboard the schooner* LaFayette *from Alexandria, Virginia, to Natchez, Mississippi, and New Orleans to be purchased by cotton and sugar planters. Handling the shipment was Franklin & Armfield in Alexandria, the South's largest slave-trading operation.*

ADMINISTRATOR'S SALE OF NEGROES!!

The undersigned will, on the first day of January, 1850, offer for sale, to the highest bidder, at Flint Hill, in the county of St. Charles, a negro woman and child, and two likely boys from five to eight years of age, belonging to the estate of Joseph McCoy, dec'd., to be sold in obedience to an order of the County Court of St. Charles, made at the November term 1849.

TERMS.--Twelve months credit, the purchaser giving bond with approved security.   A. BROADHEAD,
        adm'r. of Joseph McCoy, dec'd.
Nov. 28, 1849.

AVAILABLE ON CREDIT
An advertisement in Missouri offers a woman and three children for sale to settle the estate of their deceased owner—a common practice when slaveholders died—and promises a year's credit to purchasers willing to post bond. Traders who served as brokers or middlemen between sellers and buyers often locked slaves in jails or pens before transporting them in shackles like the leg irons below.

Early nineteenth–century leg shackles

SLAVE PEN *The dismal cell shown at left held victims of the slave trade from 1828—when brokers Isaac Franklin and his nephew John Armfield established their headquarters in Alexandria at 1315 Duke Street—until 1861, when Union troops occupied the town and seized the building from another slave-trading firm. Armfield purchased slaves and confined them here before they were transported to the Deep South, where Franklin sold them to new owners. At its peak, the firm had agents in most major Southern cities, owned a fleet of ships, and trafficked in over a thousand slaves annually. In the process, both partners became enormously wealthy. During the Civil War, the Union Army used this building alternately to house deserters and to accommodate freed slaves, who worshipped here and went on to found nearby Shiloh Baptist Church.*

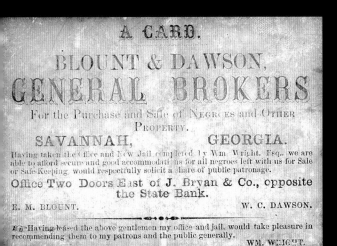

A CARD.

BLOUNT & DAWSON,
GENERAL BROKERS
For the Purchase and Sale of NEGROES and OTHER PROPERTY.

SAVANNAH,   GEORGIA.

Having taken the Office and New Jail completed by Wm. Wright, Esq., we are able to afford secure and good accommodations for all negroes left with us for Sale or Safe-Keeping, would respectfully solicit a share of public patronage.

Office Two Doors East of J. Bryan & Co., opposite the State Bank.

E. M. BLOUNT.   W. C. DAWSON.

☞ Having leased the above gentlemen my office and jail, would take pleasure in recommending them to my patrons and the public generally.
WM. WRIGHT.

SOLD AS "PROPERTY" *The business card above announces that brokers Blount & Dawson have leased the office and jail of another slave trader in Savannah, Georgia, and are ready to buy and sell "Negroes and Other Property." Such notices belied claims made by Southern apologists that slavery was a benign institution and caught the attention of indignant Northerners, who portrayed the brutal, dehumanizing nature of the slave trade in sermons, essays, novels, plays, editorials, cartoons, and cartes de visite (pictures resembling calling cards) like the one at right, showing a youngster for sale on the auction block.*

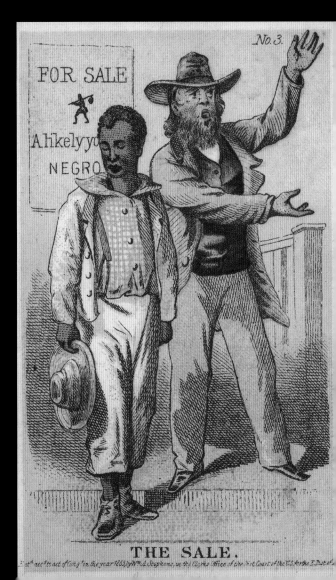

THE SALE.

7

SKILLED SLAVE WORKERS

FROM THE 1830S TO THE 1860S, DAVID DRAKE worked as a potter around Edgefield, South Carolina, a region renowned for its stoneware. Judging from the great size and unique form of the storage jars he made, he was a powerful and exceptionally skilled craftsman. He signed and dated many of his pieces and often added an inscription in verse, thus asserting his identity and literacy. Those were bold assertions for a man in his position, for Drake was a slave, as he noted on a jar in 1840: "Dave belongs to Mr. Miles / wher[e] the oven bakes and the pot biles." Today, his utilitarian ceramic pieces are displayed in prestigious museums and often sell for $100,000 or more on the antiques market.

"Dave the Potter" was among those artisans who used their training and skills to move beyond the limits imposed on many slaves. Most of those held in bondage in the South performed agricultural or domestic labor, but plantations also needed skilled workers to construct or repair buildings, furnishings, tools, and machinery. As one observer wrote, it was a rule among planters in the Deep South "never to pay Money for what can be made upon their Estates, not a Lock, a Hing[e] or a Nail if they can avoid it." Skilled slaves performed such work not only on plantations but also in towns and cities. Many were hired out by planters when their talents were not required at home, or were leased by urban slave owners to local businesses. Some were allowed to hire themselves out and shared the wages they earned with their owners. Occasionally, skilled slaves managed to purchase their freedom and join the ranks of free blacks in the South, who lived mostly in cities.

Slaves who were hired out were issued identification badges to distinguish them from free blacks or runaways. The number of badges issued each year in Charleston, South Carolina, increased from one or two thousand a year in the early 1800s to more than five thousand as the Civil War loomed. Many badges were for servants or porters, but some were for fishermen, mechanics, or other skilled workers. Their services were in demand because many white Southerners considered manual labor beneath them. Authorities made it difficult for skilled slaves to escape or achieve freedom legally by monitoring them and by enacting laws like the one adopted in South Carolina in 1820, stating that no slave could be freed without the legislature's consent. Those limitations help explain why a man as gifted as David Drake remained enslaved until the South was defeated and slavery was abolished. ✛ WSP

A SLAVE'S MASTERWORK *David Drake crafted the impressive jar at left, which he inscribed and signed "Dave." This and other works by Drake are held at the National Museum of American History and the National Museum of African American History and Culture. These identification badges, listing the vocation of slaves who were hired out, were all issued in Charleston.*

Know All men by these presents that I Tobias Hanson of the City of washington for the Consideration of a loan of the sum of one Hundred & fifty five dollars to me in hand paid By Henry Evans the receipt whereof I do hereby acknowledge have granted Bargained And sold unto the said Evans my Slave Daughter mary which said Slave I warrant and defend against all persons whomsoever The Condition of the above obligation is such that if the aboved named Tobias Hanson give the services of the said mary to the said Evans four days in each & every week hereafter until the said ~~~~~~~~ Tobias Hanson shall return to the said Evans the sum of one Hundred and fifty five dollars then the above obligation null & void otherwise in full force & virtue of Law Given under my hand this Twenty Seventh day of mary one thousand eight hundred & Thirty Three Signed Seal & delivered

in the presence of

                                 his

                             Tobias x Henson Seal

                                 mark

8

THE PRICE OF FREEDOM

MOST AFRICAN AMERICANS HELD IN SLAVERY were unable to purchase their freedom because laws in some Southern states made that difficult, if not impossible, or because their owners asked too high a price. Securing liberty for oneself could be prohibitively costly, but Tobias Henson, a resourceful slave born around 1770 in Maryland, managed to purchase not just his own freedom but that of several family members.

> *Know All men by these presents that I, Tobias Henson. . . . give the services of the said mary to the said evans four days in each & every week.*
>
> **HENSON FAMILY PAPERS,**
> **ANACOSTIA COMMUNITY MUSEUM**

Henson's owner, Philip Evans, lived on land just east of the Potomac and Anacostia Rivers. That land was ceded to the District of Columbia in 1790 but remained for some time under the laws of Maryland, which imposed fewer restrictions on manumission, or freeing slaves, than nearby Virginia did. It was not uncommon in Maryland for diligent workers like Henson to receive part of what their owners earned for hiring them out to other employers and to accumulate more in savings than they were worth to their masters. Upon Evans's death in 1817, Henson was valued at $350, and his ownership passed to Philip Evans Jr. On Christmas Eve 1818, Henson bought his freedom from his new owner at the inflated price of $400.

That was just the first step toward Henson's larger goal of freeing and supporting his family, including his two daughters. In 1826 he brought property called "The Ridge," located adjacent to land belonging to the widow of Philip Evans Sr. In 1832 he purchased his elder daughter Matilda and granddaughter Mary Jane from Henry Evans, the younger brother of Philip Evans Jr. A year later, Henson purchased his younger daughter, Mary Ann, from her owner, James Middleton, for $300. He evidently paid for her in part with a loan of $155 obtained that same day from Henry Evans, for whom Mary Ann was required to work four days a week until the loan was repaid, as detailed in the promissory note shown here. He soon paid Evans back and released her from that obligation.

Henson did not free his daughters immediately after purchasing them. Retaining ownership of them gave him some economic and legal leverage, which he used to sell Mary Ann's services to Henry Evans. But he was also shielding his daughters from hardships and restrictions imposed on free African Americans in and around the nation's capital. A law enacted in 1820, for example, stated that free blacks could not become residents of Washington, D.C., unless two sponsors—in most cases, their former white owners—each posted a $500 bond guaranteeing their good conduct.

In November 1837 Tobias Henson transferred all his property to Matilda, upon her promise that he and his wife would not "suffer for the necessities of life," and at the same time freed Matilda, Mary Ann, and their children. Henson is not listed in the 1840 Federal Census; it is believed that he passed away shortly after fulfilling those last legal commitments to his family. The price of freedom had indeed been high, but he was more than equal to it. ✣ AMA

HIS WORD AND BOND *As shown in detail above, Tobias Henson could not write, but he endorsed his promissory note to Henry Evans (OPPOSITE) by signing it with an X and honored its terms to the letter.*

9

FREDERICK DOUGLASS

NO ONE IN THE NINETEENTH CENTURY UNDER-stood the contradictions of American society better than the escaped slave, newspaper editor, and civil rights leader Frederick Douglass. In a long life of impassioned advocacy, Douglass fought to end slavery and free African Americans from its bitter legacy of discrimination and intimidation. He drew attention to the disparity between the bright promise of liberty and equality offered in the Declaration of Independence and the harsh reality for millions of Americans living in bondage. "What to the slave is the 4th of July?" he asked in a speech delivered in 1852. "I answer: a day that reveals to him, more than all other

> *I appear before you this evening as a thief and robber. I stole this head, these limbs, this body from my master, and ran off with them.*
>
> **FREDERICK DOUGLASS**

days in the year, the gross injustice and cruelty to which he is the constant victim. To him, your celebration is a sham; your boasted liberty, an unholy license." Douglass knew that such contradictions would persist until Americans of every complexion had secured their right to "life, liberty, and the pursuit of happiness," and he worked tirelessly to hasten that day.

Born Frederick Bailey in 1818 on a plantation in Maryland, he learned to read and write as a child at a time when laws required that slaves remain illiterate. Constantly testing the limits of bondage both physically and intellectually, he escaped from Baltimore in 1838 and found freedom in the North, where he took the name Douglass and joined the growing antislavery movement. He became a follower of abolitionist William Lloyd Garrison and began speaking publicly on the evils of slavery

with the conviction of one who knew what it was like to be whipped by a master intent on breaking him body and soul. His autobiography, *Narrative of the Life of Frederick Douglass*, published in 1845, broadened the scope of his attack on the South's "peculiar institution" and helped make him an international celebrity who lectured to rapt audiences in Europe.

By 1847 Douglass had moved to Rochester, New York, where he founded the crusading newspaper, *North Star*, so named for the pole star that guided escaping slaves to freedom. The *North Star* became a rival to Garrison's *Liberator*. Unlike Garrison, who remained a pacifist until the Civil War erupted, Douglass argued that force was necessary to end slavery and urged African Americans to fight for their freedom. In 1863 he helped recruit black soldiers to defend the Union and met with Abraham Lincoln at the White House to protest discrimination against those troops, who were paid less than white soldiers.

Douglass's prominence owed much to his persuasive oratory, which was echoed in his writing style. He was plain, direct, and passionate. His speech had the rhythms of the African Methodist Episcopal church, of which he was a member. He also understood the power of photography to project his presence. He sat for many portraits over his long career, but none was more expressive of his strength and determination than the image shown here, taken in 1856.

After the Civil War, Douglass witnessed with dismay the failure of Reconstruction and efforts to protect the newly won constitutional rights of African Americans. He died in 1895 as the nation was beset by racial segregation. His last major campaign was against lynching. He did not live to see America become a true land of liberty, but he left a legacy of moral and political activism on which the twentieth-century civil rights movement would build. ✛ DCW

LIBERATOR *Made when Douglass was in his late thirties, this ambrotype (a glass negative with a dark background reflecting a positive image), conveys his fierce commitment to liberty and justice for all.*

10

JOHN BROWN

JOHN BROWN (1800–1859) WAS A NORTHERNER BY birth, but he was no stranger to the brutality of slavery. In his youth, he witnessed the vicious beating of an enslaved boy, and the memory never left him. Years later, in November 1837, when a proslavery mob murdered newspaper editor and abolitionist Elijah Lovejoy, Brown rose at a public meeting and vowed to devote his life to the destruction of slavery. In private, he prayed with his wife and sons and secured a pledge from them to support him in "fighting slavery by force of arms."

By 1846, when Brown arrived in Springfield, Massachusetts, to open a wool brokerage business, he had developed a radical plan for liberating those held in bondage. Eager to share that plan with African American leaders who possessed "the energy of head and heart to demand freedom for their whole people," he sought out black activists, including

> *Here, before God, ...*
> *I consecrate my life to*
> *the destruction of slavery!*
> JOHN BROWN

clergyman Henry Highland Garnet, and took them into his confidence. Impressed by Brown and the audacity of his plan, Garnet and others spoke of him to Frederick Douglass, who traveled to Springfield to see him. When the two men met privately in November 1847, Brown revealed his vision for an escape route to freedom through the Appalachian Mountains.

Arguing that slavery would never be defeated except by force, Brown proposed to station armed companies of men at intervals along a line extending southward through the Virginia mountains and beyond. Those liberators would carry out raids and free slaves, who would either join the raiding parties or be guided to safety in the North along his

"Subterranean Pass Way." He proclaimed that if he were to be killed while conducting that campaign, he "had no better use for his life than to lay it down in the cause of the slave."

Douglass doubted that such a plan would succeed, but he was struck by Brown's fervor and commitment. After the two men met for the second time in February 1848, Douglass declared to the readers of his *North Star* newspaper that Brown was "as deeply interested in our cause as though his own soul had been pierced with the iron of slavery."

A daguerreotype portrait of John Brown, made not long after his arrival in Springfield, conveys his antislavery zeal. In this riveting image, Brown stands erect with one hand raised as though repeating his earlier pledge to dedicate his life to slavery's destruction. The banner he grasps is not an American flag but what is believed to be the standard of his proposed campaign to liberate slaves.

Brown's wool business failed, and he left Springfield without implementing that militant plan. In May 1856 he led four of his sons and three other followers in an attack that claimed the lives of five proslavery men along Pottawatomie Creek in Kansas. Some abolitionists recoiled, but others hailed Brown and backed his ill-fated assault on the federal arsenal at Harpers Ferry in October 1859. Brown hoped that the raid would ignite an insurrection by slaves armed with pikes and guns he had purchased as well as weapons seized at the arsenal. U.S. Marines led by Colonel Robert E. Lee soon retook Harpers Ferry, however, and Brown went to the gallows on December 2, 1859, warning that "the crimes of this guilty land will never be purged away but with blood." ⊹ AMS

FOMENTING REBELLION *The pike at left was among 950 pikes that John Brown acquired to arm slaves incited to rebel by his raid on Harpers Ferry. The raid grew out of an earlier plan he devised in the mid-1840s around the time that this daguerreotype—one of the earliest images of him—was taken in Hartford, Connecticut, by African American photographer Augustus Washington.*

.44-caliber Sharps sporting rifle

.52-caliber Sharps Model
1853 carbine

.31-caliber six-shot Massachusetts
Arms Co. revolver

ARMED AGAINST SLAVERY *John Brown—shown at left in one of the last
pictures taken of him, around 1858—obtained the firearms above for use in
Kansas against proslavery forces or in his subsequent raid on Harpers
Ferry. This six-shooter (ABOVE, BOTTOM) was among two hundred revolvers
Brown purchased from the Massachusetts Arms Company, which offered
the guns to him at half price to protect "the free state settlers of Kansas."
Helping to finance such deals was the wealthy Massachusetts abolitionist
George L. Stearns, who received the letter opposite from Brown in 1857
after he fled Kansas, where he was wanted for murdering proslavery settlers
at Pottawatomie Creek. Finding refuge in Tabor, Iowa, Brown began for-
mulating plans to launch a slave insurrection in Virginia and asked Stearns
for help: "I am in immediate want of from Five Hundred to One Thousand
Dollars for secret service & no questions asked." Such aid enabled Brown to
buy weapons for the Harpers Ferry attack, including carbines such as
the Sharps .52-caliber (ABOVE, MIDDLE) that were shorter, lighter, and more
suitable for raiders than rifles like the Sharps .44-caliber (ABOVE, TOP),
carried by Brown in Kansas.*

Tabor. Freemont Co, Iowa. 10th Aug. 1857.

George L Stearns Esqr
   Boston Mass   My Dear Sir

          Please find enclosed first
number of a series of tracts lately gotten up here. Would be glad to know how
you like it.   I am now waiting further advice from Free State friends in
Kansas with whom I have speedy _private_ communication lately started.
I am at this moment unable to move _very_ _much_ from an injury of my back:
but getting better fast.   I am in _immediate_ want of from Five Hundred
to One Thousand Dollars for _secret_ _service_ & _no_ _questions_ _asked_.
Will you exert yourself to have that amount, or some part of it, placed in
your hands subject to my order?   / I have learned with gratitude
what has been done to render my Wife & Children comfortable. May God
himself be the everlasting portion of all the _contributers_." This generous
act has lifted a heavy load from my heart.   Rather interesting times were
some expected in Kansas at last accounts: but no great excitement is reported.
Our next advices may entirely change the aspect of things. I _hope_ the friends
of Freedom will respond to my call: & "prove me now herewith." This is
intended for any friends to whom you may _think_ _propper_ to show it.
Please write me at once (directing _Envelope_ to Jonas Jones, Esqr; Tabor. Freemont Co.
Iowa.) He will forward to me when I leave.
             Respectfully Your Friend
                John Brown

$1000

REWARD!

RAN AWAY from the subscribers, on the night of the 5th inst. a NEGRO MAN named

George,

aged 22 or 23 years, 5 feet 7 or 8 inches in height—color, a dark black, a long or double head, had a variety of clothing, among which may be found a green frock cloth coat, with a black velvet collar, a low-crowned white silk hat.

One negro BOY, aged 25 or twenty-six years; 5 feet 10 or 11 inches high,, named

Jefferson---

he is a dark molatto, slim and spare made, had on a fine Janes coat and a variety of other clothing.

One negro girl, named ESTHER, (nicknamed *Puss*,) aged 17 or 18, black, tall, slim and regularly proportioned,—diffident and serious, embarrassed when addressed, and at the same time picks or plays with fingers. She is about 5 feet 6 or 8 inches high, and sister to the boy named George.

A girl named AMANDA, aged 15 or 16, a dark copper colored mulatto, thick and heavy set, 5 ft. 4 inches high, has a sullen and impudent look, a large head of hair, and a green lincy dress. She and Esther both have a variety of clothing.

☞ The above reward will be given if the said negroes can be apprehended or secured so that we can get them; or will give $300 for either of s'd negro boys, or $200 for either of s'd girls.

Of the two boys the mulatto is the tallest. And of the girls the black one is the taller.

Germantown, Mason Co. Ky. }
20th January, 1840.

ANDERSON DONIPHAN,
JOSEPH FRAZEE,
JOHN D. MORFORD.

11

FUGITIVES OR FREEDOM SEEKERS?

CONTRARY TO CLAIMS BY SOUTHERN PLANTERS and politicians that slaves were happy and well treated, many of them fled bondage at great risk. Their overt resistance to oppression threatened the social and psychological foundations of Southern society and led slave owners to seek drastic legal remedies that heightened antislavery sentiment in the North and swelled the ranks of abolitionists.

Handbills offering extravagant rewards for the return of so-called fugitives—a term that defined the runaways as outlaws—suggest that their acts of defiance took a toll on slaveholders not just financially but personally by deflating their egos. Running away gave slaves a taste of freedom and the satisfaction of outmaneuvering their master, even if they did not remain at liberty for long. Newspapers regularly ran columns of ads calling for the return of escaped slaves alongside ads describing captured runaways held in local jails, waiting to be reclaimed. Those who sought freedom in the "Promised Land" up North were greatly outnumbered by those who sought refuge just a few miles from home. Some went to "lie out" in nearby woods or swamps for a while or fled to Southern cities, hoping to blend into the free black population there. Others ran off to reunite with family members who had been sold off—or to avoid being sold themselves, especially when a master died and those he owned were about to be parceled out to heirs or auctioned off. Many absconded to avoid the whip, if only briefly, or to avoid other injuries and indignities inflicted on them daily.

Runaways relied largely on their own resources and on aid from other slaves or free blacks in the South. Those seeking liberty in Northern states or Canada were also helped by a loose organization of black and white abolitionists who formed a covert system of routes, safe houses, and guides or "conductors" that became known as the Underground Railroad. Slave owners pursued runaways, using paid slave catchers or posses organized by sheriffs or other officials and guided by dogs that tracked escaped slaves and could tear their flesh if allowed.

Slave catchers had both state and federal laws on their side. In 1787 the nation's founders included in the Constitution a provision requiring states to return slaves who had escaped from bondage in another state. The Fugitive Slave Act of 1793, enacted by the U.S. Congress and signed by President George Washington, made it a crime to assist an escaped slave. Northern states that outlawed slavery were required to enforce the slave laws of Southern states, but officials often hesitated to do so. Proslavery legislators in Congress responded by pushing through the incendiary Fugitive Slave Act of 1850, which made the federal government responsible for capturing and returning runaways. Federal marshals could now force citizens who opposed slavery to serve on posses as slave catchers.

Many Northerners were deeply offended by the law and came to view slavery as a threat to their own rights. The abolitionist movement gained strength as growing numbers of Americans recognized those who fled slavery or aided them not as disreputable fugitives or lawbreakers but as freedom seekers and liberators. ✛ WSP

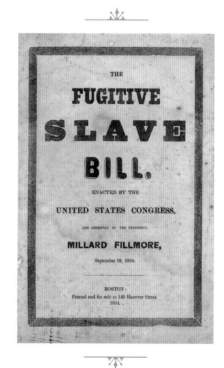

THE
FUGITIVE
SLAVE
BILL.

ENACTED BY THE

UNITED STATES CONGRESS,

AND APPROVED BY THE PRESIDENT,

MILLARD FILLMORE,

September 18, 1850.

BOSTON:
Printed and for sale at 145 Hanover Street.
1854.

ENFORCING SLAVERY *A handbill issued in Kentucky in 1840 (OPPOSITE) seeks the return of four runaways in their teens and twenties. Copies of the Fugitive Slave Act of 1850 (INSET) were printed by abolitionists to encourage public opposition to it.*

12

HARRIET BEECHER STOWE

WHEN PRESIDENT ABRAHAM LINCOLN MET Harriet Beecher Stowe (1811–1896) in 1862, he reportedly said to her, "So you're the little woman who wrote the book that started this great war!" By dramatizing the evils of slavery in her best seller, *Uncle Tom's Cabin*, Stowe made that issue more emotionally charged and widened the rift between Northern foes of slavery and Southern proponents. She was moved to write the novel by the Fugitive Slave Act of 1850, which placed escaped slaves in free states like her native Connecticut at increased risk of being seized and returned to their owners. After discussing the issue with her brother, abolitionist Henry Ward Beecher, she resolved to take up her pen against slavery. "Up to this year I have always felt that I had no particular call to meddle with this subject," Stowe wrote in 1851 to Gamaliel Bailey, editor of the antislavery newspaper the *National Era*. "But I feel now that the time is come when even a woman or a child who can speak a word for freedom and humanity is bound to speak."

Stowe proposed "to set forth the sufferings and wrongs" endured by slaves in a serialized novel, which appeared in the *National Era* in forty installments between June 5, 1851, and April 1, 1852. First published as a book in March 1852, *Uncle Tom's Cabin* sold more than 300,000 copies within a year. The novel stirred readers and, in Stowe's words, converted to "abolitionist views" many who had been put off by the "bitterness of feeling in *extreme abolitionists*." In 1853, Alexander H. Purdy, owner of New York City's National Theatre, staged a play based on the novel and commissioned Alanson Fisher to produce the portrait of Stowe shown here. Installed in the theater's lobby, the painting conveyed the inner resolve of this remarkable "little woman" who had a large impact on the nation's conscience. ✛ DM

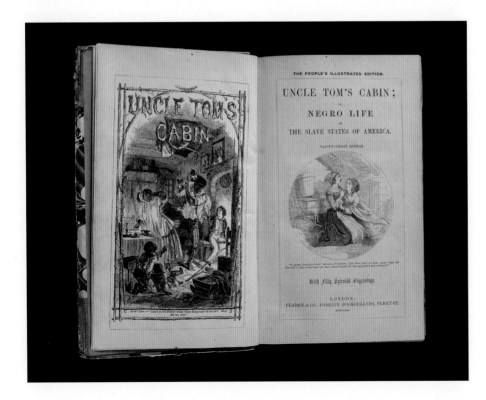

UNCLE TOM'S AUTHOR *Harriet Beecher Stowe was an international celebrity by the time she sat for this portrait by Alanson Fisher in 1853. She had just returned from a wildly successful tour of the British Isles, where* Uncle Tom's Cabin *was even more popular than in America. The London edition (LEFT) replaced her original subtitle,* Life among the Lowly, *with* Negro Life in the Slave States of America. *The novel's emotional appeal stemmed in part from Stowe's experiences in Cincinnati where she lived for many years and encountered slaves from nearby Kentucky. She empathized with those whose loved ones were taken from them when her young son died of cholera in 1849. "It was at his dying bed and at his grave that I learned what a poor slave mother may feel when her child is torn away from her," she wrote.*

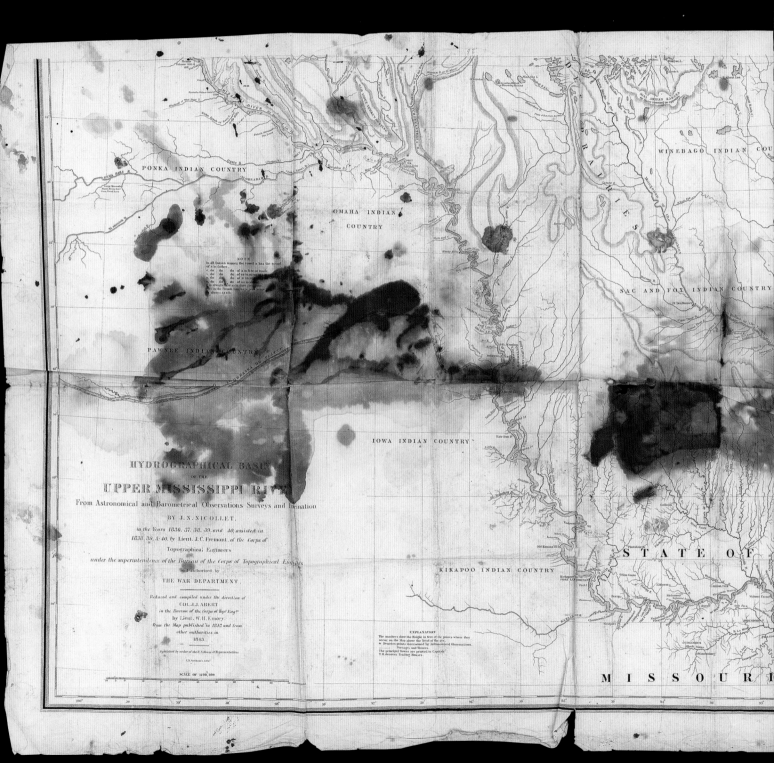

13

BLEEDING KANSAS

I N THE MID-1850S KANSAS BECAME A BATTLEGROUND for forces fiercely at odds over slavery. The Kansas-Nebraska Act of 1854 repealed the Missouri Compromise of 1820, which had admitted Missouri as a slave state but barred slavery in other western territories above latitude 36° 30′, an area including Kansas and Nebraska. The new act allowed settlers in the two territories to decide for themselves whether to allow slavery. That caused little trouble in Nebraska where Northern "free-soilers" predominated, but it convulsed "Bleeding Kansas" where settlers from Missouri and other slave states clashed with those from free states.

Abolitionists eulogized those who died fighting to keep slavery out of Kansas, including Frederick Brown, who had joined his father, John Brown, in the deadly assault on proslavery men at Pottawatomie Creek. Another free-soil martyr was David Starr Hoyt of Massachusetts, who set out for Kansas in early 1856 with a cache of rifles that was seized by opposing Missourians. He was killed that August outside Fort Saunders, a proslavery stronghold near Lawrence. This map of the region stained with Hoyt's blood was found on his body.

Violence over slavery was not confined to America's frontier. A few months before Hoyt was slain, South Carolina congressman Preston Brooks beat Massachusetts senator Charles Sumner repeatedly with a cane for a speech in which he blasted South Carolina Senator Andrew Butler—a relative of Brooks and a supporter of the Kansas-Nebraska Act—for taking as his mistress "the harlot, Slavery." Sumner was left bloodied, unconscious, and nearly dead on the Senate floor. The fate of Kansas was not settled until January 1861 when it was admitted by Congress as a free state, from which Southern secessionists were fast departing. ✣ PG

FATAL TERRAIN *After David Starr Hoyt was killed in Kansas by proslavery foes on August 12, 1856, his body was returned to his family along with this geological map of the region with a large blood stain on the back.*

14

DOUGLAS AND LINCOLN

STEPHEN DOUGLAS (1813–1861), PORTRAYED BELOW in a wood carving, was the nation's preeminent politician in the decade before the Civil War. Born in Vermont, he represented his adopted state of Illinois in the U.S. Senate from 1846 until his death soon after armed conflict between North and South erupted. He had tried to prevent this struggle by forging uneasy political compromises that ultimately did more to exacerbate the crisis than ease it.

The central issue dividing the nation was slavery and its expansion into western territories and future states. Douglas's solution for the conundrum was "popular sovereignty," or leaving the issue of slavery in those emerging states to be decided by the people there. He first applied that doctrine to the sparsely populated territories of Utah and New Mexico when hammering out the intricate congressional Compromise of 1850, which also admitted California as a free state, ended the slave trade in Washington, D.C., and instituted a harsh new Fugitive Slave Act that infuriated abolitionists. Douglas caused further controversy by pushing through the Kansas-Nebraska Act of 1854, which set Kansas ablaze over slavery and made popular sovereignty increasingly unpopular with partisans on either side of that issue.

Campaigning in 1858 for a third term in the Senate, Douglas, a stalwart Democrat, faced Abraham Lincoln (1809–1865) of the young Republican Party, founded in opposition to the westward expansion of slavery. Although Lincoln did not yet have a national reputation like his opponent, their paths had crossed often enough for Douglas to declare, "I shall have my hands full." Indeed, Lincoln followed Douglas on the stump speech circuit and forcefully rebutted his arguments for popular sovereignty soon after he delivered them. When Lincoln suggested that they meet on the same stage, Douglas could not refuse without looking weak and proposed seven debates across the state. Those historic face-offs, held between August 21 and October 15, 1858, offered a sharp contrast in appearance and substance between the tall, gangly Lincoln and the short, stout Douglas, known as the "Little Giant." Douglas declared that the Union could "endure forever, divided into free and slave states as our fathers made it." Lincoln's memorable words earlier in the race proved more prophetic: "A house divided against itself cannot stand. . . . this government cannot endure, permanently half slave and half free."

Douglas won the election in 1858, but Lincoln won the argument by eloquently denouncing slavery as a "vast moral evil" that must not be allowed to spread beyond the South. He had gained recognition nationwide, and he would continue to define and shape the antislavery platform of the Republican Party. Just two years after losing the Senate race in Illinois, he would secure his party's nomination for president and go on to defeat Douglas and other candidates in a contest that fractured the nation. ✣ JGB

"LITTLE GIANT" *This painted wooden image of Stephen Douglas, measuring about eighteen inches high and inscribed with his name at the base, was carved by an unidentified folk artist around 1858. After Douglas died in 1861, he was memorialized in a carte de visite (OPPOSITE, RIGHT), sold to admirers of the "Little Giant," who was more than a foot shorter than Abraham Lincoln, shown in a photograph (OPPOSITE, LEFT) taken around the time he debated Douglas.*

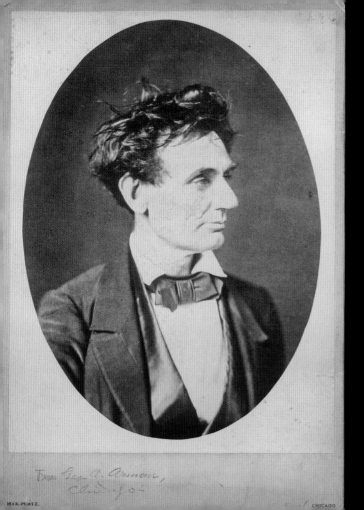

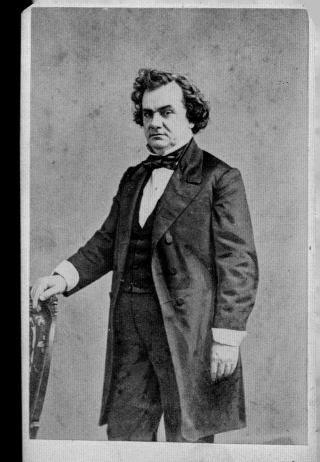

Born April 23, 1813. Died June 3, 1861.

From Carbutt's Gallery, 131 Lake Street, Chicago.

"THE ANIMAL HIMSELF"

IN APRIL 1860 CHICAGO SCULPTOR LEONARD W. VOLK learned that Abraham Lincoln was trying a prolonged court case in that city and invited the prominent lawyer and politician to sit for him. The two had met earlier in 1858 during the heated Lincoln-Douglas senatorial debates. Volk was then working on a statue of Stephen Douglas and asked to portray his opponent as well. Lincoln agreed but was too busy to fulfill Volk's request. Now in 1860, with Lincoln emerging as a Republican presidential prospect, Volk once again broached the topic. Lincoln, who often sought opportunities to be photographed at key moments in his life, made time to be immortalized by one of the city's leading artists.

For a week in April, Lincoln arrived at the sculptor's studio first thing in the morning and left before the court opened and the trial resumed. On the second day, to aid his work on the sculpture, Volk made a mold of Lincoln's face by applying wet plaster and prying it loose when it dried—a procedure Lincoln found "anything but agreeable." From that mold the artist produced an evocative plaster cast

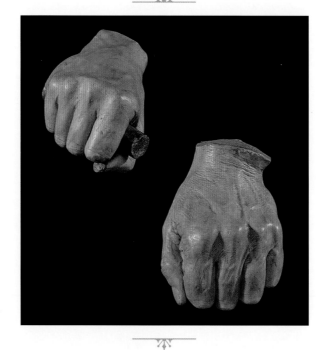

of Lincoln's face, pictured opposite and on the following pages from various angles. This life mask captured Lincoln as he looked when he rose to prominence on the national stage, with every line and wrinkle on his face recorded. Later when Volk presented Lincoln with a copy of the final bust, he remarked wryly, "There is the animal himself."

Volk was in Springfield, Illinois, with Lincoln on May 18 when word arrived by telegraph that he had been nominated for president at the Republican convention in Chicago. On that festive occasion, Volk asked to cast the nominee's powerful hands and proceeded to set up shop in his house. When the sculptor suggested that Lincoln grip something in his right hand, the candidate went out to his shed and sawed off part of a broomstick. He then began smoothing the rough edges of the sawn piece. Volk told him that was unnecessary, to which Lincoln replied, "I thought I would like to have it nice." Volk kept that wooden prop after the plaster mold was removed and inserted it into his cast of Lincoln's right hand (inset).

In addition to sculpting a bust of the clean-shaven Lincoln as he appeared in the spring of 1860, Volk later produced a full-length statue of the bearded president, which was placed in 1877 within the rotunda of the Illinois State Capitol at Springfield near Volk's statue of Douglas. In 1886 Stephen Volk, the artist's son, sold the original plaster casts of Lincoln's face and hands to a group that commissioned sculptor Augustus Saint-Gaudens to make a limited set of replicas. In 1888 that group presented bronze copies fashioned by Saint-Gaudens to the Smithsonian along with the originals from which they were made, on condition that those "plaster casts should never be tampered with" or copied again. ⊹ HRR

CAPTURING LINCOLN *These plaster casts of Lincoln's face and hands were made on separate occasions in 1860, before and just after the Republican convention, respectively. Lincoln's right hand was swollen from shaking the hands of the many supporters who came to congratulate him in Springfield for winning the presidential nomination.*

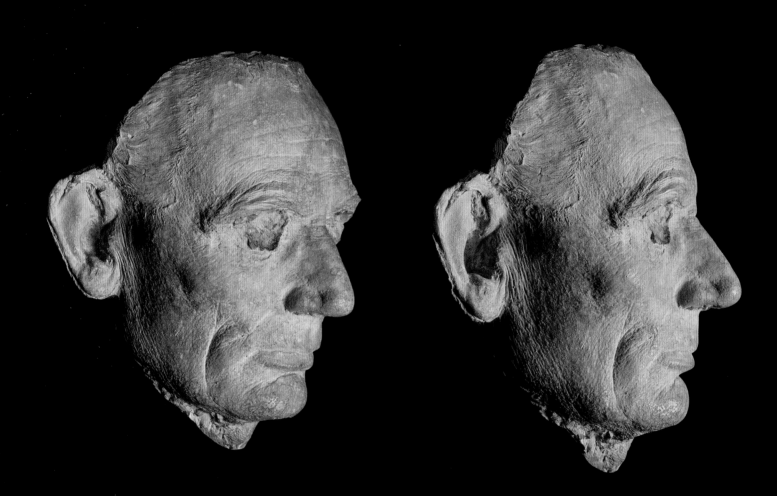

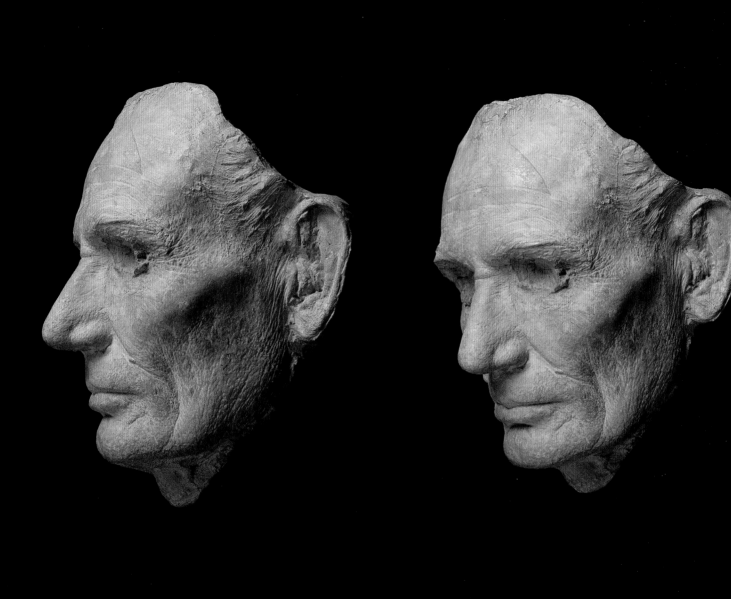

16

THE ELECTION OF 1860

THE PRESIDENTIAL CAMPAIGN OF 1860 WAS FULL of all the pageantry and hoopla that characterized mid-nineteenth-century elections. Party spokesmen stumped across the country and political clubs organized picnics, rallies, and torch-light parades.

The Republicans crafted a campaign around a frontier depiction of Abraham Lincoln that had just enough truth behind the image to captivate the public. The idea of portraying Lincoln as "the rail splitter" was the inspiration of Illinois politician Richard J. Oglesby, who sought to find "one thing in Mr. Lincoln's unsuccessful career as a worker that could be made an emblem . . . [to] make enthusiastic the working people." In May 1860 Illinois Republicans met to select their state's presidential nominee. Lincoln's supporters capped off a demonstration in the meeting hall with John Hanks, Lincoln's cousin, carrying in two fence rails supposedly split by Lincoln and Hanks. Suspended from the rails was a banner that read, "Abraham Lincoln the Rail Candidate for President in 1860." Delegates wildly cheered the theatrics, and Lincoln handily won nomination. One observer described the banner as "the 'Battle flag' in the coming contest between 'labor free' and 'labor slave,' between democracy and aristocracy." In that moment, Lincoln became a symbol of the self-made frontiersman and representative of honest, free, enterprising labor.

With Lincoln as their candidate, Republicans decorated their headquarters with fence rails. Their political clubs, including the Wide Awakes, organized massive rallies where they marched behind banners pulling miniature log cabins and carrying props such as this oversized axe with printed paper labels declaring on one side "Old Abe is Ours" and "Good Time Coming Boys" on the other.

The carnival atmosphere masked a deadly serious dispute over extending slavery westward that split the old political parties into warring factions. Many in the North shared the concern voiced by Lincoln in 1858 when he warned that if slavery was not contained, "its advocates will push it forward, till it shall become alike lawful in all the States, old as well as new—North as well as South." Southern slaveholders responded by insisting that banning slavery in the western territories would lead to its abolition across the country.

The Republican Party, largely created out of the remnants of the northern Whig Party, called for a complete prohibition of the extension of slavery. In 1860 the Democratic Party split over the issue of slavery. Northern Democrats nominated Stephen Douglas for president. His platform called for residents of each territory to decide whether to permit slavery. Southern Democrats nominated John C. Breckinridge and called for slavery's expansion into the West. Members of the new Constitutional Union Party and their nominee John Bell tried to avoid taking any controversial positions and simply promised to maintain the Constitution, the Union, and the laws.

Lincoln won the election but received less than 40 percent of the popular vote and not a single electoral vote in the South, where the response to his victory was swift and defiant. One day after the results were announced in South Carolina, the *Charleston Mercury* reported that a rebellion was brewing against Lincoln and his party: "The tea has been thrown overboard—the revolution of 1860 has been initiated." ✛ HRR

BOOSTER'S BLADE *This ax touted Abraham Lincoln as a rail-splitting frontiersman—a hard lot he gladly escaped as a young man by studying law and settling comfortably in Springfield, Illinois. He campaigned for president in 1860 under Republican banners, like the one opposite, with Hannibal Hamlin of Maine as his running mate.*

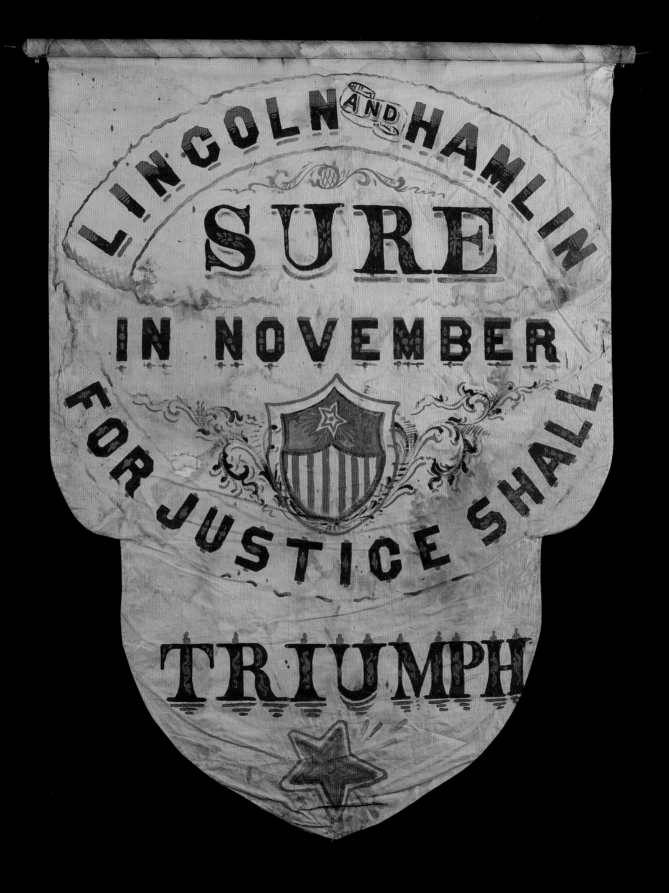

REPUBLICAN GUARDS *A sketch published in the* Illustrated News of the World *in late 1860 portrays Wide Awakes—who wore Lincoln badges like the one shown below—parading in uniform on behalf of their candidate and holding aloft their emblem, a watchful eye symbolizing their role as guardians of the Union and its free soil. Marchers in such rallies carried transparencies that were lit from within by oil lamps and glowed at night. The example below hails Lincoln as a patriot embodying the spirit of 1776 and refers to him as "Old Abe," a nickname of long standing that made the former one-term U.S. congressman seem more experienced and venerable than he was at fifty-one.*

Lincoln parade transparency

Wide Awake badge

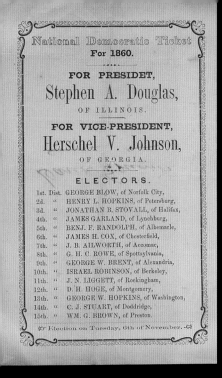

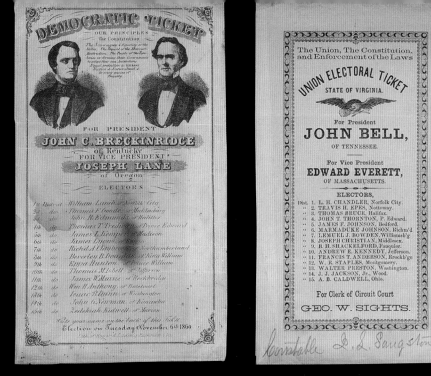

1860 Douglas ticket

1860 Breckinridge ticket

1860 Bell ticket

ALSO-RANS *The three parties that lost to Lincoln and the Republicans in 1860 offered the tickets above, identifying the candidates and their electors in Virginia. Northern Democrats (also known as National Democrats), who sought Southern votes by teaming Stephen Douglas with vice-presidential nominee Herschel Johnson of Georgia, received 29 percent of the popular vote but won only Missouri and a few electoral votes in New Jersey. Southern Democrats matched John C.*

Breckinridge with running mate Joseph Lane of Oregon and swept most of the South but lost the free states of Oregon, California, and the populous North to the Republicans. The short-lived Constitutional Union Party paired John Bell with Edward Everett of Massachusetts and edged out the Southern Democrats to win three slave states in the upper South where Unionist sentiment remained strong: Virginia, Kentucky, and Tennessee.

17

DISSOLVING THE UNION

NOWHERE WAS THE OUTCRY AGAINST ABRAHAM Lincoln's election in 1860 more strident than in South Carolina, where many called for their state to leave the Union. The secession movement had its roots there in 1832 when Senator John C. Calhoun invoked the constitutional theory of states' rights to justify South Carolina's attempt to nullify a despised federal tariff. That crisis ended when the tariff was reduced, but as debate later turned to fugitive slaves and the regulation of slavery in the territories, South Carolina politicians frequently invoked Calhoun's language in their threats of secession. Fear of abolition was particularly strong among whites in states such as South Carolina, where those held in bondage made up more than half the population.

Three days after Lincoln's victory, the general assembly in South Carolina called for a secession convention. Dissenting voices were barely heard amid the clamor for independence. Although rain poured on the convention's opening day, the fervor among the 169 delegates could not be dampened. On December 20, 1860, at St. Andrew's Hall in Charleston, they voted unanimously to secede from the Union and declare their state an independent commonwealth.

Outside the hall, crowds clapped and cheered, the bells of St. Michael's Church chimed, palmetto flags unfurled, and The Citadel cannons fired. "The Union Is Dissolved!" proclaimed the *Charleston Mercury* in an extra edition rushed into print that day (right). A later edition boasted, "In less than fifteen minutes our Extras, containing the long looked for Ordinance, were being thrown off the fast presses and distributed among the eager multitude that thronged under the great banner of the 'Southern Confederacy.'"

The secession of one state did not in fact create that Confederacy, but revelers in Charleston trusted that other Southern states would soon join them. Amid the excitement, few paused to consider what lay in store for those who defied a Union that President Lincoln would defend with all his might. ✦ SMC

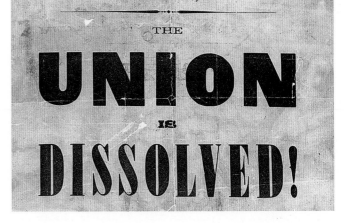

CONFEDERATE DAWN *This* Charleston Mercury *broadside printed and distributed on December 20, 1860, announces the first act of secession that fractured the American nation. Only the union between South Carolina and the United States was dissolved on this date, but defiant Southerners foresaw a larger blow to the Union as a whole as more states declared independence and joined with South Carolina to form the Confederacy.*

18

PASSAGE THROUGH BALTIMORE

On his way to Washington, D.C., for his inauguration in 1861, Abraham Lincoln was warned of an assassination plot in Baltimore: secessionists reportedly planned to attack him in broad daylight as he changed trains. He was advised to alter his plans and pass through the city at night, riding incognito in a sleeping car. Lincoln reluctantly heeded the advice and arrived unannounced in the nation's capital. He regretted doing so when the incident was publicized and he was ridiculed for sneaking into Washington. Among those who lampooned him was Adalbert J. Volck (1828–1912), a German immigrant who practiced dentistry in Baltimore while expressing his Southern sympathies in scathing sketches like the one at right, which shows a disguised Lincoln peeking out anxiously from a boxcar—encountering the "menace" of a hissing cat.

The Civil War prints by Volck held at the National Portrait Gallery are rare and vivid documents of Confederate sentiment in Maryland, where Lincoln imposed martial law during the conflict and suspected secessionists were jailed. Volck later explained that he was motivated to produce his drawings after "seeing the illustrated papers of the North filled with one-sided pictures of the war."

To counter "villainous caricatures" of Confederates by Thomas Nast and other Northern artists, Volck surreptitiously published his sketches under a pseudonym in a limited edition for two hundred subscribers. "The drawings, etching and printing were all done by myself at night, after the day's unintermittent professional labor," he confided. "Of course entire secrecy had to be preserved." Not content simply to portray Union troops as brutal occupiers and Lincoln as the devil incarnate, Volck also conducted covert missions, including smuggling medical supplies to Confederates in Virginia. ✢ JGB

The drawings, etching and printing were all done by myself at night, after the day's unintermittent professional labor. Of course entire secrecy had to be preserved.

ADALBERT J. VOLCK

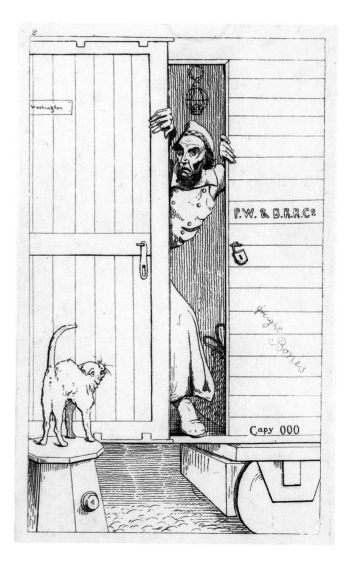

LINCOLN INCOGNITO *Adalbert J. Volck derides Lincoln in "Passage through Baltimore," one of thirty drawings in the artist's privately published collection,* Sketches from the Civil War in North America.

19

LINCOLN'S FIRST INAUGURATION

O N MARCH 4, 1861, ABRAHAM LINCOLN TOOK THE PRESIDENTIAL OATH of office on the steps of the Capitol. No other president of the United States entered office with the nation in such peril. Two weeks earlier, Jefferson Davis had become president of the Confederate States of America. In Washington, D.C., fear of violence hung in the air. Soldiers blocked off cross streets, and sharpshooters manned the roofs along Pennsylvania Avenue. The unfinished Capitol dome loomed in the background as if to symbolize the nation's uncertain future. Photographer Alexander Gardner recorded the historic event, capturing Lincoln, wearing his iconic tall hat, under a wooden canopy built for the occasion (right).

In his inaugural address, Lincoln promised not to interfere with slavery where it already existed. Yet he warned secessionists that he would honor his oath "to preserve, protect, and defend" the Constitution and the Union. His speech, which concluded with an appeal for those on both sides of the sectional divide to be guided by "the better angels of our nature," struck some Northerners as too conciliatory. To many Southerners, however, it sounded like a declaration of war. ✛ HRR

MIXED MESSAGES *Lincoln appears above alternately as Pax, the goddess of peace, and Mars, the god of war, in this cartoon by Thomas Nast (1840–1902) published in the* New York Illustrated News *on March 23, 1861, satirizing the contrasting reactions to Lincoln's inaugural address.*

20

THE FIRE-EATER'S WAR

EDMUND RUFFIN (1794–1865) WAS THE VERY epitome of the Southern "fire-eater," as radical defenders of slavery and the society on which it was based were known. Convinced that their plantation system was a positive good for both slaves and the South, fire-eaters opposed any compromise with the North that would limit the extension of slavery and might lead to its extinction. After 1850, as political efforts to resolve differences between slave states and free states broke down, each side in the sectional crisis stepped up rhetorical attacks on the other. In that violently charged political atmosphere, disunion became not just a very real possibility but one welcomed by fire-eaters.

A Virginia plantation owner, Ruffin had deep roots in the slave South. By 1860, his family held some two hundred people in slavery. He first came to public notice as an agricultural reformer, proposing ways to improve farming practices and replenish exhausted soil. Moving on from agricultural reform, he turned to politics and offered a defense of the South as a civilization superior to the North by touting the presumed benefits of the plantation system for both whites and blacks. Underlying his argument was the racist assumption that African Americans were naturally suited for slavery and unfit for freedom. Furthermore, Ruffin and other fire-eaters claimed that the emancipation of slaves—which they suspected was Abraham Lincoln's hidden agenda—would reduce Southern whites to menial status and make Northerners their masters. The presidential election of 1860, Ruffin wrote, would decide "whether these southern states are to remain free, or to be politically enslaved."

After Lincoln's election, Ruffin moved to Charleston, South Carolina, thrilled by the leadership role that the Palmetto State was taking in the secession movement and disgusted by the lukewarm response in Virginia. Ruffin was in Charleston during the "secession winter" of 1860–61 as battle loomed. A war for Southern independence was the consummation of his dreams. Fittingly, the sixty-six-year-old fire-eater attached himself to the Palmetto Guards and in the early hours of April 12, 1861, pulled the lanyard on a cannon that fired what may have been the first shot aimed at Fort Sumter in Charleston Harbor

Too old and infirm for extended military duty and temperamentally unsuited for office-holding, Ruffin spent the Civil War at a farm west of Richmond, following the ebb and flow of battle, which engulfed his family's property east of Richmond. With the Confederacy defeated and his hopes for an independent South dashed, Ruffin faced a bleak future. On June 17, 1865, he wrapped himself in a Confederate flag and committed suicide with a musket. Credited with firing the first shot of the Civil War, Ruffin can also be said to have fired its last. But in a suicide note declaring his "unmitigated hatred of Yankee rule," he foreshadowed the bitter conflicts of Reconstruction and its aftermath, when an unrepentant South rejoined the Union. ✢ DCW

OPENING FIRE *Edmund Ruffin, pictured around 1861, urged an attack on Fort Sumter and helped launch it. The attack unfolded within view of Charlestonians, portrayed on rooftops in an illustration from* Harper's Weekly *(OPPOSITE) showing dark smoke billowing from Fort Sumter.*

SECRETS IN LINCOLN'S WATCH

ABRAHAM LINCOLN WAS NOT AN OUTWARDLY VAIN man, but in the late 1850s he decided to purchase a fine gold watch from George Chatterton, a jeweler in Springfield, Illinois. It was probably the single-most expensive personal item Lincoln had bought for himself. Acquired when his law practice was flourishing, this watch, consisting of an English lever movement inside an American case, was a conspicuous symbol of his success.

After arriving in Washington, D.C., Lincoln sent his watch for repair to M. W. Galt & Company on Pennsylvania Avenue. Jonathan Dillon, a young watchmaker who was by his own account the only Union sympathizer in the shop, had just completed his work on the timepiece when news of the attack on Fort Sumter reached Washington on April 13, 1861. Dillon recalled that unsettling day in an interview published in the *New York Times* in 1906 when he was eighty-four years old: "I was working upstairs when Mr. Galt came up. He was much excited, and gasped: 'Dillon, war has begun; the first shot has been fired.' At that moment I had in my hand Abraham Lincoln's watch, which I had been repairing. . . . I unscrewed the dial, and with a sharp instrument wrote on the metal beneath." In the excitement of the moment, Dillon recorded the news and his support for Lincoln. He scratched across the inside plate, "Jonathan Dillon / April 13–1861 / Fort Sumpter was attacked / by the rebels on the above / date J Dillon" and "April 13–1861 / Washington / thank God we have a government / Jonth Dillon." In the following years, other watchmakers also left behind notes. In 1864 L. E. Gross signed his name, and at some point a Southern supporter wrote "Jeff Davis" across one of the metal pieces. It is unlikely the Lincoln ever knew about the messages that he carried in his pocket. If he did, he certainly would have had the name of his Confederate rival removed.

In 1958 Lincoln's great-grandson, Lincoln Isham, donated the timepiece to the Smithsonian. The museum's staff never needed to remove the dial, and the inscriptions on the inner workings remained hidden. As years passed, the unconfirmed

April 13–1861 / Washington / thank God we have a government Jonth Dillon

MESSAGE IN LINCOLN'S WATCH

story was known only within Dillon's family. In 2009 Dillon's great-great-grandson, Doug Stiles, contacted the museum to see if anyone knew of the existence of the watch or had heard of the story that his ancestor had often recounted. On March 10, 2009, the museum arranged to have the dial removed. Before a small gathering of Dillon family members, reporters, and staff members, the watch's movements were taken out of their case, and Doug Stiles was invited to be the first to read the words inscribed on the fateful day. ✝ HRR

MESSAGES UNCOVERED *Nothing on the surface of Lincoln's watch (ABOVE) indicated that those who repaired it had left messages. Not until its interior was exposed (OPPOSITE) could one see the inscriptions made by Jonathan Dillon in 1861 and other watchmakers—one who signed his name in 1864 and another who wrote "Jeff Davis."*

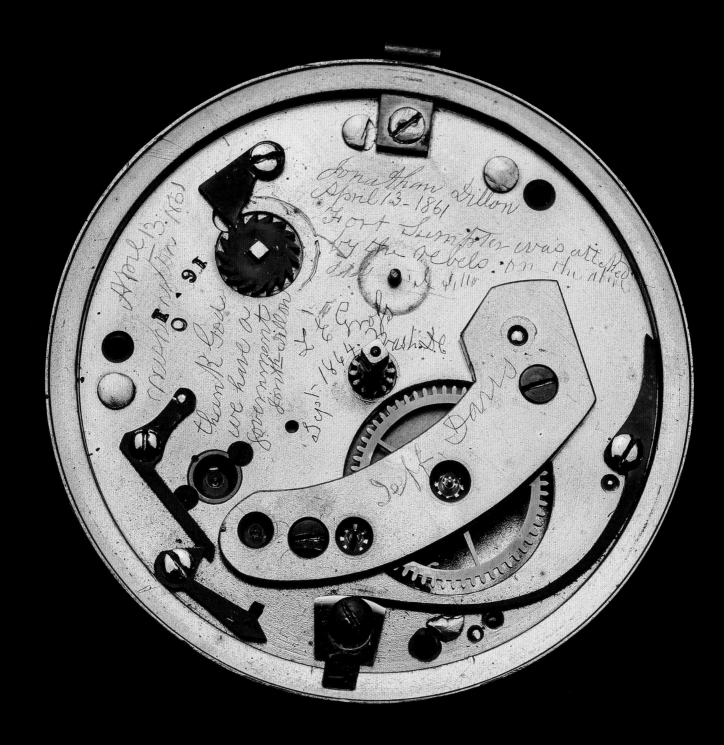

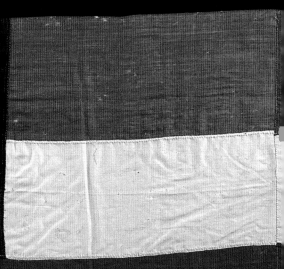

FLAGS FOR A NEW NATION

WHEN SOUTHERN DELEGATES CONVENED AT Montgomery, Alabama, in February 1861 to establish the Confederate government, they faced the challenge of devising not only a new constitution but also a new flag for their nation. William Porcher Miles, a former U.S. congressman who represented South Carolina at the convention, proposed a design quite unlike the U.S. flag, which he considered a symbol of tyranny. Other delegates, however, preferred a flag based on the Stars and Stripes.

Many Confederates considered themselves revolutionary patriots like George Washington, Thomas Jefferson, and other founders who declared independence in 1776. They proclaimed their American heritage by taking the U.S. Constitution and the Stars and Stripes as models for their own constitution and flag while making changes that signaled their distinct identity.

The First Confederate National Flag, also known as the "Stars and Bars," was adopted on March 4, 1861—a date chosen defiantly to coincide with Abraham Lincoln's inauguration—and had seven stars for the seven original Confederate States of America (South Carolina, Mississippi, Florida, Alabama, Georgia, Louisiana, and Texas). The number of stars on that banner increased as Virginia joined the Confederacy in April 1861, followed by Arkansas, North Carolina, and Tennessee. The U.S. government refused to accept secession and continued to represent all the Southern states on its national flag, which acquired its thirty-fourth star when Kansas entered the Union in January 1861. The number of stars expanded again with the admission of West Virginia as the thirty-fifth state in July 1863.

The similarity between the Stars and Stripes and the Stars and Bars caused confusion and calamity during the First Battle of Bull Run (known to Confederates as First Manassas) in July 1861. As opposing troops clashed amid the dust and smoke, they found it hard to distinguish their own national flag from the enemy's. That contributed to deadly incidents of friendly fire that were particularly costly for the Confederates. Although they prevailed at Manassas, Confederate generals P.G.T. Beauregard and Joseph Johnston concluded that their forces needed a battle flag that was distinct from their national flag and would not be confused with the Stars and Stripes. William Miles revived his earlier design for the Confederate national flag featuring an X-shaped cross of St. Andrew, which was incorporated in the battle flag of the Army of Northern Virginia. Introduced in November 1861, it had three stars on each arm of the cross and one in the center. The thirteen stars represented the eleven official states of the Confederacy as well as Kentucky and Missouri, where Confederates were challenging Unionists for control. The Army of Northern Virginia went on to achieve lasting fame under General Robert E. Lee, and its battle flag became an enduring symbol of Southern defiance. ✣ JLJ

OPPOSING STANDARDS *Among the Civil War–era banners in Smithsonian collections are a thirty-four-star U.S. flag (OPPOSITE, TOP), introduced when Kansas joined the Union; an eight-star Confederate national flag (OPPOSITE, BOTTOM), which was probably made to signal Virginia's entry as the eighth Confederate state; and a thirteen-star Confederate battle flag of the Army of Northern Virginia (INSET).*

23

GENERAL SCOTT AND COLONEL LEE

IN APRIL 1861, A FEW DAYS AFTER THE FALL OF FORT Sumter, Virginia governor John Letcher sent envoys to Washington, D.C., to urge Winfield Scott (1786–1866), commanding general of the U.S. Army, to join his fellow Virginians in embracing the Confederacy. Scott refused. "I have served my country, under the flag of the Union, for more than 50 years," he said, "and so long as God permits me to live, I will defend that flag with my sword, even if my own native state assails it."

Although Scott was too infirm at seventy-four to command troops in the field, it would have been demoralizing to the Union if he had joined the Confederates. Elevated by Congress in 1852 to the rank of lieutenant general, Scott shared that distinction with only George Washington. He had been actively engaged in all major American military conflicts since the War of 1812, spanning thirteen presidential administrations from James Madison to Abraham Lincoln. In a masterful campaign during the Mexican War, he had clinched victory by capturing Mexico City, which earned him a gold medal from Congress in 1848 and the Whig Party's presidential nomination four years later. Though he lost the presidential election to Franklin Pierce, he remained a national war hero, whose obsession with military etiquette and protocol had earned him the nickname "Old Fuss and Feathers."

Not long before the Civil War began, while headquartered in New York City, Scott visited photographer Mathew Brady, most likely at his new studio on Broadway called the National Portrait Gallery, near Scott's brownstone residence on Twelfth Street. Since 1856, Brady had been making large photographs measuring about eighteen by fifteen inches, called "Brady Imperials." Scott's commanding presence—he stood just

over six feet, four inches and weighed nearly three hundred pounds—clearly called for the Imperial-size image shown here, which captured "the grand old man of the army" in physical decline. A fancier of rich foods and fine wines, he could no longer ride a horse and walked haltingly, afflicted as he was with gout, dropsy, rheumatism, and vertigo. He could be arrogant and contentious, bold and benevolent, petty and jealous, thoughtful and sage. Famous for his vanity, he favored a dress uniform adorned with yards of gold braid.

Some whispered that Scott was growing senile, but his military judgment remained sound. President Lincoln, facing what he called "this giant insurrection," sought Scott's recommendation for field commander of the fledgling Union Army. He could think of no one better for the task than Colonel Robert E. Lee (1807–1870), a fellow Virginian who had served as a staff officer under him in Mexico before becoming superintendent at West Point. Scott considered Lee "the very best soldier that I ever saw in the field" and was deeply disappointed when he turned down the command, explaining that he could not draw his sword against his own state. On April 20 Lee left the U.S. Army to serve Virginia and the Confederacy. In his letter of resignation to Scott, the dedicated Virginian politely severed ties with that faithful old Unionist: "To no one Genl have I been as much indebted as to yourself for uniform kindness & Consideration.... your name & fame will always be dear to me." ✣ JGB

DIVIDED VIRGINIANS *Robert E. Lee (INSET)—a model officer like his superior Winfield Scott (OPPOSITE)—posed for a daguerreotype in civilian dress as a captain of engineers in the early 1850s. Later this copy of the photograph was altered to depict Lee in uniform.*

PARTING WAYS AT WEST POINT

George Armstrong Custer

John Pelham

I N THE SPRING OF 1861, THE DRUMBEATS OF WAR reverberated at the U.S. Military Academy, where cadets from North and South now had to choose sides. For John Pelham (1838–1863), the son of an Alabama planter who opposed secession but stood by the South, the choice was agonizing. Torn in his allegiance, young Pelham wrote Confederate President Jefferson Davis to ask what he should do. On April 22, eight days after Fort Sumter fell and just two weeks before his graduation, he left West Point to join the Confederate Army.

George Armstrong Custer (1839–1876) was one class behind Pelham. The son of an Ohio farmer, he excelled at military drills but neglected his studies and finished last in his class. Because the Union needed officers, Custer and his classmates graduated a year early. Most cadets remained loyal to the United States, but more than a quarter of those in the two graduating classes joined the Confederate Army.

Both Pelham and Custer became famous for the manner in which they fought and died. During the first two years of the war, Pelham led artillery in more than sixty engagements and was promoted to major by age twenty-four. "It is really extraordinary to find such nerve and genius in a mere boy," Thomas "Stonewall" Jackson remarked. "With Pelham on each flank I believe I could whip the world." Off duty when fighting erupted at Kelly's Ford, Virginia, on March 17, 1863, Pelham rushed into the fray and was killed. His body lay in state at the Confederate Capitol in Richmond before burial in Alabama.

Custer rose even higher in the Union Army, becoming a brigadier general at twenty-three. Yet the "Boy General" remained controversial during and after the Civil War. In 1876 his reckless daring led to disaster at the Little Bighorn, where Sitting Bull's Lakota warriors killed him and more than 250 of his men. ✤ FHG

SOLDIERS IN TRAINING *Two ambrotypes portray George Armstrong Custer (LEFT, TOP) and John Pelham (LEFT, BOTTOM) during their West Point days. Custer wears a cadet coatee similar to the one owned by Ulysses S. Grant (OPPOSITE), a member of the class of 1843.*

MILITIA UNIFORMS

THE COLORS BLUE AND GRAY ARE FOREVER associated with the Civil War. When the first shots were fired at Fort Sumter, however, most of the soldiers on which the Union and Confederacy would rely in the coming months were members of state or local militia companies who wore uniforms of sundry colors and patterns. Many continued to do so after they enlisted to fight for the opposing armies. More than a few battles were waged between North and South before either side established a regular uniform for its troops and the Civil War became an iconic confrontation between the blue and the gray.

When the conflict began, it was widely assumed that the outcome would be determined quickly in one big clash. But the Union could not wage even a short war if it relied solely on the Regular U.S. Army, which numbered only about 16,000 men and lost more than one fourth of its officers to the Confederacy. Abraham Lincoln initially asked for 75,000 volunteers to serve for ninety days, and Jefferson Davis requested 100,000 twelve-month volunteers. Many men who answered those calls wore their militia uniforms; others received uniforms of various patterns from local depots or tailors, resulting in considerable variation in dress even among companies in the same regiment. A journalist described one Union camp in Ohio where companies gathered for training as "an Eastern bazaar, in which every variety of clothing under heaven is to be found."

The Union and Confederate quartermaster departments foresaw the need for regularity in uniforms but found it hard to implement. In April 1861 the Confederate quartermaster general called for blue coats, which were not yet standard for Union troops, and a number of Confederates wore blue early on. Other Southerners went to war in outfits of different colors or in civilian dress.

Among the conspicuous items worn by militiamen when the conflict began were shakos—tall hats that could make soldiers prominent targets in battle. The prevailing tactics, however, called for opposing ranks to open fire on each other at close range, in which case even soldiers wearing inconspicuous clothing were plainly visible to their opponents. A greater danger was the deadly confusion that resulted when troops in motley dress were unable to tell friends from foes. Bitter experience taught both sides to forsake variety for uniformity, which had the further advantage of making the production of clothing for troops more consistent and efficient. A war that dawned with a bright medley of colors and costumes evolved into a stark struggle between men in blue and gray. ✛ JLJ

MILITIA GARB *This faded, well-worn, long-tailed coatee was like that worn by many militiamen during drills in the years leading up to the war. As shown by the examples at right, their headgear was as diverse as the men themselves—volunteers of various origins and descriptions who went off in 1861 to fight for the Union or the Confederacy in their militia uniforms.*

Dragoon helmet, First Troop, Philadelphia City Cavalry, 1835
(missing horsehair crest)

Chapeau worn by a member of the Portland Rifle Company, late 1850s

Charleston Light Infantry cap, 1860

1st Regiment of Artillery, Pennsylvania Militia shako, ca. 1861
(missing pompon)

26

THE SEAMSTRESS AND THE FIRST LADIES

ALTHOUGH MARY LINCOLN AND VARINA DAVIS NEVER met, the first ladies of the United States and the Confederate States were connected through another notable woman: Elizabeth Keckly (1818–1907), the gifted African American seamstress and dressmaker who worked for them both. Keckly used her skill with a needle to purchase her freedom from slavery and, in 1860, moved to Washington, D.C., where she established a successful dressmaking business. The fashionable Varina Davis—whose husband, Jefferson Davis, served in Washington as secretary of war and subsequently as senator from Mississippi before taking charge of the Confederacy—became Keckly's foremost client. Keckly later recalled that she went to the Davis house every afternoon to work for that family of "late risers." She was surprised when Varina invited her to leave Washington with the Davises, who took up residence at the Confederate White House in Richmond in the summer of 1861. Keckly chose not to return to Virginia, where she had been born into slavery, and decided instead "to cast my lot among the people of the North."

Keckly's reputation as Varina Davis's dressmaker, and her promise of fine work at reasonable rates, won her the job as Mary Todd Lincoln's "modiste," fulfilling a cherished ambition to work at the White House in Washington. Addressed as "Lizabeth" by the first lady and as "Madame Elizabeth" by the president, Keckly became a valued and trusted member of the Lincoln household. For the next four years, she shared daily intimacies with the first family as she brushed the president's hair before

receptions and helped care for his dying son, Willie. But it was Mary who relied on her most. While fashioning clothes for the first lady and dressing her, Keckly soothed Mary, who fretted about money, politics, and Washington gossip, of which she was often the target. Keckly, now a member of the city's black middle class, drew the first lady's attention to the plight of the many impoverished African Americans who flocked to Washington seeking freedom, shelter, or work. At war's end, she traveled with Mary to Richmond and toured the Confederate White House just a week after the Davises evacuated that mansion. The visit took place barely a week before Abraham Lincoln was assassinated. His death cast his widow into mourning so deep and desperate that not even Keckly could do much to comfort her.

Elizabeth Keckly recounted her experiences with the two first ladies in her 1868 memoir, *Behind the Scenes*. Although she wrote the book hoping to shine a sympathetic light on Mary Lincoln, it drew further attention to the former first lady's extravagance and her notorious attempt in 1867 to cover her debts by selling clothes and jewels from her copious White House wardrobe. She felt betrayed by the book's personal revelations. Mary Lincoln never again spoke to the woman she had once called "my best and kindest friend." ⚜ LKG

WHITE HOUSE COUTURIER *Elizabeth Keckly, pictured around 1890, received President Lincoln's inkwell (INSET) from Mary Lincoln, for whom she made this purple velvet dress (OPPOSITE).*

VARINA DAVIS *Shortly before her husband became leader of the Confederate States, Varina Davis (1826–1906), portrayed at right in 1849, told a friend: "I would rather remain in Washington and be kicked about, than go south and be Mrs. President." Although she played her role as the South's first lady dutifully, her abiding affection for friends and relatives on the Union side led some to question her devotion to the Confederacy. After the war, the Davises became embodiments of the "Lost Cause." Her jewels (BELOW), including a crown-shaped ruby brooch presented to her by the Women of the Confederacy in 1902, reinforced the image of fallen Southern royalty.*

Diamond and ruby brooch

Howell crystalline wedding set of necklace, brooch, and bracelet

Emerald and diamond engagement ring

MARY TODD LINCOLN "I must dress in costly materials," the first lady told Elizabeth Keckly. "The people scrutinize every article that I wear with critical curiosity." Indeed, Mary Lincoln (1818–1882), pictured at right by Mathew Brady in 1861, drew scathing criticism. Her manners, clothing, costly accessories (BELOW), and Confederate relatives in Kentucky were all fodder for gossip. Meanwhile, her charitable acts, including visits to wounded soldiers and support for African American war refugees, went unnoticed. Even after her husband's death, public sympathy was tempered by the belief that she was not conducting herself as Abraham Lincoln's widow should.

MRS. LINCOLN.

Entered according to Act of Congress in the year 1861, by M. B. Brady, in the Clerk's office of the District Court of the U.S. for the So. District of New-York.

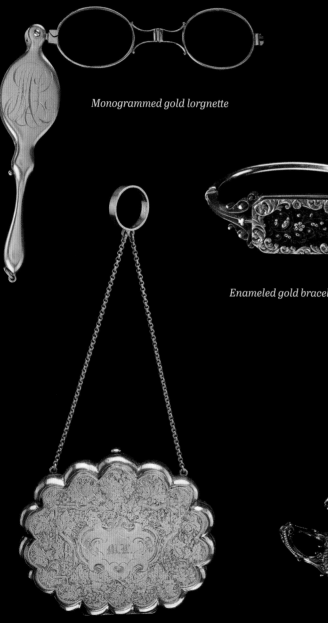

Monogrammed gold lorgnette

Enameled gold bracelet watch

Monogrammed gold evening purse

Silver coffee and tea service

CONFEDERATE MONEY MADE IN NEW YORK

CONFEDERATE AUTHORITIES WERE WELL AWARE that money is an emblem of sovereignty and that proclaiming their independence meant producing their own currency. Yet the first paper money they issued was not produced in the South, and that did not bode well for the future fortunes of this aspiring nation.

When secession occurred, Southerners were using U.S. and foreign coins for many transactions, and those coins remained legal tender in the Confederacy. The new government did not anticipate much need for paper currency and ordered an initial printing of only a million dollars' worth. The notes would pay interest at 3.65 percent per annum and would function more like bonds than like bills, as indicated by their large denominations: $50, $100, $500, and $1,000 (above). They were issued from Montgomery, Alabama, the first Confederate capital, but were engraved and printed in New York City by the National Bank Note Company, which had an expertise and reputation that no Southern company then could match.

Once the war began, Northern companies were forbidden to do business with the South. The embattled Confederacy soon required more currency and had to print notes within its borders. New firms arose to fill that need, including the Southern Bank Note Company in New Orleans, formerly a branch of the New York–based American Bank Note Company.

The Confederacy as a whole, however, lagged far behind the Union economically. Unable to raise enough revenue to finance its costly war effort, the Confederate treasury tried to cover the deficit by issuing vast amounts of paper money that rapidly depreciated. Counterfeit Confederate notes smuggled in from the North added to the glut, resulting in ruinous inflation. A nation that first had to prove its sovereignty by issuing money created in the heart of enemy territory went on to produce homemade currency, but it was all but worthless by war's end. ✛ RD

TOP NOTE *The highest-denomination currency issued by the Confederacy, this $1,000 note was engraved and printed in New York in 1861. Pictured are Senator John C. Calhoun of South Carolina (*LEFT*) and President Andrew Jackson of Tennessee (*RIGHT*), under whom Calhoun served as vice president for one term.*

28

THE BOWIE KNIFE

BOWIE KNIVES LIKE THE ONE AT RIGHT, LOST BY A Confederate in battle, were traditional in the South. Named for legendary frontiersman Jim Bowie, who wielded a weapon of this sort in a famous fight in Mississippi in 1827 and later died in Texas at the Alamo, the bowie knife was used for hunting and butchering as well as close combat. Such was its popularity that large numbers were manufactured in Britain for export to the United States. By 1861, Samuel Colt's revolver surpassed it as a sidearm, but many Confederates and some Federals carried bowie knives when they went to war and used them as tools in camp and as weapons of last resort. During the First Battle of Bull Run in July 1861, Louisianans known as "Tigers," led by Major Roberdeau Wheat, threw down their muskets, which took time to reload, and charged their startled foes with bowie knives in hand.

The knife shown here belonged to a member of another Louisiana outfit also known as "Tigers"—the Fifth Company, Washington Artillery of New Orleans. Named for George Washington, that volunteer artillery battalion originated in the early 1800s and fought in the Mexican War. In the years leading up to the Civil War, service in the Washington Artillery was popular among wealthy young men in New Orleans. That helps explain why such a well-crafted, costly bowie knife, with a foot-long blade that could be honed to razor sharpness, was carried by an artilleryman in the Fifth Company. The Fifth joined General Braxton Bragg's Confederate Army of the Mississippi in 1862 before it entered battle at Perryville, Kentucky, on October 8. Eighteen of the Tigers were killed or wounded there. The soldier who owned this knife probably lost it as the company pulled back hastily from its position under pressure from Union troops, one of whom recovered the weapon after the Confederates withdrew. The Washington Artillery outlasted the Civil War. It eventually became the 141st Field Artillery Regiment and is now part of the Louisiana National Guard. Its unit insignia still bears the snarling face of a tiger and the motto, "Try Us." ✢ DDM

A FIGHTING EDGE *Bowie knives similar to this one, found with its sheath at Perryville, Kentucky, were purchased and often carried into battle by Confederates, few of whom were issued revolvers as sidearms.*

A CALL TO ARMS

I N 1861 THE AMERICAN PEOPLE, NOW FIRMLY DIVIDED into two hostile camps, experienced the greatest outbreak of war fever in their history. "I never knew what a popular excitement can be," wrote Harvard professor George Ticknor. "The whole population, men, women, and children, seem to be in the streets with Union favors and flags." In Goldsboro, North Carolina, British journalist William H. Russell witnessed a raucous celebration when news arrived that Fort Sumter had fallen. Revelers with flushed faces and wild eyes yelled hurrah "for 'Jeff Davis' and the 'Southern Confederacy,'" he reported. "Here was the true revolutionary furor in full sway."

Tens of thousands of Northerners and Southerners, more than had served in any previous American conflict, eagerly answered the call to arms. Volunteers on both sides believed that they were defending their country against aggression. James A. Garfield of Ohio, whose decision to fight for the Union would later help propel him to the presidency, thought the North had no other choice after Southerners opened fire at Charleston than to subjugate the rebellious Confederacy. "I hope we will never stop short of complete subjugation," he wrote. "Better to lose a million men in battle than allow the government to be overthrown."

Confederates like Charles C. Jones of Georgia, on the other hand, viewed Abraham Lincoln as the aggressor because he denied the right of Southerners to secede, as American colonists did from the British Empire in 1776. "Can you imagine a more suicidal, outrageous, and exasperating policy than that inaugurated by the fanatical administration at Washington?" Jones wrote his parents after enlisting at Savannah. "Heaven

forbid that they ever attempt to set foot upon this land of sunshine . . . and of liberty."

Another motive for enlistment was the desire of young men on both sides to prove their courage and conviction to friends and neighbors who volunteered with them, to local leaders who organized their regiments, and to the public at large. Many immigrants from Ireland and Germany, hoping to gain full recognition as American citizens, joined the Union Army. Few men in the North volunteered to help win liberty or citizenship for slaves. But many fought to preserve free labor on free soil and defeat the "slaveocracy," or Southern planters and politicians who hoped to extend slavery across the continent.

Most Americans had a romantic image of war not yet dashed by the harsh realities of life in squalid camps and death on dismal battlefields. In time, enlistments would decline and both sides would resort to conscription. For now, however, the opposing armies had no trouble filling their ranks with volunteers. Lincoln speculated on why so many rushed to enlist and cited among the reasons "patriotism, political bias, ambition, personal courage, love of adventure, want of employment, and convenience." Whether to repel an invasion, protect the homeland, or preserve the Constitution, the Confederate and Union volunteers of 1861 felt compelled to enlist to fulfill a duty to themselves and their country. ✢ RL

FRESH RECRUITS *Like the Union soldier in this portrait, which features a hand-tinted U.S. flag, thousands of volunteers posed for photographs in uniform after enlisting. Some answered appeals like the broadside above, issued by Colonel Joshua T. Owen, who raised a regiment in Philadelphia to serve in Colonel Edward Baker's brigade.*

30

PATRIOTIC PRINTS FOR THE UNIONISTS

CIVILIANS TRYING TO VISUALIZE THE CIVIL WAR AS IT UNFOLDED HAD access to photographs but obtained some of their most dramatic and colorful views of the conflict through lithography, a printing process using stones or metal plates to impress designs in ink on paper. Inexpensive, mass-produced lithographs or chromolithographs (color prints) graced many parlor walls during the Civil War and served as conspicuous displays of patriotism. Often purchased by women, whose domestic duties routinely included decorating the home, they provided family members with constant reminders of the cause for which their men in uniform were fighting. Most were printed in Northern cities such as Boston, Hartford, New York, and Philadelphia. These prints were often proudly pro-Union like the chromolithograph at right, originally published as a sheet-music cover for an updated version of the old song "Yankee Doodle," which remained wildly popular during the Civil War.

> *I know only two tunes: one of them*
> *is "Yankee Doodle," and the other isn't.*
>
> **ULYSSES S. GRANT**

Many lithographs celebrated military heroes and martyrs or indulged in other forms of flag-waving. To follow progress on the battlefield, civilians were able to obtain a few maps featuring useful charts or panoramas, including bird's-eye views inspired by the ballooning craze. Elaborate prints such as the "Union Military Chart" (overleaf) combined patriotic emblems like the U.S. Capitol with enough geographical detail to allow people to follow the progress of distant campaigns. For the most part, however, lithographers were less concerned with informing the public than with inspiring them. Their battle scenes sheltered viewers from the harsh realities of combat by minimizing the gore and maximizing the glory. ✛ DSJ

YANKEE VOLUNTEERS MARCHING INTO DIXIE *In this print by Boston lithographer John Henry Bufford, a Union officer leads recruits dressed as Uncle Sam in red, white, and blue to war. In addition to serving as a sheet-music cover for "Yankee Doodle," Bufford's 1862 chromolithograph was published for display in homes and recruitment halls. This print and those on the next two pages are from the Harry T. Peters "America on Stone" lithographic collection at the National Museum of American History. About one-third of the 1,686 prints in the collection were produced during the Civil War or soon afterward as commemoratives.*

J.H. BUFFORD'S, LITH. BOSTON.

KEE VOLUNTEERS MARCHING INTO DIXIE.

"YANKEE DOODLE KEEP IT UP, YANKEE DOODLE DANDY."

PUBLISHED BY C.F. MORSE 456 PENN. AY WASHINGTON CITY, & G.A. MORSE 13 COURT ST. BOSTON.

UNION MILITARY CHA

HARDEE'S TACTICS.

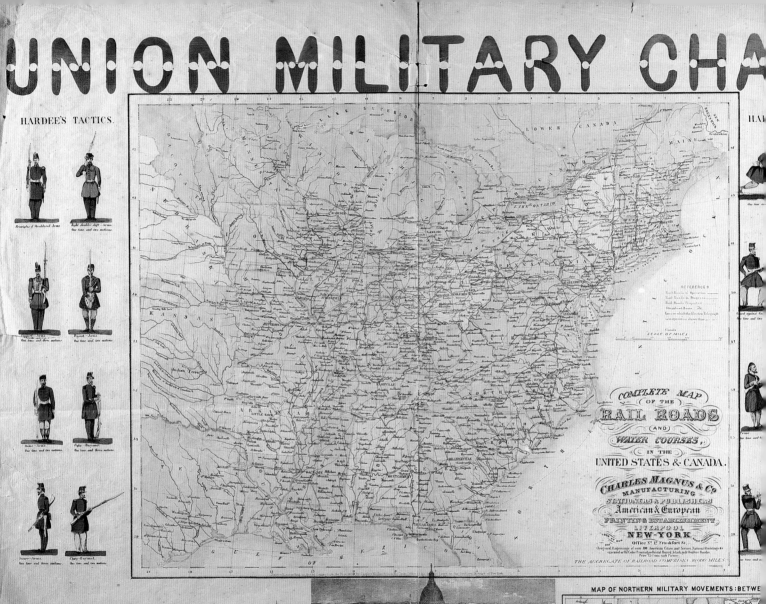

COMPLETE MAP
OF THE
RAIL ROADS
AND
WATER COURSES
IN THE
UNITED STATES & CANADA.

CHARLES MAGNUS & Co.
MANUFACTURING
STATIONERS & PUBLISHERS
American & European
PRINTING ESTABLISHMENT,
LIVERPOOL
NEW-YORK
Office No 12 Frankfort St.

THE AGGREGATE OF RAILROAD COMPRISES 30,000 MILES.

HARDEE'S TACTICS

MILITARY MAP OF MARYLAND & VIRGINIA.

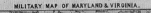

MAP OF NORTHERN MILITARY MOVEMENTS : BETWE

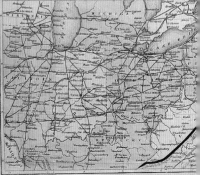

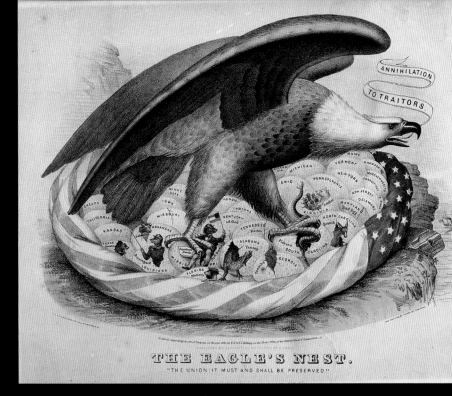

THE EAGLE'S NEST.
"THE UNION IT MUST AND SHALL BE PRESERVED."

BATTLE OF BULL'S RUN, VA, JULY 21ST 1861.
Colonel Corcoran leading the gallant "Sixty Ninth" to the charge on the Rebel Batteries

UNION MILITARY CHART *Published in New York in 1861 by Charles Magnus & Co., this functional and decorative print (FAR LEFT) features an 1859 map of the eastern United States and four smaller charts, including one of Pensacola, Florida, where Union troops aided by the U.S. Navy held Fort Pickens. Adorning the print are illustrations from* Hardee's Tactics *(by former West Point commandant William Hardee, who joined the Confederates) and allegorical figures of Liberty and Justice next to the U.S. Capitol, envisioned with its dome completed.*

THE EAGLE'S NEST *In this 1861 political cartoon printed by lithographers E. B. and E. C. Kellogg of Hartford, Connecticut (LEFT, TOP), an eagle perches on a nest made from a U.S. flag and filled with thirty-four eggs representing all the states claimed by the Union as war loomed. Northern eggs remain intact while Southern eggs are cracking and disgorging noted secessionists. The print's subtitle is from an 1830 toast by President Andrew Jackson: "The Union! It Must and Shall Be Preserved."*

BATTLE OF BULL'S RUN *The Kelloggs firm made another print after the bitter Union defeat at Bull Run in July 1861 (left, bottom). This lithograph offers Northerners solace by portraying Colonel Michael Corcoran on horseback during that battle, holding aloft the emerald flag of the 69th Regiment, New York State Militia and urging his men forward in a heroic charge. Wounded and captured, Corcoran was released in 1862 and hailed as a hero before he died the following year.*

31

THE DEATH OF ELLSWORTH

No UNION OFFICER WAS CLOSER TO HIS commander in chief when the war began than twenty-four-year-old Elmer E. Ellsworth (1837–1861), colonel of the New York City 1st New York Fire Zouaves and a frequent guest at the White House. Abraham Lincoln "loved him like a younger brother," wrote presidential secretary John Hay. A charismatic drillmaster who clerked in Lincoln's law office in Illinois before raising his brightly clad regiment of firefighters in New York City, Ellsworth figured prominently when several thousand Union troops advanced from Washington, D.C., into northern Virginia to occupy Alexandria and environs on May 24, 1861, one day after Virginians voted to secede. He and his Zouaves, now designated the 11th New York Infantry, crossed the Potomac River by boat and reached the Alexandria wharf at dawn. Goaded by the sight of a large Confederate flag flying over the Marshall House on King Street, Ellsworth entered the hotel with Corporal Francis E. Brownell and several other soldiers, made his way to the rooftop, and pulled down the banner. He was descending the staircase with flag in hand when the innkeeper, James W. Jackson, confronted him with a shotgun and killed him instantly with a blast to the chest. Jackson was then shot and bayoneted to death by Brownell.

Reports of Ellsworth's death at the hands of an ardent secessionist caused a sensation throughout the North. Church and fire bells tolled, and flags flew at half-mast to honor the first Union officer killed during the Civil War. As Lincoln stood with other mourners before Ellsworth's open casket in the East Room of the White House, he was heard to say: "My boy! My boy! Was it necessary that this sacrifice be made?"

Throughout the conflict, Ellsworth's name, face, and martyrdom were memorialized on stationery and in patriotic lithographs and sheet music. After the war, Francis Brownell petitioned Congress on his own behalf for the Medal of Honor. In 1877 he received the coveted medal, which he later bequeathed to the Smithsonian Institution, along with the weapon he used to cut down Ellsworth's assailant (overleaf). ✣ JGB

MARTYR'S SHRINE *The Marshall House (LEFT), a run-down hotel described as "the resort of rowdies and loafers," became a mecca for sightseers after the Ellsworth-Jackson shootings. Thousands of Union soldiers passing through Alexandria toured the site, and many carried away relics from the building.*

REQUIEM *Among many tributes to the deceased Ellsworth was the "Funeral March" (OPPOSITE), published as sheet music in Philadelphia in 1861. Pictured wearing Union blue and Zouave red in a chromolithograph based on a portrait by Mathew Brady, Ellsworth is treading on the artist's rendition of the Confederate national flag.*

COL. ELLSWORTH.

FUNERAL MARCH.

Philadelphia, LEE & WALKER, 722 Chesnut St

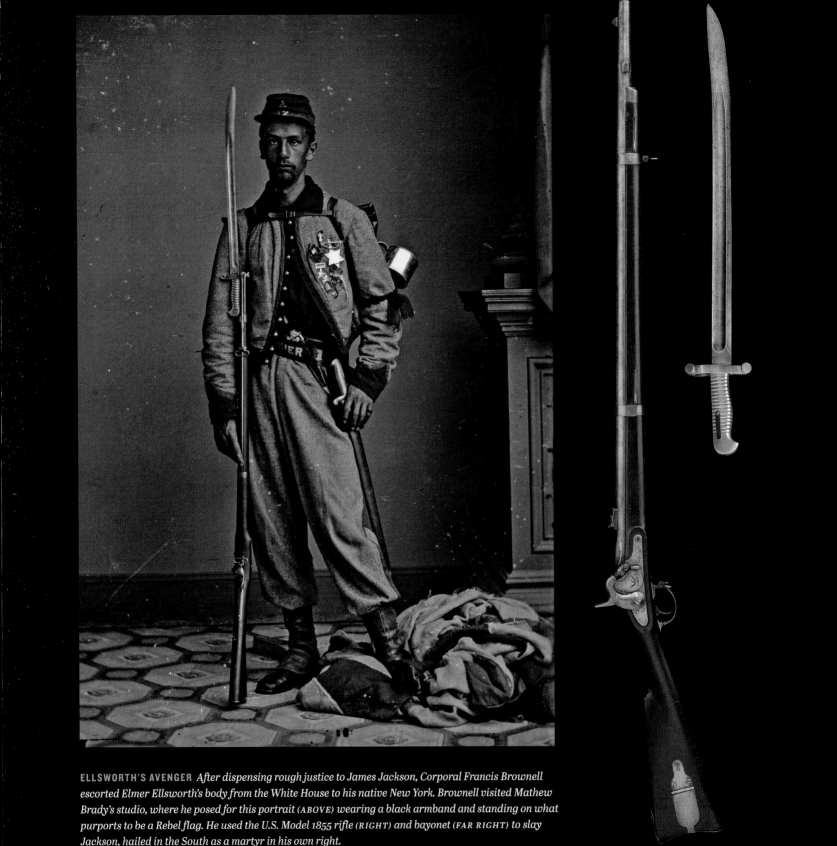

ELLSWORTH'S AVENGER *After dispensing rough justice to James Jackson, Corporal Francis Brownell escorted Elmer Ellsworth's body from the White House to his native New York. Brownell visited Mathew Brady's studio, where he posed for this portrait (ABOVE) wearing a black armband and standing on what purports to be a Rebel flag. He used the U.S. Model 1855 rifle (RIGHT) and bayonet (FAR RIGHT) to slay Jackson, hailed in the South as a martyr in his own right.*

DASHING ZOUAVES

THOUSANDS OF CIVIL WAR SOLDIERS ON BOTH sides wore colorful and distinctive Zouave uniforms inspired by the exotic outfits of French North African troops. The original Zouaves were mountain-dwelling Berbers recruited by the French in the 1830s as they occupied and colonized Algeria. There, as elsewhere in the nineteenth century, imperial forces interacted with frontier inhabitants in ways that altered the customs and material culture of both groups. The valiant Zouaves and their alluring costume greatly impressed French soldiers, who eventually took the place of Algerians in Zouave regiments but retained a uniform based on that of the original Berber recruits. The uniform consisted of a short jacket, baggy trousers, and a tasseled fez. Local women who served them as sutlers, laundresses, and cooks also wore Zouave jackets.

The dashing Zouave units in their colorful North African dress won international renown when they joined Anglo-French forces fighting Russian troops in the Crimea in the mid-1850s. Correspondents and artists covering the Crimean War publicized their fighting spirit and their sartorial flair, triggering a Zouave craze that reached the United States in the late 1850s and added a new dimension of "orientalism" to American popular culture. Zouave figures were portrayed by renowned artists such as Winslow Homer and Eugène Delacroix and proliferated in the decorative arts, photography, and theater. Elmer E. Ellsworth helped spread the cult after encountering Frenchman Charles DeVilliers, a former Zouave officer who came to America as a fencing instructor. Ellsworth transformed an obscure volunteer militia company in Chicago into the flashy U.S. Zouave Cadets, who went on tour in 1860 and performed precision drills, often defeating rival drill clubs. A reporter who watched them dazzle crowds in New York City wrote: "Their bronzed features, sharp outlines, light, wiry forms, muscular developments and spirited, active movements, give them an appearance of dashing ferocity."

By the time Ellsworth entered the Union Army as colonel

of the New York City 1st New York Fire Zouaves and was killed in May 1861, numerous Zouave units had enrolled to fight for the North or the South. Enthusiasm for the cult receded in the Confederacy, largely because manufacturing the fancy uniforms proved too costly there, but it persisted in the North. In 1864 the Union Army of the Potomac fielded an entire Zouave Brigade. Soon after the conflict ended, the War Department exhibited Union Zouave uniforms in a celebratory retrospective at the Schuylkill Arsenal in Philadelphia. Those uniforms, sampled above and on the following pages, are held now at the National Museum of American History and testify to a heroic era when soldiers flaunted their colors not just by waving flags but by donning conspicuously colorful outfits. ✚ MV

ZOUAVE JACKET *This wool jacket was worn by a member of the 41st New York Infantry Regiment, also known as the DeKalb Zouaves, composed of German immigrants from New York and Pennsylvania.*

Prewar Zouave militia units wore various outfits, and wartime Zouave regiments often chose uniforms without regard for army regulations or what other Zouaves favored. The basic outfit consisted of a tasseled fez, a short jacket and vest, a sash around the waist, baggy trousers, and leggings. Many units wore some but not all of those items, and regimental variations resulted in a colorful array of Zouave garb.

Zouave wool jacket and trousers

Red felt fez

Blue felt fez

Red felt fez with white turban

Sash from uniform of the 155th Pennsylvania Infantry Regiment Zouaves

62nd New York Zouave jacket

155th Pennsylvania Zouave jacket

HOMER'S ZOUAVE An 1864 drawing by Winslow Homer portrays a soldier of the 5th New York Infantry, known as Duryée's Zouaves for Colonel Abram Duryée. These jackets are from the 62nd New York Infantry (RIGHT, TOP)—known as the Anderson Zouaves for Major Robert Anderson of Fort Sumter fame—and the 155th Pennsylvania Infantry Regiment (RIGHT, BOTTOM), part of the Zouave Brigade.

Vivandière skirt

WOMEN IN UNIFORM *Some Zouave regiments provided uniforms to vivandières— women who sold food and drink to soldiers and sometimes aided the wounded. The basic outfit was a knee-length skirt, worn over trousers, as well as a tunic or jacket and a hat. These examples of vivandière clothing display the red-and-blue color scheme favored by Union Zouaves.*

PLAYING SOLDIER *In this photograph (OPPOSITE), produced around 1863 when the Zouave craze in the North had yet to subside, three boys appear in Zouave uniforms against the painted backdrop of a Union tent.*

Vivandière uniform, with skirt over trousers

WARTIME PHOTOGRAPHY

I N THE 1850S NEW PHOTOGRAPHIC PROCESSES MADE PRODUCING PICTURES less expensive and allowed multiple prints to be made. Photography became a more flexible and accessible medium, enabling many people during the Civil War to obtain portraits of friends and family members and visualize the conflict by collecting prints of leading figures and landmarks.

By 1861 the daguerreotype process—which typically involved exposure times of fifteen seconds or more and produced images on silver-coated copper plates that could not be reproduced—had largely given way to the wet collodion process. A viscous solution produced by dissolving guncotton in ether and alcohol, collodion could be poured onto a glass plate, which was then immersed in silver nitrate to make it light sensitive and inserted into a camera like the one shown here, with a cap over the lens to prevent exposure. The photograph had to be taken while the collodion was still wet, but the exposure time was reduced to several seconds, which was not quick enough

> *The camera is the eye of history.*
>
> **MATHEW BRADY**

to portray people in motion without blurring the image but did eliminate the need for long poses. The image on the glass plate was a negative, which the photographer could keep or discard by scraping off the collodion. Glass negatives were used to print positive images on albumen paper (coated with a light-sensitive mixture including egg whites) or were placed against a dark background to produce ambrotypes, which appeared positive. Collodion could also be poured onto iron plates, used to produce tintypes—positive images that required no printing. Itinerant photographers who turned out quick, inexpensive portraits for soldiers and civilians favored tintypes. Other photographers who visited camps and battlefields produced glass negatives, which they sent to studios for printing. Advances in equipment and technology enabled photographers to venture out and capture great events as they unfolded. In the words of Mathew Brady, the camera was now "the eye of history." ✦ STP

FIELD CAMERA *Although large and cumbersome by today's standards, field cameras and lenses like those at left let photography move outside of the studio and into the landscape, allowing for the creation of images seared into our collective memories. The wet-plate collodian process required wet and dry chemicals and processing trays to prepare the plates and develop the negatives. Photographers also needed plenty of water onsite.*

34

PORTRAITS TO KEEP LOVED ONES CLOSE

THE EXCITEMENT OF HAVING ONE'S PORTRAIT taken and the desire to share portraits with friends and family acquired new meaning and urgency with the onset of the Civil War. The pride many men in uniform felt when they visited a photographer's studio mingled with the somber thought that the photograph might be the last image their loved ones would have to remember them by. Soldiers also held portraits of their loved ones close when they headed off for battle.

The power of portraits to hold couples and families together visually even as they were being forced apart by war was enhanced by the development of ambrotypes, tintypes, and photographs on paper, which made obtaining portraits convenient and affordable for Americans of modest means. The frames and cases in which portraits made during the Civil War were set served not just to protect those images but to preserve couples and families as a symbolic unit when their members were far apart. The four photographs shown opposite were produced separately, but placing those portraits together, with links between the frames, kept those family members united in spirit, if not in reality.

While war photographers like those from Mathew's Brady's studio ventured out in wagons that served as portable darkrooms and produced negatives on glass plates that had to be printed elsewhere, itinerant tintype photographers set up their own darkrooms at military camps and produced portraits of soldiers on the spot for a small price. Many tintypes were sold in inexpensive frames, but some were purchased and sent home by troops uncased. Mailbags rattled with those metal pictures, whose sharp edges occasionally sawed through the paper envelopes.

Soldiers often went into battle with portraits of loved ones, worn around their necks or carried in their pockets or wallets. A British journalist who was touring America, George Augustus Sala, wrote in his diary of attending an exhibit at which Mathew Brady presented photographs taken by Alexander Gardner at Antietam soon after the horrific battle there on September 17, 1862. "Here before me, is one of Mr. Gardner's photographs representing a dead soldier on the field of Antietam," Sala noted. "A shell has caught him in the middle, ripped him up and scattered his bowels about." Sala noticed that the dead soldier was wearing a locket around his neck and commented: "The locket contains, perchance, the portrait of a mother, sister, sweetheart, or rubbish of that kind."

Such "rubbish" was in fact often as dear to a soldier as his own life and limbs. Writing from a military hospital late in the war, Alfred Janson Bloor, an assistant secretary for the U.S. Sanitary Commission, told of encountering a seventeen-year old soldier who had clung to his mother's portrait despite being gravely wounded in battle—and who still held her image close in his one remaining hand. ✣ STP

HELD TOGETHER *Friends and kin who were too far apart during the war to gather in a photographer's studio like the family above could bring their framed pictures together in one case like the four unidentified family members opposite, including a young man in uniform, portrayed in a tintype.*

35

COLLECTING CARTES-DE-VISITE

T HE STRUGGLE BETWEEN NORTH AND SOUTH WAS FOLLOWED WITH great interest at home and abroad, where portraits of the leading players helped those far from the action picture figures they read about in newspapers. The album shown here was kept by Karl Schenk, who became president of Switzerland in 1865. It contains small portraits known as *cartes-de-visite* because they were about the size of calling cards people presented at the door when visiting fashionable residences. Introduced in the late 1850s, when a process was devised for making multiple prints from a single glass negative, they functioned mainly as collectables to be preserved in albums.

> *The Photograph Album has become a necessity. . . . Soon we will have among us complete panoramas of passing humanity.*
>
> **ADVERTISEMENT BY STRICKLAND & COMPANY IN MILWAUKEE, 1865**

Schenk's album contains pictures of Abraham Lincoln and many other Northern political and military leaders as well as some of their Southern counterparts. Jefferson Davis appears here in a formal portrait taken by Mathew Brady along with seven prominent officers who served under him, including the elusive "Gray Ghost," John Singleton Mosby. One can imagine Schenk with newspapers, maps, and the album spread out before him, seeking to comprehend the sprawling conflict under way in America.

Cartes-de-visite were not limited to portraits of the famous. Ordinary people obtained multiple copies of their own likenesses to share with acquaintances, who collected them along with pictures of celebrities. An advertisement in 1862 for an album sold by Appleton & Company boasted that it would be "easy for the purchaser to fill all the niches, not reserved for family and friends, with a choice of the notabilities of the time." Another ad suggested that collecting pictures was now a national pastime: "The Photograph Album has become a necessity . . . Soon we will have among us complete panoramas of passing humanity, royal and humble, famed and unknown." ✢ STP

COLLECTOR'S BEQUEST *Shown here in Karl Schenk's portrait album are Jefferson Davis, Robert E. Lee, Joseph Johnston, James Longstreet, John Bell Hood, John H. Morgan, John B. Magruder, and John S. Mosby. Schenk's son Fritz gave the album to General Charles Hodges, a Civil War veteran, whose niece, Aileen Taylor, donated it to the Smithsonian in 1951.*

Lee.   Johnston.   Longstreet.

Morgan.   Magruder.   Moseby.

36

PIONEERING PHOTOJOURNALISTS

WHILE MANY PHOTOGRAPHERS DID A BRISK business during the Civil War creating studio portraits of newly uniformed soldiers, others followed armies into the field and served as photojournalists, documenting this struggle on camera in a way that no conflict had ever been covered before. Among those who ventured out was Mathew Brady, arguably the most famous photographer in America, with studios in New York and Washington, D.C. He believed that such images would complement his earlier "Gallery of Illustrious Americans" in providing a historic record of the era. Ever the entrepreneur, he also hoped to reap a financial windfall.

Granted permission to photograph war scenes by Winfield Scott, the head of the Union Army, Brady set out with assistants in a horse-drawn wagon loaded with equipment to join Federal troops led by General Irwin McDowell as they advanced against Confederate forces holding a vital rail junction at Manassas, Virginia. On July 21, 1861, the largest and bloodiest battle yet fought on American soil unfolded along Bull Run, near Manassas. Brady's plans to document the anticipated Union victory there were upset when Confederates rallied and routed their foes, who retreated to Washington in disarray. Amid the chaos, Brady secured a sword from a New York Zouave for protection and made it back to Washington safely, but his nerves were rattled and much of his equipment was lost.

After Bull Run, Brady seldom got close to the action again. Yet he invested much time and money recording the war with the help of the talented photographers he employed. The images that they and other photojournalists produced circulated widely in years to come. By portraying the woeful carnage and destruction left in the wake of battle, they altered the public's understanding of this conflict and of war itself. ✣ FHG

BLASTED BATTLEGROUND *Eight months after the First Battle of Bull Run, two of Mathew Brady's employees, George Barnard and James Gibson, visited the scene and recorded the war-ravaged landscape in photographs such as this one (LEFT), showing a ruined stone bridge across which Union troops had advanced and retreated during the fighting. The bridge was destroyed by Confederate forces when they withdrew from Manassas in March 1862.*

BRADY AFTER BULL RUN *Brady took this self-portrait (OPPOSITE) just after he returned from Bull Run, wearing a sword he acquired as Union troops and spectators fled the scene. Brady never profited as he hoped by documenting the Civil War, but he recouped some expenses by selling his negatives, many of which ended up in the Library of Congress or in Smithsonian collections.*

Photo taken
July 22nd
1861

BRADY
The Photographer
returned from
Bull Run

M. B. Brady,

Wash., D.C.
No. 2.38

LINCOLN'S AIR FORCE

THE UNION ARMY BALLOON CORPS WAS THE FIRST MILITARY aeronautical unit in American history. Thaddeus S. C. Lowe (1832–1913), a New Hampshire native and accomplished balloonist, organized the corps and was its guiding spirit. At the invitation of Smithsonian Secretary Joseph Henry, Lowe met with President Lincoln in June 1861 to discuss balloon reconnaissance, which he demonstrated by making tethered flights near the present site of the National Air and Space Museum. On June 18 Lowe ascended to five hundred feet and wired a message to the White House. "The city with its girdle of encampments presents a superb scene," he signaled Lincoln. "I have pleasure in sending you this first dispatch ever telegraphed from an aerial station." Lincoln was enthusiastic and helped foster the Balloon Corps by prevailing on General Winfield Scott to see Lowe.

> *I have pleasure in sending you this first dispatch ever telegraphed from an aerial station.*
>
> **THADDEUS S. C. LOWE TO ABRAHAM LINCOLN**

Equipped with seven new balloons, wagons carrying hydrogen gas generators to provide lift, and a flat-topped barge that enabled ascents from water, Lowe and the aeronauts he hired performed reconnaissance for Union commanders campaigning in Virginia and elsewhere. They observed enemy movements before and during battles and occasionally took part in the action by helping to direct artillery fire.

Unwilling to rely on the military judgment of civilian aeronauts, Union commanders sometimes ventured aloft themselves or ordered junior officers to do so. One reluctant balloonist in uniform was Lieutenant George Armstrong Custer. Invited to stand up and enjoy the view, the intrepid cavalryman declined. "My confidence in balloons at that time was not sufficient to justify such a course," he explained later, "so that I remained seated in the bottom of the basket with a firm hold upon either side."

Confederates also experimented with balloons, although less successfully than the Union. Lowe's corps remained active until mid-1863 when his increasing difficulties with army bureaucrats led to his departure and brought its operations to an end. ✣ TC

WARTIME AERONAUT *Thaddeus S. C. Lowe stands in a reconnaissance balloon near Richmond, Virginia, during the Battle of Seven Pines (Fair Oaks), which ended on June 1, 1862. Holding the tether lines are men of the 4th Maine Infantry, who were trained to assist Lowe.*

Will Lieut. Genl. Scott please see Profesor Lowe, once more about his balloon?

July 25, 1861,   A. Lincoln

PRESIDENTIAL ORDER *When Winfield Scott showed little interest in Thaddeus Lowe's proposal to conduct aerial reconnaissance for the Union Army, Abraham Lincoln sent Scott the note above, directing the general to see "Professor Lowe," an unofficial title he acquired as an aerial showman before the war.*

AERONAUTICAL INSTRUMENTS *Lowe used the barometer at left to gauge his altitude and the binoculars below to observe enemy positions and movements. He was often accompanied by high-ranking Union officers or linked telegraphically to ground stations that relayed his reports to commanders.*

A tethered balloon overlooks Confederate fortifications at Yorktown, Virginia, in this depiction by artist Arthur Lumley, who based the scene on an ascent he made with Lowe in April 1862 during Union General George McClellan's advance on Richmond.

PROUD PROFILE *Lowe stands beside his horse, binoculars slung over his shoulder, in this wartime portrait. At odds with superiors in Washington, D.C., over his expenses and other matters, Lowe resigned in May 1863 and the Balloon Corps was disbanded a short time later.*

38

CONTRABANDS

I
N MAY OF 1861, THREE SLAVES ESCAPED FROM A
Confederate work party near Hampton, Virginia, and
sought sanctuary at Union-held Fort Monroe overlook-
ing strategic Hampton Roads at the mouth of the James
River. The fort's commander, Major General Benjamin Butler,
a shrewd lawyer by trade, refused to return the runaways
to their masters and declared them "contraband of war," or
property confiscated from the enemy, thus suspending their
enslavement without officially emancipating them.

Congress confirmed But-
ler's declaration three months
later and went on to enact a
law in July 1862 stating that
slaves who escaped from owners in rebellious states and
found refuge within Union
lines "shall be forever free of
their servitude." By then, thousands of African Americans
had effectively emancipated
themselves by fleeing to Fort
Monroe or other Union-occupied areas. Eventually, over
400,000 slaves found freedom in that way.

Contrabands, or "freedmen," did not escape menial labor.
Many worked for the Union Army as servants, shovelers, or
washerwomen. Living in crowded contraband camps, they faced
unhealthy conditions but built homes, schools, and churches
and took the first steps toward self-government. ✛ WSP

CONTRASTING VIEWS *In this detail of a photograph (INSET) taken
in occupied Virginia by Alexander Gardner in late 1862, a contraband
named John Henry serves a Union officer much as slaves served
Confederate officers. By contrast, Winslow Homer's 1865 painting
Army Boots depicts two young freedmen employed by the army at
ease between tasks.*

39

KEEPING CONFEDERATES POSTED

WHEN THE CONFEDERACY EMERGED, IT HAD to assert its sovereignty not just by issuing its own currency but by establishing its own postal service—an essential communications network that bound societies and nations together. Postal services conveying information and opinions helped the thirteen original American states combine to stage a revolution and forge a republic. As the United States expanded, so did the U.S. Post Office Department, which became the country's largest employer. When the Civil War began, that department continued to serve Confederate states until May 31, 1861, when U.S. Postmaster General Montgomery Blair suspended service there. Blair also demonetized all U.S. postage issued before the war to prevent Confederates from redeeming stockpiles of stamps for cash to purchase weapons. A nation stitched together by its postal service had come undone.

On June 1 Confederate Postmaster General John H. Reagan officially took charge of the more than 8,000 post offices in the seceded states, but Confederate stamps were not yet available. Some Southern postmasters did without stamps temporarily by marking envelopes as "PAID," while others used provisional stamps, printed locally. The first Confederate postage stamp, issued on October 16, 1861, had a value of five cents and featured Jefferson Davis. Produced by a Southern firm, the stamp was of low quality, so Reagan looked abroad to neutral Great Britain and contracted with Thomas de La Rue & Company of London, which offered finely engraved plates with exquisite detail and good paper for printing stamps.

The Confederacy eventually issued thirteen different stamps, many of them printed in the South as facilities improved there and all of them honoring Southern heroes. Unlike Abraham Lincoln, who did not appear on a U.S. postage stamp until after his death, Jefferson Davis was often depicted on Confederate stamps, which also featured three former U.S. presidents from the South, pictured below: Andrew Jackson, Thomas Jefferson, and George Washington.

A greater challenge for the Confederacy than printing stamps was providing regular mail service, which was disrupted when Union armies invaded the South and the U.S. Navy blockaded its ports. Some ships evaded that blockade and carried mail and freight to and from Southern ports, but other vessels attempting to do so were intercepted. In the spring of 1862 the U.S. warship *Mercedita* overtook the British blockade-runner *Bermuda*, carrying nearly five million Confederate stamps printed in London by Thomas de La Rue & Company, most of which were confiscated by a boarding party from the *Mercedita* and later destroyed. One prize produced by that London firm and seized by the boarding party survived, however—a fine copper printing plate for stamps (overleaf), now held by the Smithsonian National Postal Museum. ✛ CRG & NP

C.S.A. ISSUES *Before Confederate stamps like those at left were issued, Southerners used provisionals such as the five-cent Memphis stamp on a decorative envelope honoring Jefferson Davis (OPPOSITE, TOP). The lower envelope here was mailed from Brest, France, when the C.S.S. Florida docked there, relayed by British ships to Bermuda, carried by a blockade-runner to Wilmington, North Carolina, and forwarded to Marietta, Georgia.*

CONFEDERATE STATES OF AMERICA.
JEFF. DAVIS.
OUR FIRST PRESIDENT.

ADV.

March to the battle field.
The foe is on before us.
Each heart is Freedom's shield,
And Heaven's smile is o'er us.

H. H. Williams.
New Orleans.
La.

Confederate Cruiser Florida.

WILMINGTON
MAY
6

MARIETTA
MAR
11

Fwd 10
2
22

Mrs Wm G. McAdoo,
Marietta, Cobb County
Georgia,
Confederate States of America.
Talmage

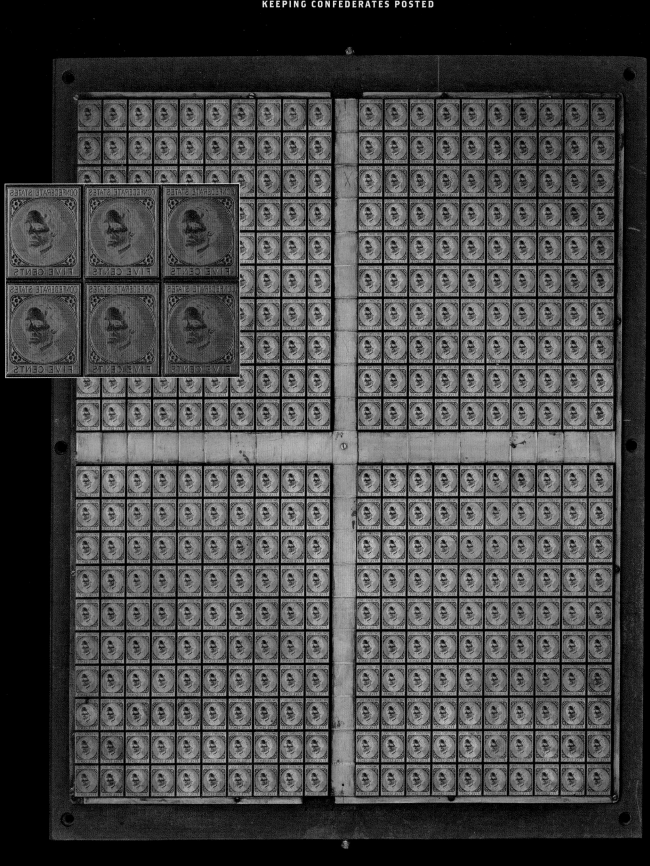

CAPTURED PRIZE *This copper printing plate—designed to produce four panes of one hundred five-cent Jefferson Davis stamps with e*
impression—was destined for Charleston, South Carolina, aboard the Bermuda when it was seized by the U.S.S. Mercedita in 1862.

CLARA BARTON

CLARA BARTON (1821–1912), FOUNDER OF THE American Red Cross, was raised in Massachusetts and began her career in education. After leaving a school she had established, where a man was appointed principal in her stead, she went to Washington, D.C., in 1854. She worked as a clerk and later a copyist at the U.S. Patent Office and she became the first woman to receive a salary equivalent to that of her male counterparts. Although political opposition led to the loss of her position in 1857, she resumed work at the Patent Office in 1860 after Abraham Lincoln's election. In April 1861, when the first trainload of wounded Union troops arrived in Washington, she tended to those Massachusetts volunteers, who had been attacked by secessionists in Baltimore. Following the First Battle of Bull Run, Barton coordinated efforts to aid Union soldiers. In 1862 she received permission to deliver food and medical supplies in wagons to field hospitals on the front lines. "I may be compelled to face danger, but never fear it," she wrote, "and while our soldiers can stand and fight, I can stand and feed and nurse them." Present at Antietam in September 1862, she demonstrated a devotion to the wounded that earned her the title "angel of the battlefield."

By the time Mathew Brady photographed her around 1866, Clara Barton was a notable figure. A series of lectures she delivered between 1866 and 1868, entitled "Work and Incidents of Army Life," enhanced her reputation as a nurse and an organizer of relief efforts. A reporter who heard Barton speak wrote of her "extraordinary powers of description and eloquence." Brady's classic image of her conveys the confidence and determination that enabled her to overcome the barriers to achievement commonly faced by women of her era. ⊹ ACG

AGENT OF MERCY *When Mathew Brady took this picture in Washington, soon after the war ended, Clara Barton was running the Missing Soldiers Office, where she received letters from concerned family members and resolved the fate of more than twenty thousand men.*

I may be compelled to face danger, but never fear it, and while our soldiers can stand and fight, I can stand and feed and nurse them.

CLARA BARTON

41

BERDAN'S SHARPSHOOTERS

WHEN THE CIVIL WAR BEGAN, HIRAM BERDAN—A MECHANICAL engineer, inventor, and expert marksman—proposed forming a unit of sharpshooters made up of volunteers from throughout the Union. To qualify, recruits had to place ten shots within five inches of a bull's-eye at a distance of six hundred feet. Berdan was appointed colonel of the 1st U.S. Sharpshooters in November 1861 and later commanded the 2nd U.S. Sharpshooters.

Berdan wanted his sharpshooters armed with .52-caliber Sharps breech-loading rifles. Instead, the Army Ordnance Department sent him Colt revolving rifles, which could fire five shots without reloading but were less reliable than the single-shot Sharps rifle and unpopular with Berdan's recruits. By his own account, Berdan strengthened his case for the Sharps rifle at a shooting demonstration attended by President Lincoln and General George McClellan. His target bore the image of the Confederate president, and Berdan later remarked that "I did not think it was exactly the thing to fire at Jeff Davis in the presence of the President of the United States. Mr. Lincoln laughed heartily and replied: 'Oh, Colonel, if you make a good shot it will serve him right.'" Berdan fired what he called a lucky shot and hit the target in the eye at six hundred yards. His men were duly equipped with Sharps rifles as requested.

Wearing green uniforms that made them hard to spot amid trees and grass, Berdan's men fought mainly as skirmishers—soldiers who led advances and probed enemy lines for weaknesses, sometimes taking cover and targeting officers or artillerymen. Sharpshooters of exceptional skill were assigned to act independently as snipers (below), using heavy target rifles that could hit their targets up to a thousand yards. ☩ DDM

LONG SHOT *An engraving by Winslow Homer in 1862 shows a sharpshooter with the Army of the Potomac perched in a tree as he targets a distant Confederate through a telescopic sight. Homer stated that such sniping "struck me as being as near murder as anything I could think of in connection with the army and I always had a horror of that branch of the service."*

I remarked that I did not think it was exactly the thing to fire at Jeff Davis in the presence of the President of the United States. Mr. Lincoln laughed heartily and replied: "Oh, Colonel, if you make a good shot it will serve him right."

HIRAM BERDAN

DRESSED TO KILL *Hiram Berdan owned the .52-caliber Sharps New Model 1859 Rifle at left, which he tinkered with and altered during the Civil War. The men of his 1st U.S. Sharpshooters wore the green woolen uniform displayed at right and above, including frock coat, pants, and forage cap. The coat's shiny brass buttons were later replaced with inconspicuous black rubber buttons.*

Hd Qrs, Army in the Field
Camp near Donelson, Feb.y 16th 1862

Gen. S. B. Buckner.
      Confed. Army,
                  Sir,

                  Yours of this date proposing
Armistice, and appointment of Commissioners,
to settle terms of Capitulation is just received.
No terms except an unconditional and immediate
surrender can be accepted.

            I propose to move immediately upon
your works.

                        I am Sir, very respectfully
                        your obt. Svt.
                              U. S. Grant
                              Brig. Gen.

42

THE EMERGENCE OF GRANT

IN FEBRUARY 1862 BRIGADIER GENERAL ULYSSES S. Grant (1822–1885) gave the Union Army its first major victory by capturing Fort Donelson in western Tennessee. That triumph and his earlier seizure of nearby Fort Henry opened up two avenues of invasion into the South, along the Tennessee and Cumberland Rivers. It also gave U. S. Grant a new nickname, "Unconditional Surrender Grant," inspired by the famous letter reproduced opposite. He wrote the letter on February 16 after his forces repulsed an attempt by Confederates to break out of Fort Donelson, prompting General Simon Bolivar Buckner to seek surrender terms from Grant. Buckner had been Grant's comrade in the Mexican War and had loaned him money in hard times. Now, however, Grant stated bluntly in his reply: "No terms except an unconditional and immediate surrender can be accepted. I propose to move immediately upon your works." War was serious business, to be fought aggressively and persistently. Buckner reluctantly accepted what he called Grant's "ungenerous and unchivalrous terms," and surrendered the fort and its fourteen thousand defenders.

Grant's uncompromising stance made him famous, earning him praise throughout the North. President Lincoln promptly promoted him to major general and showed an abiding faith in him in years to come, ultimately elevating him to general in chief of the Union Army. The letter that marked the turning point in Grant's career might have been lost had not his aide-de-camp, Major John Rawlins, noticed it among Buckner's papers following his surrender. Rawlins asked Grant if he could keep it, and Grant, unaware of how large this document would loom in his own life and in the nation's history, assented. Rawlins stored the letter in a trunk in his attic. In 1869, not long before his death, he was speaking of his war experiences with a cousin J. K. Wallace, who asked if Rawlins had a copy of Grant's signature. Rawlins went upstairs, rummaged through his trunk, found the letter, and gave it to Wallace with some good advice: "You had better be careful of that, as it will be valuable some day."

Wallace later sold the letter to Charles L. Webster, nephew of Samuel Clemens. Better known as Mark Twain, Clemens and Webster were publishing Grant's memoirs, which became a best seller and rescued Grant's family from penury after he died. In January 1918 Webster's widow, in accord with his wishes, donated the letter to the Smithsonian. Frustrated because her donation was not constantly on display, she asked in 1932 that it be given back. The staff explained to her that the paper and ink were fragile and that constant display would destroy the letter, which remained thereafter in the Smithsonian's care. Since being donated, the letter has been on view for only short periods, but even that has taken its toll. The lasting historical significance of Grant's demand for unconditional surrender—echoed forcefully by American leaders during World War II—makes this fragile document, written when the country was bitterly divided, a national treasure today. ✧ DKA

TWO-STAR GENERAL *This photograph of Ulysses S. Grant (INSET), wearing two stars as a major general, was taken after he captured Fort Donelson and earned promotion. Little-known when the war began, he won fame with this letter demanding unconditional surrender.*

43

MEN OF PROGRESS

COMMISSIONED IN 1857, CHRISTIAN SCHUSSELE'S painting *Men of Progress* (right) was completed in 1862 and portrays nineteen American technological innovators, several of whom had a significant impact on the Civil War. One late inclusion by Schussele was naval architect John Ericsson (standing just right of the column at center). He engineered the ironclad U.S.S. *Monitor*, which flew the flag below—little of which has survived—during its celebrated duel in March 1862 with the ironclad C.S.S. *Virginia* (converted by Confederates from the salvaged wooden frigate U.S.S. *Merrimack*). Others in this painting were famed for prewar inventions of military importance, including Samuel Colt (standing third from left), whose Hartford armory turned out Colt revolvers and other weapons for the Union. Elias Howe (seated farthest at right) devised the sewing machine,

which helped clothe troops and brought him profits that he used in part to equip a Connecticut regiment in which he served. Schussele pictured Samuel F. B. Morse seated with his right hand on the table beside his telegraph, which proved of great strategic value during the war. Smithsonian Secretary Joseph Henry (standing just left of the column) conducted electrical research that contributed to Morse's invention and quarreled with him over credit for it.

Although they never came together as pictured here, Schussele chose an apt setting for those innovators—the Great Hall of the U.S. Patent Office. That building now houses the National Portrait Gallery, where the painting hangs today. ✛ ACG

HALL OF FAME *Christian Schussele's* Men of Progress *may have been commissioned by New York inventor Jordan Mott (seated just left of the column). A fragment of the flag flown by the U.S.S.* Monitor *(INSET) resides at the National Museum of American History.*

THE WARTIME PATENT OFFICE

T HE LARGEST PUBLIC BUILDING IN EARLY Washington, D.C., the U.S. Patent Office was designed to celebrate and facilitate American invention and science. A fine example of Greek Revival architecture, it provided exhibit space for patent models that inventors submitted, including several that were used during the Civil War (overleaf). The government also exhibited its historical, scientific, and art collections there until they were transferred to the Smithsonian.

> *The Patent Office . . . that noblest of Washington buildings was crowded close with rows of sick, badly wounded and dying soldiers.*
> **WALT WHITMAN**

Early in the war, the building became a barracks for Union soldiers. As the conflict intensified, the building also served as a hospital and morgue for soldiers wounded at Bull Run, Antietam, and Fredericksburg. Poet Walt Whitman helped care for those patients as a volunteer. As he related, "The Patent Office . . . that noblest of Washington buildings was crowded close with rows of sick, badly wounded and dying soldiers." Reformer Dorothea Dix established the first nursing corps to care for wounded soldiers in several buildings in the capital, including the Patent Office. President Lincoln briefly struck a festive note here when he held his second inaugural ball on the third floor in March 1865, a month before his assassination at Ford's Theatre a few blocks away. ✣ PMH & JB

CULTURAL CENTER *Shown around 1865, the Patent Office Building was transferred to the Smithsonian in 1962 and is now home to the National Portrait Gallery and the Smithsonian American Art Museum.*

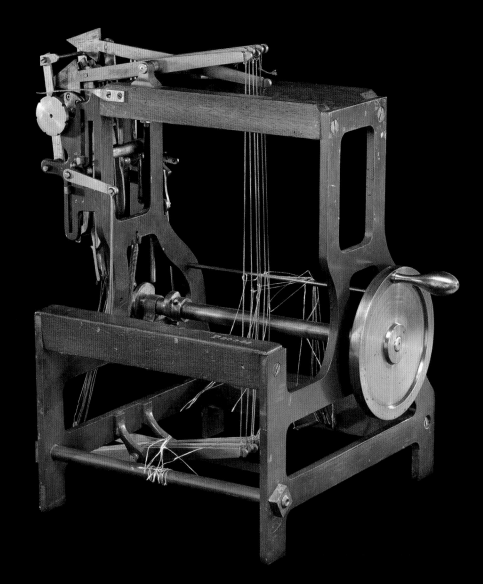

TELEGRAPH *Samuel F. B. Morse was granted a patent in 1846 for his "Improvement in Electro-Magnetic Telegraphs," shown in this model submitted to the U.S. Patent Office (LEFT). Used to send signals in Morse code, which he patented in 1840, his telegraph enabled the instantaneous transmission of news and military dispatches during the Civil War.*

ARTIFICIAL LIMB *Dubois D. Parmelee obtained a patent in 1863 for the artificial leg above, which used a valve to produce suction within a rubber device called a bucket that was molded to fit the patient and kept the artificial limb attached without straps. Some seventy thousand soldiers required prosthetics for injuries received during the Civil War.*

BROAD LOOM *Patented in 1858 by George Crompton of Massachusetts, this efficient broad loom (RIGHT) wove cloth at almost twice the rate of other machines of that type then in use. It helped meet the growing demand for cloth when the Union went to war and had to equip hundreds of thousands of soldiers with uniforms and blankets.*

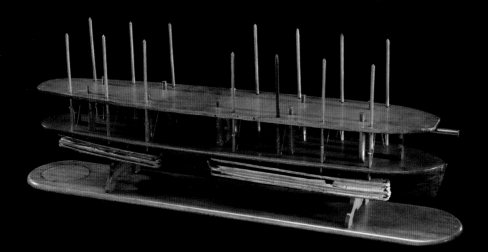

The patent system added the fuel of interest to the fire of genius.

ABRAHAM LINCOLN

LINCOLN'S BRAINCHILD *In 1849 Abraham Lincoln secured patent number 6,469 for a "Method of Buoying Vessels over Shoals." Represented by the model above, the method involved inflating flotation devices at the side of the boat to lift it off shoals. The invention Lincoln proposed was never produced, but he remained a strong advocate for the patent system, which gave inventors a financial interest in the breakthroughs they achieved.*

SEWING MACHINE *Granted patent number 4,750 in 1846, Elias Howe's innovative sewing machine (RIGHT) was used by seamstresses in homes and shops to produce clothing for soldiers during the Civil War. Between 1860 and 1865, the number of sewing machines in the United States nearly doubled.*

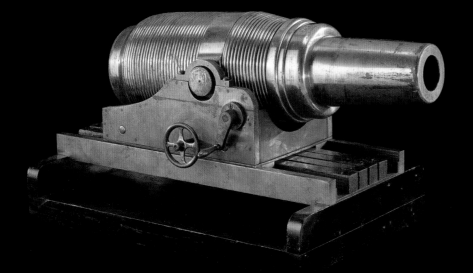

GUN CARRIAGE *John Ericsson, designer of the ironclad U.S.S. Monitor, was granted a patent in 1863 for this improved gun carriage (LEFT). It allowed the cannon to recoil backward in its tracks when fired and was made to be worked by fewer hands within a confined space such as a gun turret. Ericsson obtained another patent in 1864 for a new method of manufacturing guns.*

45

THE UNION'S CONSTRUCTIVE GENIUS

A PRECOCIOUS ENGINEER, HERMAN HAUPT (1817–1905) graduated from West Point at the age of eighteen. He soon left the army to enter the booming business of building railroads, which expanded much faster in the North than in the South. This expansion gave the Union an advantage when the Civil War erupted and troops and supplies had to be transported over long distances. Haupt became chief engineer of the Pennsylvania Railroad and an authority on bridge construction before he returned to duty in April 1862 as a colonel and took charge of the U.S. Military Railroad Construction Corps.

> *That man Haupt has built a bridge ... and, upon my word, gentlemen, there is nothing in it but beanpoles and cornstalks.*
> **ABRAHAM LINCOLN**

One of his first challenges was to build a railroad bridge over Potomac Creek in Virginia to replace a vital span destroyed by Confederates as they withdrew southward. Supervising inexperienced workers, he constructed a trestle bridge with two million feet of timber in nine days. President Lincoln came down from Washington and marveled at the structure, which was stronger than it looked. "That man Haupt has built a bridge across Potomac Creek," he remarked, "about four hundred feet long and nearly one hundred feet high, over which loaded trains are running every hour, and, upon my word, gentlemen, there is nothing in it but beanpoles and cornstalks."

Haupt proved not only a prodigious builder but also a dynamic organizer and administrator. To document his accomplishments and innovations, he turned to Andrew J. Russell (1829–1902), who formed a photographic unit and took the two pictures opposite, showing Haupt in a pontoon boat (top) and his Potomac Creek Bridge (bottom). Those were among the images in Haupt's 1863 manual, *Photographs Illustrative of Operations in Construction and Transportation*, which detailed "experiments made to determine the most practical and expeditious modes to be resorted to in the construction, destruction, and reconstruction of roads and bridges." Published in a limited edition as an album with photos inserted, the manual illustrates Haupt's constructive feats as well as methods he developed to wreck railroad tracks and otherwise deny transportation to the enemy.

For Russell, this was the beginning of a distinguished career as a documentary photographer, one whose pictures taken during and after the war—including a series portraying construction of the Union Pacific Railroad—showed how military and industrial technology altered the American landscape and ultimately reunified the country. Haupt furthered that technological transformation and was eager to resume his peacetime role as a master builder of railroads. A military nonconformist who defied protocol and never officially accepted his commission as a brigadier general, he clashed often with high-ranking commanders before he returned to civil engineering in 1863. Lincoln, who had troubles of his own with stubborn military chiefs, missed Haupt's forceful presence and his businesslike dispatches, which told the president "in the fewest words the information most sought for." ✛ LV

SIGNAL LANTERN *Train crews used this lamp (INSET) to prevent accidents on the U.S. Military Railroad, established in 1862 when the War Department took charge of all Union-controlled railroads. Herman Haupt led its Construction Corps, whose work Andrew J. Russell documented in photos like those at right.*

SAVING OLD GLORY

THE ORIGINAL "OLD GLORY" WAS A LARGE U.S. flag with twenty-four stars. William Driver, a ship captain from Massachusetts, flew it at sea. Driver took his treasured flag with him when he completed his last voyage in 1837 and settled in Nashville, Tennessee, where he raised it on patriotic occasions. He stood by that flag as the Civil War loomed and spurned those Tennesseans who pressed for their state to leave the Union in 1861. According to an account written later by his daughter, Mary Roland, he asked her and her mother to refurbish Old Glory that spring. "It's all going to pieces and needs an overhauling so that it can better weather the breeze," he told them. They updated the number of stars on the flag to thirty-four, and Driver added a white anchor in memory of his days at sea.

In June 1861 Tennessee joined the Confederacy. Driver had the flag sewn inside a quilt to preserve it from harm. As his daughter recalled, secessionists raided his house repeatedly but failed to find the flag. Then on February 25, 1862, following the surrender of Fort Donelson to Ulysses Grant, Union troops occupied Nashville. Driver removed Old Glory from the quilt, carried it through the streets to the state capitol, and hoisted it there with the help of soldiers of the 6th Ohio Infantry.

In 1873 the elderly Driver gave the flag to his daughter, Mary, who cared for it after his death and set down its story in print. She donated it in 1922 to the Smithsonian, where Old Glory has been exhibited and preserved as the forerunner of all the American flags that now bear that proud title. ✠ JLJ

"OLD GLORY" *Measuring ten by seventeen feet and held at the National Museum of American History, "Old Glory" originated as a twenty-four-star flag after Missouri became the twenty-fourth state in 1821 and was refashioned in 1861 with thirty-four stars and an anchor.*

47

TRIBES AT WAR

NATIVE AMERICANS WERE AS DIVIDED BY THE Civil War as the rest of the nation. The two Native Americans who rose to the rank of general during the conflict were on opposing sides. Ely Parker of the Senecas served on Ulysses Grant's staff and was brevetted brigadier general as the conflict ended. Stand Watie of the Cherokees earned that rank earlier as a commander of Indian cavalry in the Confederate Army of the Trans-Mississippi.

No Indian nations were more divided or devastated by the war than those known as the Five Civilized Tribes—Cherokee, Seminole, Creek, Choctaw, and Chickasaw. Native Southerners who had emigrated voluntarily or been removed from homelands east of the Mississippi to the Indian Territory, they included some slave owners. By late 1861 Confederate agent Albert Pike had negotiated treaties with the five tribes, but sizable factions opposed those pacts. Stand Watie and his Confederate warriors ended up at odds with followers of Cherokee Chief John Ross, who went over to the Union. Tensions between those who had accepted removal and those who had resisted it exacerbated conflict within the Cherokee and Creek tribes.

Native Americans elsewhere enlisted to fight for various Union or Confederate states. Catawbas served in three South Carolina regiments, and Iroquois formed a company in the 5th Pennsylvania Infantry. Company K of the 1st Regiment, Michigan Sharpshooters, consisting of Objibwas, Ottawas, and men of other tribes, served under Grant in 1864 at the Wilderness, Spotsylvania, and Petersburg, where they fought in the calamitous Battle of the Crater. "Some of them were mortally wounded," an officer recalled, "and drawing their blouses over their faces, they chanted a death song and died—four of them in a group." ✛ TC

FROM WARRIOR TO CHIEF *Lieutenant Pleasant Porter (LEFT), pictured around 1863 with a Colt pistol in hand, served under General Stand Watie with McIntosh's Creek Volunteers. Although the Civil War set Confederate Creeks like Porter at odds with those who favored the Union or neutrality, he later helped restore tribal unity and became principal chief of the Creek Nation.*

PROUD VETERAN *Like many Native Americans, Joe Tasson (RIGHT) of the Meskwaki (Fox) served as an interpreter during the Civil War. Although the details of his service are unknown, he lived on the Sac and Fox reservation in Tama County, Iowa—where this picture was taken after the war— and probably aided Union officers campaigning in tribal territory.*

THE YOUNG NAPOLEON

B Y THE SPRING OF 1862, MAJOR GENERAL GEORGE B. McClellan (1826–1885) had taken the demoralized Union throng that retreated in disarray from Bull Run the year before and transformed it into the formidable Army of the Potomac, a disciplined force of more than 120,000 men. Great things were expected of this precocious thirty-five-year-old commander, dubbed the "Young Napoleon" by the press and referred to affectionately by his troops as "Little Mac." Trained as an engineer at West Point, where he

graduated second in his class, he served with distinction under General Winfield Scott during the Mexican War and was one of the nation's most promising young officers when he resigned in 1857 to run a railroad, the civilian equivalent of running an army. Not long after he wed Mary Ellen Marcy, the daughter of a former commander, he was summoned to Washington, D.C., to lead the Army of the Potomac. Confident that he was destined for glory, he wrote her proudly: "Who would have thought, when we were married, that I should so soon be called upon to save my country?"

McClellan's exceptional engineering and managerial skills were in evidence as he transported his vast army to Fort Monroe in March 1862 and prepared to advance up the Virginia Peninsula and take Richmond. His men were well organized and well supplied. They were not, however, well used. He greatly overestimated the size of the army opposing him and advanced tentatively, giving his foes time to strengthen defenses around their capital. McClellan's inertia, coupled with his incessant demands for more soldiers, dismayed President Lincoln, who recalled him in July following bloody battles in which Confederates led by Robert E. Lee seized the initiative and drove the Army of the Potomac back from Richmond. Lincoln soon restored McClellan to active command after Lee inflicted another defeat on the Union in the Second Battle of Bull Run and advanced into Maryland. No one could "lick these troops of ours into shape half as well as he," Lincoln remarked of McClellan. "If he can't fight himself, he excels in making others fight." The Young Napoleon would have one last chance to save his country and his reputation at the tumultuous Battle of Antietam. ⊹ KG

A MODEL GENERAL *George McClellan (pictured with his wife) was a small man who loomed large in the eyes of his troops. Among his possessions at the Smithsonian shown opposite are the nonregulation coat, with buttons in groups of three signaling his rank as major general; a Colt Model 1861 Navy revolver, given to him by Samuel Colt; and chess pieces stored in a box engraved with his name.*

If he can't fight himself, he excels in making others fight.

LINCOLN ON MCCLELLAN

49

CHICKAHOMINY FEVER

AS MCCLELLAN'S TROOPS APPROACHED RICHMOND IN 1862, THOUSANDS were felled by disease in swamps along the sluggish Chickahominy River. Colonel Wesley Brainerd, a Union engineer who helped bridge that river, wrote that many of those toiling there contracted so-called "Chickahominy fever, for which there seemed to be no antidote but quinine in immense quantities. The Army lost far more men by this disease than by the bullets of the enemy."

Such costly efforts produced the bridge shown here and other spans, which enabled McClellan's invaders to close in on the Confederate capital. But they themselves were prey to an invisible invader—something noxious that seemed to emanate from the swamp and its foul air, afflicting them with fever and chills. Not until later would scientists determine that this debilitating disease called malaria (meaning "bad air") was in fact caused by a parasite introduced into the bloodstream by mosquitoes. Malaria infected many troops defending Richmond as well. One Confederate recalled how "the big swamp mosquitoes would stick their long bills through our clothes, to get a last farewell taste of our blood."

All that was known at the time was that quinine helped those suffering from malaria get back on their feet. Made from cinchona bark harvested in the Andes, shipped to New York, and processed into pills for Union troops, quinine was scarce in the Confederacy, which had to smuggle that drug and other medicines through the Union blockade. Victims who lacked quinine found that malaria could be a deadly enemy. ✛ DW

PLAGUES OF WAR
For Federals who bridged the Chickahominy River (LEFT) and Confederates who opposed them, falling in battle presented just one risk in a war that exposed soldiers to malaria, dysentery, typhoid, and other diseases afflicting men living in unsanitary camps and unprotected from mosquitoes, flies, and other pests. Quinine, held in tins like the one at center right, was one of the few effective drugs available to troops during the conflict.

In camp '64 & '65

Civil War
1st O.V.A.
Co. B.

Hard-tack

A. B. Hayes
taken winter of '64 & '65
Age 20

50

HARDTACK AND COFFEE

THE MEN CALLED THEM "TEETH-DULLERS," "jaw-breakers," "sheet-iron crackers," and "worm castles." They emerged from the oven as hard as bricks, three-inch square crackers, or hardtack, made with six parts flour to one part water and perforated to speed baking time. Crammed into boxes left outdoors in camp, the crackers were exposed to the elements and often infested with insects. Many Civil War soldiers echoed the familiar complaint that hardtack was "imperishable, indestructible, and practically inedible," but it was often the staple of their diet.

Regulations on both sides called for men to receive varied rations, including beef or pork in either fresh or salted form, beans, rice, vinegar, and sugar. In practice, however, some of those items were often unavailable or reached camp in such poor condition that only someone with more culinary skill than most soldiers possessed could make them palatable. Hardtack became easier to chew when it was dipped or simmered with other ingredients to produce "hell-fired stew." One soldier complained that the vermin lurking in hardtack were "all the fresh meat we had," and added: "I, preferring my game cooked, used to toast my biscuits."

One of the few savory items that soldiers could look forward to was coffee. It was fairly plentiful in the Union Army, although men were often issued green coffee beans, which they had to roast over fire and grind with their rifle butts. Confederate troops frequently had to accept roasted chicory, peanuts, or corn as additives or substitutes for coffee, which grew scarce when Union ships blockaded Southern ports. During lulls in the fighting, Northerners would sometimes fraternize with their foes and barter their coffee beans for Southern tobacco.

Poor rations left some troops malnourished and contributed to diseases such as scurvy and dysentery that afflicted both sides. Efforts were made to improve the diet of soldiers, and by 1863 many Union troops were receiving fresh meat and bread in camp and had to put up with hardtack only when on the march. Even when their food was paltry or barely edible, men took comfort in sharing meals around campfires and found their humble fare a source of amusement if not nourishment. Augustus B. Hayes, who joined the 1st Ohio Light Artillery at the age of seventeen, was one of many soldiers who had his portrait taken in uniform during the war. He distinguished himself, however, by placing that tintype in a unique frame (opposite), fashioned from hardtack issued to him in 1864—a memento preserved by the Smithsonian as a fine example of a soldier making the most of what the army doled out to him. ✛ RL

CULINARY ART *Signed and dated, this hardtack frame made by Augustus Hayes to hold his portrait was an ingenious use of those tough crackers. Shown below is a typical Union soldier's mess kit, including a kettle and tin cup, a twist of tobacco, and bags that held rations of sugar and coffee—prized pick-me-ups that seldom went bad.*

51

UNION INFANTRY GEAR

TO MEET THE DEMAND OF THE FAST-EXPANDING Union Army, the War Department in 1861 awarded contracts for uniforms to various manufacturers. Some maximized their profits by using "shoddy"—a cheap cloth substitute made of glued and pressed fabric scraps—and produced clothing that barely lasted a month. Union soldiers received a monthly uniform allowance of $3.50, which they overspent when their shoddy jackets and trousers fell apart. Arms and equipment issued in the war's first months were often of poor quality as well, including shoddy blankets. Some soldiers received obsolete .69-caliber smoothbore muskets. Others were issued rifle muskets, whose grooved barrels made them more accurate than smoothbores, but troops had to make do with an odd assortment of American and European models until Northern arms makers stepped up production.

By 1862 the supply problems were being remedied. The colorful assortment of militia and locally tailored uniforms worn by Union troops early on gave way to the familiar dark blue coat and sky-blue trousers. Dependable weapons such as the Springfield Model 1861 rifle musket were issued to many infantrymen. Other equipment of good quality was produced, but soldiers still suffered from occasional shortages, sometimes of their own doing. On warm days, inexperienced soldiers might jettison overcoats and other items to lighten their loads. As one private stated, "In the afternoon the heat became so intolerable that I tore off my dress coat and threw it away." But men learned not to dispense with clothing they might need again, and officers eased their burdens by hauling excess gear in baggage trains. ✢ KG

TRUE BLUE *The Union infantryman's standard outfit included the Pattern 1858 forage cap (INSET), a dark blue sack coat (RIGHT, TOP), and sky-blue kersey trousers (RIGHT, BOTTOM).*

Sack coat and trousers

After we had gone three or four miles, the men began to throw off blankets, coats and knapsacks, and towards night the road was strewn with them.

A SOLDIER IN THE 83RD PENNSYLVANIA INFANTRY

Infantryman's Hardee hat

IDENTIFICATION TAG
Union troops sometimes purchased unofficial identification tags like the one at right, with the soldier's name inscribed on the front or back. The U.S. Army did not introduce official I.D. tags until the early 1900s.

Union identification tag

Enlisted man's frock coat

DRESSED UP *In addition to a sack coat and a forage cap, some Union men were issued a frock coat and a Hardee hat like those worn in this portrait of infantryman Thomas Anthony. Like the Hardee hat shown above, his hat is pinned up on his left side to denote infantry, and he wears an enlisted man's single-breasted frock coat.*

EQUIPPED FOR ADVERSITY *Greatcoats like the one at left kept Union infantrymen warm in the winter, and metal canteens like the Model 1861 below helped slake their thirst on the march. When battle loomed, many Northern troops relied on the Model 1861 Springfield rifle musket, to which a bayonet could be attached.*

Model 1861 canteen

Model 1855 bayonet

Union infantry greatcoat

SOLDIER'S LUGGAGE *Union infantrymen carried essential items in knapsacks like the one below. Soldiers were issued up to sixty rounds of ammunition in the form of cartridges, held in a cartridge box that was slung over the shoulder or attached to the waist belt. They also carried a wool blanket to sleep under at night or wear as a cloak in cold, damp weather.*

U.S. cartridge box

U.S. belt plate

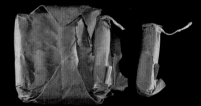

Cartridges

Knapsack

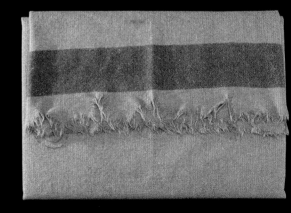

Wool blanket

52

CONFEDERATE INFANTRY GEAR

*Slouch hat of Private George W. Ramsay,
17th Virginia Infantry*

CONTRARY TO THE STEREOTYPE OF THE TYPICAL Confederate infantryman as ragged and shoeless, most Southern soldiers were fairly well appointed, if not always uniform in appearance. Like Northern infantrymen, they wore various outfits initially, furnished by the soldiers themselves or by their communities or states. In 1862 the Confederate Quartermaster Department set up depots around the South and supplied clothing to soldiers. Severe shortages resulted at times when Southern armies engaged in grueling campaigns like Robert E. Lee's advance into Maryland in September 1862. But such ordeals for threadbare Confederates were the exception rather than the rule.

The basic Confederate uniform consisted of trousers and a coat or jacket. As cloth grew scarce in the South, the long frock coat gave way to a shorter sack coat or more often to a shell jacket, which became standard. Colors ran the gamut from dark blue—favored by some Southerners before it became identified with the Union—to lighter shades of gray, brown, or butternut, produced using vegetable dyes that faded over time from brown or gray to tan. The infantryman's standard headgear, the kepi, provided little protection from the weather and was often exchanged for a slouch hat.

The shoes of hard-marching Southerners wore out quickly and were sometimes replaced with those scavenged from dead Yankees. Like Union troops, they carried a haversack for food, a knapsack for clothing and personal items, and a cartridge box. Lacking much industry, the South and its soldiers relied largely on imported or captured weapons, notably British-made Pattern 1853 Enfield rifle muskets and Union-made Springfields. ✦ KG

SOUTHERN ATTIRE *Most Confederates wore either a kepi (INSET) or a slouch hat (RIGHT, TOP). As the war went on, frock coats like the one at right were replaced by shell jackets like the one opposite.*

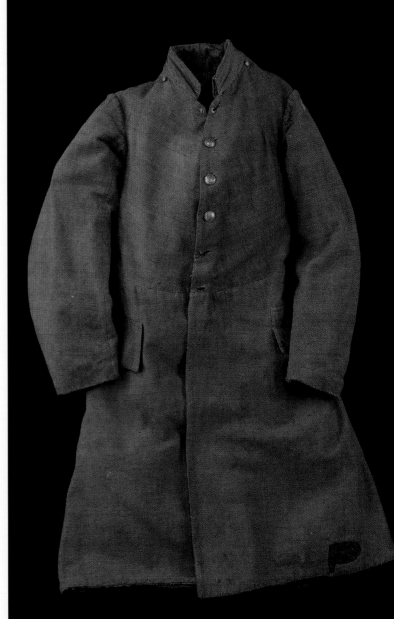

*"Butternut" frock coat of Frank B. Gibson,
26th South Carolina Infantry*

Homespun shell jacket

> *The men were good-sized, healthy and well clothed, although without any attempt at uniformity in color or cut.*
>
> **BRITISH OBSERVER A.J.L. FREMANTLE, DESCRIBING CONFEDERATE TROOPS, 1863**

Woolen trousers

Brass C.S. belt plate

Confederate buttons

VARIED OUFIT *Confederates sometimes wore homespun clothing like the shell jacket at upper left, and their trousers were gray, butternut, or blue like the pair above, which belonged to Private George W. Ramsey of the 17th Virginia Infantry. Confederate belt plates and many Confederate buttons were made of metal, although wooden buttons were also used.*

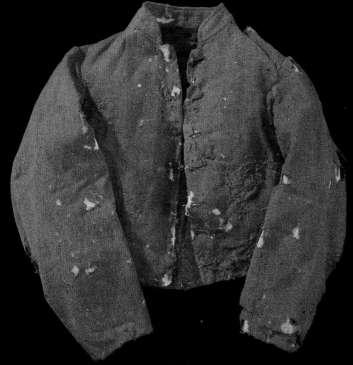

Shell jacket

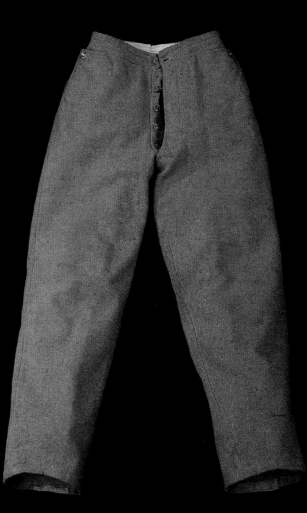

Trousers

Shoes

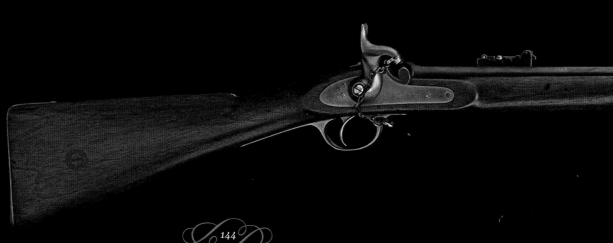

VITAL CONTAINERS *Most Confederate canteens were made of wood and were heavier than metal canteens. Soldiers often carried food in a canvas haversack like the one shown below. They also each carried a cartridge box containing a regulation forty cartridges.*

Wooden C.S.A. canteen

Haversack

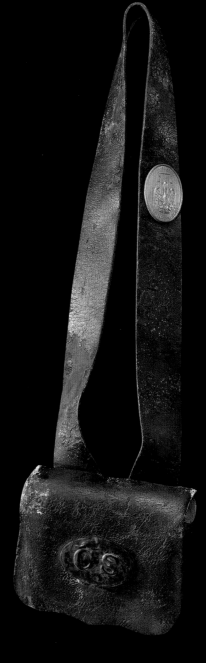

C.S. cartridge box

Pattern 1853 Enfield rifle

53

LINCOLN'S HENRY RIFLE

THE MAGNIFICENT HENRY RIFLE BELOW, WITH its engraved gold-plated frame (detail above) and polished rosewood stock, was presented to President Lincoln in 1862 by armsmaker Oliver Winchester. An innovative repeating rifle, the Henry had a magazine holding fifteen rounds that could be fired in rapid succession with a flick of the lever, which ejected the spent case and cocked the weapon. Based on a design patented by Horace Smith and Daniel Wesson and obtained by Winchester when he bought them out in 1855, the rifle and its metallic cartridges were refined by Benjamin T. Henry for Winchester's company. Despite efforts to promote the weapon by presenting engraved rifles to Lincoln and others in office, the Union purchased only 1,700 during the war. Yet Federals who obtained the weapons cherished them, and Confederates quipped that one could load the rifle "on Sunday and shoot all week." Enhanced in 1866 with an improved loading system, the Winchester repeating rifle became legendary as the gun that won the West. ✢ DDM

54

CIVIL WAR BELT PLATES

CIVIL WAR SOLDIERS HAD PLATES OF VARIOUS shapes and designs that were used to fasten the belts that they wore around their waists or slung over their shoulders to hold swords or cartridge boxes. Plates were also affixed to those cartridge boxes. The plates were stamped with letters or figures signaling which side a soldier was on or which state or unit he belonged to. Handsome and durable items handed down by veterans to their descendants or excavated at camps and battle sites, a wide array of these relics survive and are prized by collectors. Union regulations called for oval "US" plates to be used on most waist belts and on cartridge boxes, and for circular eagle plates to be used on shoulder belts. Union cavalrymen, however, used a rectangular eagle plate (opposite, bottom right) on the waist belt that held their sword.

Some Confederate troops had oval belt plates marked "CS" or "CSA," but many had state plates instead, stamped with the initials or emblem of their home state such as "NC" for North Carolina, the Lone Star for Texas, or the Palmetto for South Carolina. Adding to the mix were regimental plates worn by some troops on either side, as shown here in examples from the 1st Virginia Infantry (to which the initials "CSA" were added) and the Philadelphia Fire Zouaves (P.F.Z.) of the 72nd Pennsylvania Infantry. Other soldiers continued to use their old militia plates from before the war. Southerners had a greater assortment of plates than Northerners, most of whom by late 1863 had conformed to regulations and were using the prescribed "US" and eagle plates, which the Union with its greater manufacturing capacity produced in large numbers. ✢ JLJ

PRESIDENTIAL MODEL *This Henry rifle, serial number 6, was made for Abraham Lincoln by Oliver Winchester's New Haven Firearms Company and engraved with the words "Lincoln / President / U.S.A." His great-grandson, Robert Lincoln Beckwith, donated this treasure to the Smithsonian in 1963.*

North Carolina

Texas

South Carolina

1st Regiment Virginia Volunteers

Philadelphia Fire Zouaves

Model 1851 U.S. Cavalry Sword Waist-Belt Plate

55

THE MUSIC OF WAR

NOT ALL THOSE WHO WENT TO WAR FOR THE Union or Confederacy wielded weapons. Some dedicated recruits carried only bugles, drums, or other musical instruments. Serving as non-combatants, those morale-boosting musicians set the tempo for soldiers as they marched in stirring dress parades, regulated life in camp from reveille to taps, urged men to battle, and shared in the risks of combat by sounding commands to troops in the field or serving as medics.

Most companies had a drummer, fifer, or bugler to provide cadence on the march or signals in battle. Many regiments or brigades also had a band consisting of as few as eight or as many as two dozen musicians, most of whom played brass or percussion instruments. The majority of bandsmen were in their twenties and thirties, but a few brave boys in their early teens enlisted as drummers. Buglers figured prominently in battle because their shrill horn could be heard above the din and was used to communicate orders from commanders. As bullets ricocheted and cannons blasted, however, entire bands could sometimes be heard playing rousing tunes such as "The Battle Cry of Freedom" on the Union side and "Dixie" on the Confederate side. Frank Rauscher, leader of the 114th Pennsylvania Infantry Regiment regimental band, wrote that musicians like his helped maintain "the discipline and soldierly bearing of the men. True, they do not go into battle and charge the enemy's strongholds with a flourish of trumpets and the clashing of cymbals; and yet the precision and accentuation of step, as a preliminary to decisive action and unison of movement, owes much to the inspiriting strains of music in camp and on the march."

Between battles and campaigns, music helped relieve the tedium of life in camp and comfort lonely, homesick men. Sentimental songs of love and devotion were performed by bandsmen as well as soldiers, singing to the accompaniment of banjos, guitars, or fiddles. On the home front, composers raised morale and stirred emotions with patriotic tunes and nostalgic ballads, sold as sheet music with decorative covers and performed in homes where people pined for distant loved ones in uniform.

Soldiers of all ranks found solace in music, which brought precious moments of harmony to their often harsh and discordant existence. After being serenaded by the band of the 26th North Carolina Infantry, a grateful Robert E. Lee told the regiment's colonel: "I don't believe we can have an army without music." In his poem "Music in Camp," Virginia-born John Reuben Thompson told of an occasion when bands from opposing Union and Confederate armies, camped on either side of the Rappahannock River, set aside their animosities and serenaded each other:

> But memory, waked by music's art,
> Expressed in simplest numbers,
> Subdued the sternest Yankee heart,
> Made light the Rebel's slumbers.

Music and instruments of the Civil War survive today as testaments to the shared heritage of Americans, who had much in common even when divided into warring camps. ✛ SLK

ARMY BRASS *Musicians with the Union infantry wore dark-blue frock coats and standard infantry forage caps with a horn insignia like those shown opposite. Unlike the high-pitched bugle (INSET), the E-flat flugelhorn (OPPOSITE) was a mellow, valved instrument. This one was sold by New York bandleader and merchant Harvey B. Dodworth.*

UNKNOWN DRUMMER *The name of the Union drummer who posed for this tintype has been lost, but a story recorded in the Smithsonian accession file states that he was one of two teenage brothers who served as drummers at Gettysburg.*

SNARE DRUM *This U.S. snare drum with a stenciled spread eagle, played by a soldier with the 22nd New Jersey Infantry, was made by Ernest Vogt of Philadelphia, who in late 1864 contracted to produce two thousand of these regimental drums.*

56

ADMIRAL FARRAGUT

NEW ORLEANS AT THE START OF THE CIVIL WAR was one of the busiest ports in the world. Its strategic location near the mouth of the Mississippi River made it a prime target for Union commanders, who resolved not just to halt its lucrative trade in cotton and other goods with a blockade but to capture the city. The seasoned officer assigned to take New Orleans was David Glasgow Farragut (1801–1870) who had seen action as a boy during the War of 1812 while serving as a midshipman under his accomplished foster father, Captain David Porter.

When the Civil War began, Captain Farragut was stationed in Norfolk, Virginia. Although born in Tennessee and married to a Southerner, he was a dedicated, fifty-year veteran of the U.S. Navy and bristled when secessionists invited him to join their cause, telling them: "You fellows will catch the devil before you get through with this business." He packed up his family and moved to New York, where he held a desk job until Secretary of the Navy Gideon Welles decided not to hold his Southern background against him and made him flag officer in charge of the West Gulf Blockading Squadron, tasked with seizing New Orleans.

To take that city, Farragut's squadron had to pass between two forbidding enemy bastions at the mouth of the Mississippi, Forts Jackson and St. Philip, and contend with Confederate gunboats, ironclads, and fire rafts. When a prolonged bombardment failed to neutralize those forts, Farragut forged ahead. Advancing before dawn on April 24, 1862, he ran the gauntlet and broke through, losing just one of his seventeen ships. On April 25 he reached New Orleans and forced the surrender of the city. His feat was rewarded that summer when Congress authorized the rank of admiral, which had been denied to the U.S. Navy because admiralty was associated with royalty and aristocracy. Farragut was promptly promoted to rear admiral and later became the navy's first full admiral.

Farragut enhanced his reputation as a daring commander on August 5, 1864, when his fleet entered Mobile Bay, one of the last coastal inlets still under Confederate control and laced with underwater mines called torpedoes. Lashed to the rigging of his flagship, U.S.S. *Hartford*, to get a better view of the action, he watched in dismay as the ironclad U.S.S. *Tecumseh* hit a mine and sank, stalling his advance. "Damn the torpedoes!" he shouted, and went full speed ahead, with his flagship in the lead. Victory at Mobile Bay was Farragut's last engagement and his crowning achievement. He was idolized not only by the Northern public at large but also by men close to him, including the *Hartford*'s paymaster, William Meredith, who hailed him in verse as "Daring Dave Farragut." Gideon Welles wrote that he would "more willingly take great risks to obtain great results than any officer in either army or navy." ✛ KG

BRED TO COMMAND *David Farragut, shown as a rear admiral after his promotion in 1862, advanced on New Orleans with his foster brother, Commander David Dixon Porter, whose father assumed responsibility for young Farragut and took him to sea as a midshipman.*

HERO'S RELICS *In April 1864 the Union League Club of New York presented this jeweled sword and scabbard to Admiral Farragut, who wore the service dress coat and the cap above during the Battle of Mobile Bay that August.*

57

THE VANITY OF BEAST BUTLER

WHEN MAJOR GENERAL BENJAMIN F. BUTLER (1818–1892) arrived in New Orleans in May 1862 as commander of Federal forces occupying that city, he was already a controversial figure. An influential Massachusetts politician with negligible military experience when he received his lofty commission, he was prickly, argumentative, and inordinately vain about his looks, which were dour, and his accomplishments, which were few. Butler's earlier decision to proclaim slaves who escaped to Fort Monroe in 1861 "contraband of war" and refuse to return them to their masters earned him no credit among the white citizens of New Orleans. He proceeded to infuriate them with his General Order No. 28, which declared that any lady showing disrespect to Union soldiers occupying the city would be "regarded and held liable to be treated as a woman of the town plying her vocation." Contemptuous New Orleanians were soon referring to him as "Beast Butler" or "Spoons Butler," which signified that he was out to plunder their homes and steal their silverware, among other valuables. After Butler antagonized several foreign consuls in the city, President Lincoln recalled him in December 1862.

During a hiatus between assignments in 1863, Butler tried to repair his battered public image by encouraging an admirer to publish a flattering book about him and by posing for sculptor Edward A. Brackett, who managed to make his pouting features look almost presidential in the bust shown opposite. Sent back to Fort Monroe later that year, Butler wrote his wife: "Do you want to see me? Do the next best thing. Send down to Brackett and get the marble bust which he has done. Get up a handsome pedestal for it—he has been paid for it." ✛ EWP

BEAUTY AND THE BEAST *Benjamin Butler, who was lampooned by the press, took comfort in Edward Brackett's impressive bust of him, which was reproduced as an engraving in James Parton's admiring book,* General Butler in New Orleans *(1863), and in the general's autobiography,* Butler's Book *(1892). Butler thought he looked better in profile and adopted that pose for the 1864 photograph at right. The photograph was taken after he was given command of the Army of the James in Virginia, where he remained largely on the sidelines. General Grant, instead, bore the brunt of the fighting against Lee's forces. Shown here wearing slippers, General Butler seldom ventured far afield in the latter part of the war.*

58

A GIFT FOR SECRETARY CHASE

ON JUNE 22, 1862, U.S. TREASURY SECRETARY Salmon P. Chase received a gift from Benjamin Butler, the Union commander in occupied New Orleans—a package sealed in wax with Butler's own stamp (below). The package contained four engraved steel plates (opposite) used to print Confederate notes, the South's financial lifeblood. The loss of those plates, seized after New Orleans fell in late April 1862, was a blow to Confederate sovereignty and solvency.

Before the outbreak of war, the Confederacy relied on the National Bank Note Company in New York to design and print interest-bearing notes with values up to $1,000, yet these had proven inadequate to pay troops, purchase weapons, and keep cash circulating in the South. After the conflict began and the Union cut off trade with the South, Confederate Treasury Secretary Christopher G. Memminger found that he could no longer rely on Northern printers. He turned instead to the New Orleans branch of the American Bank Note Company, the only shop in the South with the skilled engravers and printing equipment required to produce high-quality bills that were hard to counterfeit.

Samuel Schmidt, general manager of that New Orleans branch, changed its name to the Southern Bank Note Company and promised to fulfill his contract within fifty days, but his company fell far behind. Schmidt's loyalty to the South was called into question, and Memminger ordered him to cease work and hand over the job and related materials to a rival company in Richmond. Schmidt paid little attention to that order and forged ahead, intent on honoring the contract and upholding his reputation. On April 12, 1862, less than two weeks before New Orleans fell, he shipped the last batch of 2,760 notes to Memminger. They were of value to the Confederacy, but the precious plates that produced them—and could have been used to print more high-quality currency—fell into Butler's hands and were sent as trophies of war to Secretary Chase in Washington, D.C. ✛ NB & MN

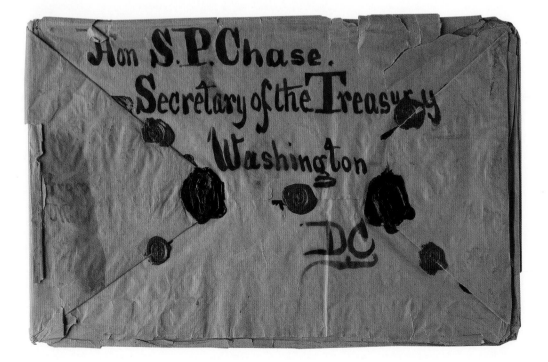

SEALED AND DELIVERED *Eager to curry favor in Washington, D.C., General Butler sent these finely engraved plates, used to produce Confederate $5 and $10 bills, to Secretary Chase at the Treasury Department in the envelope at left. Bills printed by the Southern Bank Note Company with these plates before they were confiscated by Federal forces in New Orleans are considered among the best ever produced in the Confederacy and are prized by collectors today. Some other Southern companies used lithography to produce notes that were of lower quality and were more easily counterfeited, worsening the financial condition of the Confederacy.*

59

EARLY PRISONERS OF WAR

BY 1862, WITH NO END TO THE CONFLICT IN SIGHT, Federal and Confederate authorities faced the problem of how to handle the increasing number of prisoners of war in their custody. Opposing commanders sometimes arranged to exchange prisoners after battles, but no formal agreement regarding captives was reached until July 1862 when the two sides negotiated a cartel (a deal in writing between belligerents). Under its terms, prisoners of war were to be held briefly in parole camps until they were officially exchanged and allowed to return to duty.

Until that deal collapsed and prisons became overcrowded, conditions in most camps were tolerable and inmates enjoyed some of the same diversions that had occupied their leisure time as soldiers. At Salisbury Prison in North Carolina, inmates played baseball (overleaf), attended services on Sundays, and performed in plays and concerts. Some men held there and at other Southern camps served as journalists and wrote articles for their fellow prisoners that were later published under the title *The Stars and Stripes in Rebeldom.* One reporter at Parish Prison in New Orleans noted humorously that inmates there "appeared for the review on Saturday without arms" and added that it was better to be "without arms than without legs at Manassas." At Johnson's Island, off Sandusky, Ohio, Confederates staged shows and formed their own branch of the Young Men's Christian Association (YMCA), which met weekly. One officer there kept the autograph book shown opposite, containing names, addresses, and other information on fellow prisoners—a good way to keep track of men whose whereabouts were often unknown to family members and officials.

The Union suspended prisoner exchanges in 1863 for reasons that included the refusal of Confederate authorities to release captured black troops. That suspension occurred as fighting intensified and more prisoners of war were taken than could be adequately housed and fed in the camps, some of which became notorious "hell holes." ✛ KG

OFFICERS' CONFINES *Conditions for Union officers held at Richmond's Libby Prison, pictured here amid guards' tents (BELOW, LEFT), grew worse as the war went on. One Libby inmate, Colonel John Crocker, was lucky to have his own plate and utensils (BELOW), which other prisoners lacked. This autograph book of Confederate officer Woodbury Wheeler, held on Johnson's Island, lists fellow inmates, some of them captured at Fort Donelson.*

Ft Donelson

Ft Donelson John

John

John

C. A

Woodbury Wheeler
1st Lt Latham's Battery
Co A. 40th N. C. T.

W. L. Pond 1st Lt Company C. 30th Regt
Tennessee volunteers Post office
Holliston Tennessee Surrendered
at Fort Donelson Feb 16 1862
Age 28 years

Mrs A. Donelson Col 2nd Tenn 1st
Mss (R. A) C. S. A. Surrendered at Ft Donelson
16th Feby 1862, Age Thirty six
Residence Clarksville, Tennessee.

James L. Jones Cpt. Co. B. 30th Reg
Tenn Vol Grapevine Post office
Robertson County Tennessee
Surrendered at Fort Donelson Feb 16. 1862
Age 44 years

60

BASEBALL IN PRISON

SALISBURY PRISON, PORTRAYED HERE AS IT LOOKED in 1862, held around 1,500 Union prisoners of war that summer. They were confined at this camp in North Carolina until they could be exchanged for Confederate prisoners of war. Provided with adequate medical care, fresh water from wells, and sufficient food, they passed the time by whittling, writing letters, putting on shows, gambling with dice or cards—and playing baseball, as documented in this print. In their letters and diaries, prisoners described baseball games as almost-daily occurrences.

This hand-colored lithograph was based on a drawing by Otto Botticher, a Prussian immigrant who worked as an artist before enlisting as captain in the 68th New York Infantry in July 1861. He was captured near Manassas, Virginia, in March 1862 and sent to Libby Prison in Richmond before being transferred to Salisbury. Released in a prisoner exchange on September 30, 1862, he rejoined his New York regiment and was wounded at Gettysburg before his discharge in 1864.

Botticher may have been familiar with baseball before he enlisted. The sport evolved in metropolitan New York, where rules were established for a club called the Knickerbockers in 1845. During the Civil War, players from New York and elsewhere introduced baseball to others at camps and prisons and helped popularize the sport. At Salisbury, prisoners formed competing teams, and guards sometimes joined in games.

Conditions deteriorated in 1863 after prisoner exchanges were suspended. By late 1864 Salisbury held over 8,500 famished inmates, whose mortality rate in the disease-ridden camp exceeded 25 percent. What was once a playing field became a battleground that November when a massive escape attempt by prisoners resulted in the death of nearly 250 men. ✣ DSJ

PRISONERS' PASTIME *Inmates play ball in this detail from "Union Prisoners at Salisbury, N.C.," a lithograph based on Otto Botticher's sketch and produced in 1863 by Sarony, Major & Knapp. One of the earliest baseball prints, it sold well on both sides of the Atlantic.*

61

CIVIL WAR HEADGEAR

AS THE WAR PROGRESSED AND THE CLOTHING WORN by troops on either side became increasingly more uniform, Union and Confederate soldiers continued to wear an impressive assortment of hats and caps. That variety stemmed in part from the prewar precedent of equipping each soldier with two kinds of headgear. An order issued by the U.S. War Department in 1858 called for enlisted men to receive each year one dress hat such as the Hardee hat shown below, with a tall, stiff crown and a broad brim; and a fatigue or forage cap with a visor like those pictured on the following pages. During the Civil War, some soldiers proudly wore such dress hats, but others found them too awkward and uncomfortable and favored the kepi: a forage cap modeled loosely on the French *képi*. Union infantrymen, cavalrymen, and artillerymen wore kepis with different insignia, and many soldiers customized those caps by giving them distinctive shapes and wearing them with an attitude and flair exhibited with no other article of military clothing. The kepi defined the Civil War soldier, and the soldier placed his personal imprint on the kepi.

Rivaling the kepi in popularity, particularly among Confederates, was the slouch hat—a soft, broad-brimmed hat that could be molded to the wearer's preference. Many soldiers on both sides purchased slouch hats, and some simulated them by reshaping their dress hats. The slouch hat's broad brim offered more protection against the elements than did the kepi's visor, although some men were issued waterproof covers for their caps.

Officers wore a variety of headgear, ranging from kepis and slouch hats that differed little from those worn by enlisted men to fancy chapeaux: narrow, elongated hats that protruded in front and in back and distinguished high-ranking navy and army officers from their subordinates on formal occasions. No men who fought in the Civil War donned more conspicuous headgear than Zouaves, who wore tasseled red fezzes not just for parades or reviews but when entering battle. ✛ JLJ

Hats with trimmings complete will be issued to enlisted men at the rate of one a year. For Fatigue purposes Forage Caps ... will be issued ... at the rate of one a year.

GENERAL ORDER NO. 13, WAR DEPARTMENT, NOVEMBER 30, 1858

UNION ARTILLERY DRESS HAT *This Pattern 1858 Army Hat, also known as a Hardee hat, was authorized by the War Department three years before the Civil War began and was worn by some soldiers during the conflict, including the Union artilleryman pictured opposite. Made of stiff black felt, it replaced the Pattern 1851 Army Hat. This example and the hat worn by the soldier in the photograph are stamped with the crossed-cannons insignia of the artillery branch.*

CONFEDERATE OFFICER'S KEPI *This gray wool Confederate forage cap is decorated with faded gold quatrefoil and three lines of lace, signifying that it was worn by a major or colonel.*

ZOUAVE FEZ *Made of red wool with blue tassels, this characteristic Zouave fez is from the Smithsonian's Schuylkill Arsenal collection.*

CONFEDERATE OFFICER'S BLUE KEPI *This well-preserved blue cap with gold quatrefoil and lace was worn by Colonel Robert W. Harper of the 1st Arkansas Mounted Rifles, who also owned the slouch hat shown overleaf.*

MCCLELLAN CHASSEUR CAP *Worn by General George McClellan, this well-tailored kepi, also known as a chasseur cap, was a taller type than most Civil War kepis and popular with soldiers of all ranks, who sometimes placed a wet sponge or handkerchief under the crown to keep cool.*

MCCLELLAN CHAPEAU *Adorned in gold with the U.S. coat of arms, this ceremonial chapeau was authorized for staff officers in 1858 and worn by General McClellan.*

UNION INFANTRY "MCDOWELL" KEPI *This Union officer's forage cap, with the infantry's bugle insignia, is of a type associated with General Irwin McDowell, who commanded Union troops at the First Battle of Bull Run.*

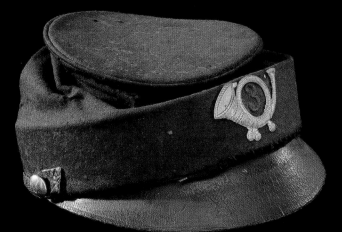

GOSLINE ZOUAVE FORAGE CAP *Men of the 95th Pennsylvania Volunteer Infantry, known as the "Gosline Zouaves," wore this chasseur pattern cap of blue broadcloth with red piping, from the Schuylkill Arsenal collection.*

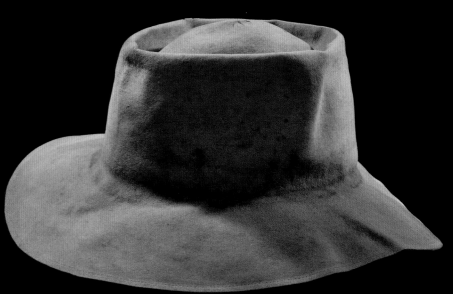

CONFEDERATE SLOUCH HAT *Like many soldiers on both sides, Colonel Robert Harper had both a kepi and a hat—in his case, the comfortable slouch hat shown here. Harper died in battle at Chickamauga on September 20, 1863, cut down by cannon fire.*

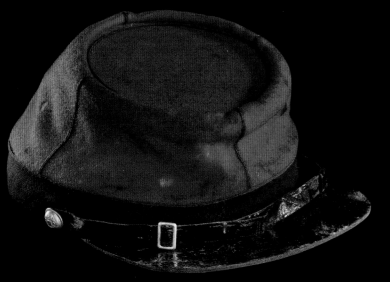

BALTIMORE MOUNTED RIFLEMAN CAP *Purchased from Canfield Bros. & Company in Baltimore, this forage cap was worn by militiaman Thomas Hill of the Maryland National Guard when he went to fight for the Union.*

KEPI WITH WATERPROOF COVER *Waterproof glazed-cotton covers for caps like the one shown at right over a Confederate kepi were purchased by both sides during the war. Not many were worn, however, and photographs of them in use are rare.*

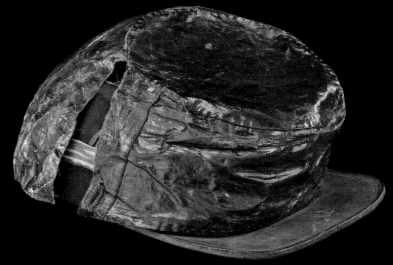

OFFICER'S CAMPAIGN HAT *Also known as a "Burnside Pattern" hat, this softer version of the Hardee hat was much like a slouch hat in appearance and comfort. It was worn by Lieutenant Nathan Levy of the 10th Michigan Infantry.*

UNION KEPI WITH CORPS BADGE *Decorated with the diamond badge of the Third Corps, this was one of many Union caps displaying such corps insignia, introduced by the Army of the Potomac in 1863.*

62

THE TELEGRAPH AT WAR

IN 1862, AS ABRAHAM LINCOLN WAITED ANXIOUSLY IN Washington for news from distant commanders, he had a distinct advantage over earlier American presidents in wartime. Less than two decades after Samuel F. B. Morse sent his pioneering telegraph message, "What Hath God Wrought," from Washington, D.C., to Baltimore on May 24, 1844, the country was crisscrossed with wires carrying electronic signals at lightning speed. On the eve of the Civil War, the United States had fifty thousand miles of telegraph lines. Much of that network was in the North, and it was now rapidly expanding to keep Union generals in touch with their subordinates in the field and their superiors in Washington. Lincoln was so eager for news from the front that he often visited the War Department, where military telegrams were received.

The Civil War became a testing ground for electronic communications on the battlefield and between front lines and rear areas. The Confederate government confiscated the Southern lines of Northern-based telegraph companies. William Morris, a Southern-born official of the American Telegraph Company, was placed in charge of those lines and quietly assured the company that he would try to protect its property. That proved difficult because both sides regularly cut telegraph lines to disrupt enemy communications.

The Union had two organizations involved in wartime telegraphy—the Signal Corps, established by the U.S. Army in 1860, and the U.S. Military Telegraph (USMT), authorized by Congress in April 1861. The USMT employed civilians and used conventional telegraph equipment that included batteries, keys, relays, and sounders that made the dots and dashes of Morse code audible. The Signal Corps, led by Major Albert Myer,

consisted of army men who were trained to serve as battlefield observers and use visual signals such as semaphore flags, which could be combined with telegraphy to relay messages in areas where stringing wires was difficult if not impossible. Few of Myer's operators knew Morse code, and he was wary of the fragile, acid-filled glass batteries that powered conventional telegraphs. Instead, Myer adopted the Beardslee Magneto-Electric Telegraph (opposite), which produced an electrical current without batteries and had a dial with letters that required only that operators be literate.

Myer organized wagon trains to transport Beardslee units to the front lines. His field telegraph service was used in Virginia during the Fredericksburg Campaign in late 1862 to link the army commander at headquarters with corps commanders whose troops engaged the enemy. The Beardslee telegraph proved unreliable, however, and had a limited range of transmission. It was abandoned in 1863 when the USMT took over the field telegraph service and the Signal Corps was relegated to using visual signals only. Civilian telegraphers of the USMT now operated close to the front lines at some risk. Meanwhile, USMT construction crews worked feverishly to expand the Union's network. By 1865 about fifteen thousand miles of military telegraph wire had been erected by the Union, and only about a thousand miles by the Confederacy, giving Lincoln and other leaders in Washington a strategic advantage over their counterparts in Richmond. ⚔ HW & CH

HIGH-WIRE ACT *Union operatives like this signalman, clinging to a pole in occupied Virginia, had to be strong and agile to repair telegraph lines and perform other tasks.*

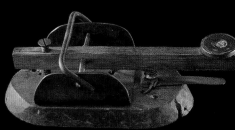

FLAWED ALTERNATIVE *Patented by George Beardslee, the Beardslee Magneto-Electric Telegraph (LEFT) allowed operators who did not know Morse code to send messages by placing the handle over a letter or number on the dial. The machine's magnetos took the place of troublesome batteries. Despite that advantage, the slow, bulky device proved inferior to conventional telegraphs that sent signals in Morse code, which the Signal Corps adopted before the USMT took over all military telegraphy. Equipment being in short supply, one Signal Corps operator made his own key (ABOVE) for Morse code transmissions.*

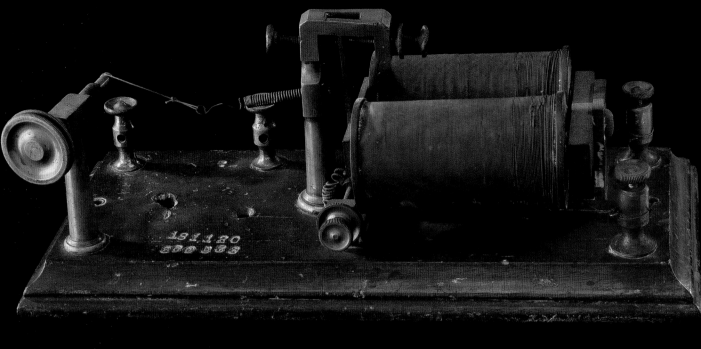

EXTENDING THE LINE *Men of a USMT construction corps attached to the Army of the Potomac are shown at left putting up telegraph wire during the war. Among the equipment they installed were relays like the one above, which received a weak electrical signal and retransmitted it as a stronger signal.*

63

WRITING THE EMANCIPATION PROCLAMATION

IN 1862 ABRAHAM LINCOLN CONCLUDED THAT TO restore the Union, slavery must end. He had always opposed slavery but had never sided with abolitionists who called for its immediate end. Instead, he sought solutions that might make slavery wither away such as restricting its spread into the western territories, offering compensation to owners who freed slaves, and relocating those who were emancipated outside the country. He eventually concluded that the war made those measures woefully inadequate.

Lincoln faced pressure on all sides—from African Americans fleeing bondage and pouring into Union camps, from Radical Republicans demanding an end to slavery, and from proslavery Unionists who threatened to oppose the war if it became a fight for abolition.

In June 1862, while awaiting news at the War Department telegraph office, Lincoln began writing an executive order on slavery. For several weeks he sat at the desk of Major Thomas T. Eckert, using the inkstand below to pen the document. After completing the draft, he explained to Eckert that he had been composing an order "giving freedom to the slaves of the South, for the purpose of hastening the end of the war."

Although Lincoln's order would not take effect until the first day of 1863, he prepared the public for it by announcing his Emancipation Proclamation on September 22, 1862. As of January 1, he declared all persons held in slavery in areas still in rebellion would be "then, thenceforward, and forever free."

Lincoln believed he had the authority as commander in chief to free only those who were enslaved within the eleven rebellious states. The order did not free slaves in Union-controlled areas, but it was widely understood that a Union victory would mean the end of slavery in the United States. "If my name ever goes into history it will be for this act," Lincoln said, "and my whole soul is into it." ☩ HRR

FREEDOM'S FONT *Abraham Lincoln used this brass inkstand to draft the Emancipation Proclamation. He waited until after Union forces prevailed at Antietam to issue his preliminary proclamation, which was finalized on January 1, 1863.*

64

LINCOLN AT ANTIETAM

SEPTEMBER 17, 1862, AT ANTIETAM WAS THE bloodiest single day in American history. Robert E. Lee had invaded western Maryland, taking the war into Union territory to demoralize the North and force the Army of the Potomac into a potentially decisive battle. Abraham Lincoln restored command of that army to George B. McClellan, who moved slowly. When he met Lee's heavily outnumbered army at Antietam Creek, his attacks were

> *I said I would remove him if he let Lee's army get away from him, and I must do so.*
>
> **ABRAHAM LINCOLN ON GEORGE B. MCCLELLAN**

disjointed and poorly executed. The battle itself was ferocious. As one witness to the carnage put it, the "landscape turned red." Over twenty thousand Union and Confederate soldiers were killed or wounded. A bloody stalemate, Antietam became a Union victory when Lee withdrew into Virginia.

In November, one month after visiting McClellan in camp (right) and urging him to pursue Lee, Lincoln sacked his commander. "I said I would remove him if he let Lee's army get away from him, and I must do so," Lincoln remarked. But he also had larger, political reasons for firing McClellan. Victory at Antietam emboldened Lincoln to issue his Emancipation Proclamation, which made this a war for liberty as well as union. McClellan opposed emancipation and abhorred the idea of waging war against slavery. With his proclamation, Lincoln radicalized the conflict. He could not rely on a reluctant McClellan to smash the Confederacy and extinguish slavery. ☩ DCW

FACE-OFF *Abraham Lincoln confronts George B. McClellan at Antietam in October 1862. Lincoln faulted him for not pursuing Lee and wondered aloud if the Army of the Potomac was now just "McClellan's bodyguard."*

65

LETTERS HOME

"I FEEL THAT OUR CONTRY NEEDS MY HELP & I AM willing to do all that I can & eaven give my life for your libertys & our beloved childs." So wrote Private David W. Walters in the letter reproduced at right, written on September 29, 1862, to his wife, Rachel. This was the third letter that he sent to her during his first month in camp with Company I of the 5th Indiana Cavalry. Rachel was able to reply within a week from their home a hundred miles or so away and let her husband know how their one-year-old son, Willard, was doing.

> *Thru the mercys of a kind God I am permitted to drop you a few lines to let you no that I am well & hearty.*
>
> **PRIVATE DAVID W. WALTERS TO HIS WIFE, RACHEL, SEPTEMBER 1862**

Letters helped bridge the distance separating this couple and other friends and kin during the war. Mail service provided a vital link between soldiers and their loved ones and helped ease their concerns for each other in times of danger and distress. This letter from David Walters begins with reassuring words for Rachel. "My dear companion," he writes, "Thru the mercys of a kind God I am permitted to drop you a few lines to let you no that I am well & hearty." He and Rachel regularly sent each other news of family and friends along with photographs, money, and postage stamps to sustain their correspondence, which continued as he campaigned in Kentucky and Tennessee before advancing into Georgia with General William T. Sherman's army in 1864. In May of that year, Rachel received word that he had been captured at Resaca, Georgia. Sadly, a condolence letter followed a year later, informing her that David had died of starvation at a Confederate prison camp in Florence, South Carolina, in February 1865. ✛ LH

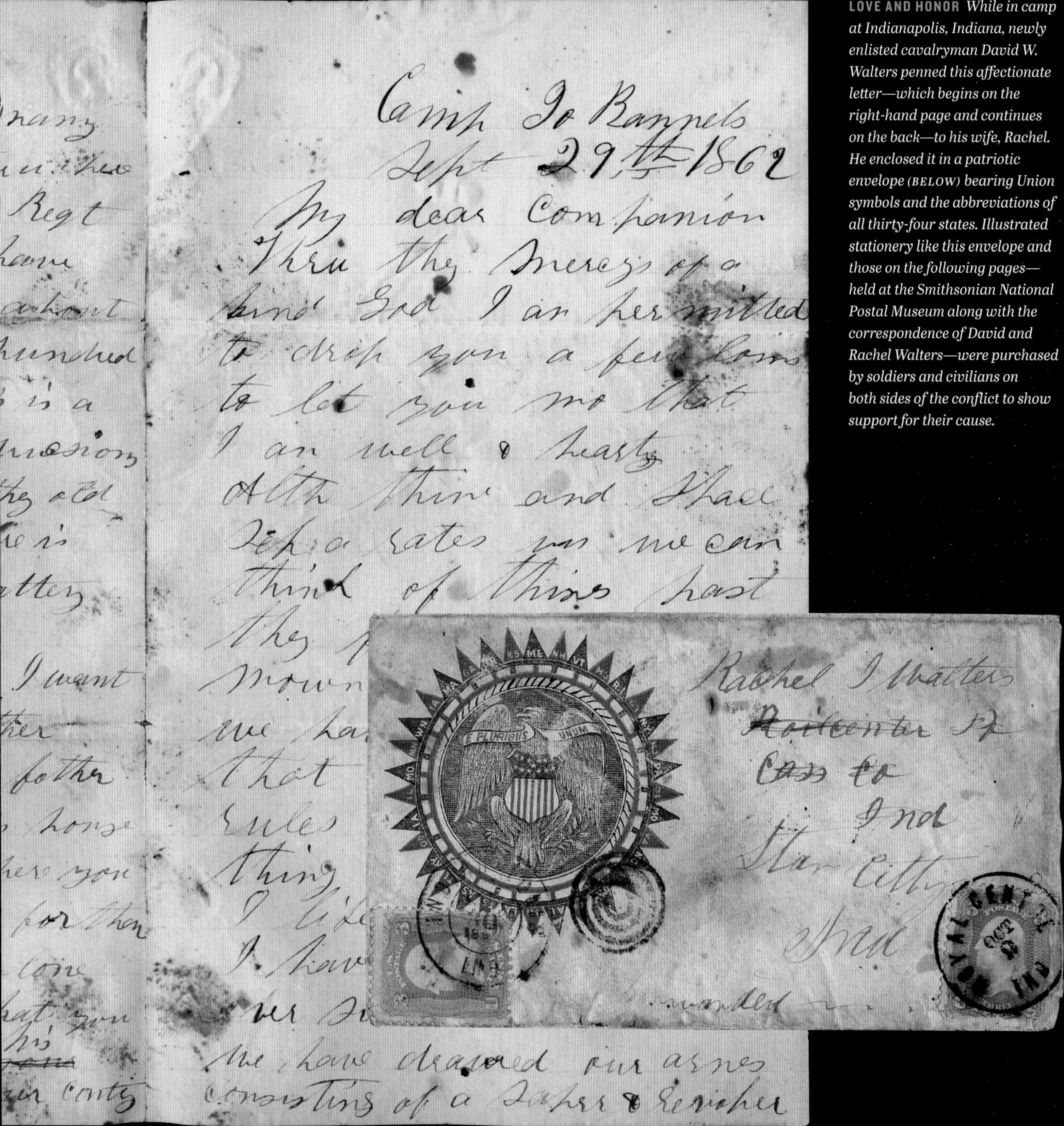

LOVE AND HONOR *While in camp at Indianapolis, Indiana, newly enlisted cavalryman David W. Walters penned this affectionate letter—which begins on the right-hand page and continues on the back—to his wife, Rachel. He enclosed it in a patriotic envelope (BELOW) bearing Union symbols and the abbreviations of all thirty-four states. Illustrated stationery like this envelope and those on the following pages—held at the Smithsonian National Postal Museum along with the correspondence of David and Rachel Walters—were purchased by soldiers and civilians on both sides of the conflict to show support for their cause.*

Camp Jo Bannets
Sept 29th 1862

My dear Companion

Thru the Mercy of a
kind God I am permitted
to drop you a few lines
to let you no that
I am well & hearty
Alth thine and I hope
these a rates you we can
think of things past

I want

other

father

house

here you

for thee

Rachel I Walters

Cass co
Ind
Star City
Ind

Map of Washington, D.C., and portrait of General McClellan, 1861

Metropolitan Fair for the U.S. Sanitary Commission, 1864

Lady Liberty with flag, 1861

George Washington as Founder of the Union, 1861

66

THE IRON MINE

THE CIVIL WAR HAD A SUBTLE YET POWERFUL impact on American landscape painting. Prior to the conflict, artists and their audience regarded the American landscape as the "New Eden," projecting their hopes for a peaceful and bountiful future. When the fighting commenced, their outlook changed. Viewers now found evidence of the war in landscapes like Homer Dodge Martin's somber 1862 painting (right), entitled *The Iron Mine, Port Henry, New York*. Iron ore extracted from such mines in the Adirondack hills along Lake Champlain and Lake George was employed to forge deadly Parrott guns used in battle by the Union during the war. Martin's work portrays a mine that appears to be abandoned after being exploited for such purposes. Rusted tailings resembling streaks of dried blood descend from the adits—cavernous mine-shaft openings that suggest entry wounds.

Viewers familiar with grim photographic images such as the pictures taken by Alexander Gardner at Antietam, showing bloated, bullet-ridden corpses decaying on the battlefield, could see such carnage reflected in Martin's portrayal of a once-idyllic landscape blasted and brutalized to provide raw materials for the Union war effort. His painting shares with those images of unburied soldiers the haunting quality of abandonment. The ravaged hillside here is left to crumble and revert to a natural state, much as an abandoned corpse decomposes and becomes part of nature. For Americans used to envisioning their landscape as peaceful and pristine, Martin's wartime landscape was a disturbing reflection of a violent upheaval that scoured the country and left few people or places untouched. ✛ EJH

ALTERED LANDSCAPE *Born in Albany, New York, in 1836, Homer Dodge Martin was associated as a young artist with the Hudson River school, whose idyllic landscapes of upstate New York often showed the countryside unaltered by civilization. In* The Iron Mine, *however, Martin portrayed the destructive impact of industry on nature and evoked the carnage caused by the Civil War.*

67

THE DESTRUCTIVE MINIÉ BALL

PRIOR TO THE CIVIL WAR, RIFLES—WHICH HAVE GROOVES INSIDE THE barrel that impart spin to a bullet to make it travel straighter and farther—were not used widely in combat because they were hard to load. Rifle balls that were big enough to engage the grooves when fired were difficult to ram down the barrel of the muzzle-loading rifles in use then. The minié ball, named after its co-inventor, Claude-Étienne Minié, was an oblong bullet, smaller than the diameter of the barrel and easy to load. Gases formed by exploding powder expanded the base of the bullet so that it engaged the rifling as it left the barrel. The invention made muzzle-loading rifles employed by both sides during the Civil War accurate and deadly. Minié balls not only traveled farther and straighter than balls fired from smoothbore muskets but also inflicted larger wounds because they mushroomed on impact. "The wound is often from four to eight times as large as the diameter of the base of the ball," wrote surgeon William T. Helmuth, "and the laceration so terrible that mortification [gangrene] almost inevitably results."

In late 1862 Union Major General Ambrose Burnside thrust his Army of the Potomac across the Rappahannock River at Fredericksburg and launched calamitous assaults on Robert E. Lee's Army of Northern Virginia, holding formidable defensive positions on Marye's Heights. During the fighting there on December 13, two minié balls fired from the opposing sides met in midflight and fused together, providing chilling evidence of what those expansive bullets could do to human flesh and bones. ✛ DDM

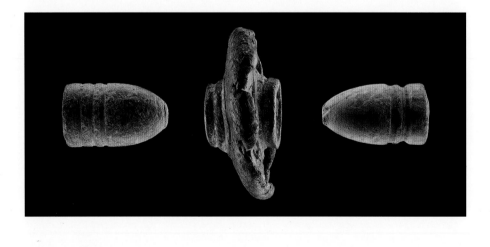

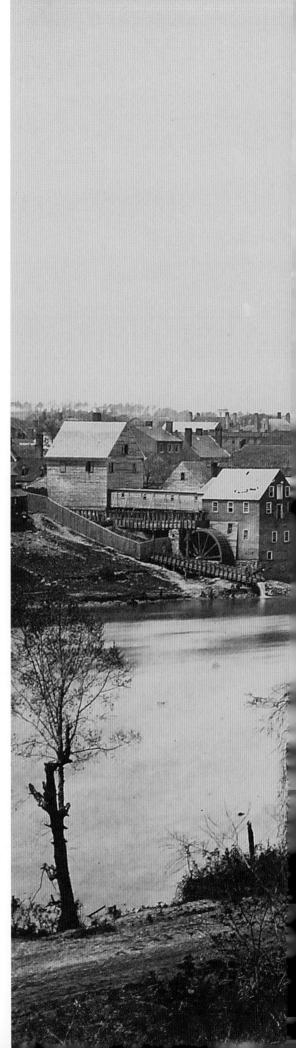

VIOLENT IMPACT *Intact minié balls are shown on either side of two that met in midflight and fused together during the Battle of Fredericksburg. The photograph of Fredericksburg at right was taken by Civil War photographer Timothy O'Sullivan.*

The wound is often from four to eight times as large as the diameter of the base of the ball, and the laceration so terrible that mortification [gangrene] almost inevitably results.

SURGEON WILLIAM T. HELMUTH ON THE IMPACT OF THE MINIÉ BALL

68

PRINTING PRESSES IN ACTION

COMMUNICATION BY VARIOUS ARMED FORCES during the Civil War was facilitated by newly invented, portable printing presses. By 1862 armies and fleets on both sides were using those tabletop models to print general orders, bulletins, and other official documents as well as more entertaining material such as unit newsletters. The Army of the Potomac purchased at least three portable presses by the end of the war. General George McClellan was making use of one even before he took command of that army. "I enclose 'Bulletin No 5' printed with our portable press," he wrote home to his wife, Mary Ellen, from Beverly in western Virginia, on July 19, 1861. "You see we have carried civilization with us in the shape of the printing press & telegraph; institutions decidedly neglected in this part of the world heretofore." Printing presses were not unknown there, in what is now West Virginia, but the new portable presses were all made in the North. One such model, the Adams Cottage press (opposite), was introduced in 1861 and marketed for military use by the Adams Press Company of New York, which ran advertisements touting the devices: "To the army and navy . . . they will be found very useful. They can be packed within the compass of a common traveling trunk, and transported any distance without injury. We have supplied quite a number of regiments with portable printing offices, and they have given universal satisfaction. Rear-Admirals Farragut, Goldsborough and Bailey have each one of our printing offices in their respective fleets." Armies and fleets also purchased chests for their printing departments like the one below, used to store type of various sizes and fonts. ✛ JB

PRINTERS' TYPE CHEST *This chest, marked "Headquarters, Army of the Potomac, Printing Department, No. 6," was made around 1863 by L. Johnson & Company of Philadelphia. Equipped with drawers to store type, it also has handles to make it easier to carry.*

> We have supplied quite a number of regiments with portable printing offices, and they have given universal satisfaction.

ADVERTISEMENT FOR THE ADAMS COTTAGE PRESS

PRINTED IN CAMP General Order No. 192 (RIGHT), intended to hasten the return of Federal convalescents and stragglers to the front lines following the disastrous Battle of Fredericksburg, was issued by command of George McClellan's successor, Major General Ambrose Burnside, from "Head-Quarters, Army of the Potomac, Camp near Falmouth, Va., Dec. 24, 1862." The size and style of the document and its "camp" address indicate that it was printed on a portable device such as the hand-operated Adams Cottage press (BELOW), patented on March 19, 1861, and regularly advertised in newspapers during the war.

Head-Quarters, Army of the Potomac,
Camp near Falmouth, Va., Dec. 24, 1862.

General Orders,
No. 192.

I. In order to facilitate the return to duty of officers and men detained at the camp of convalescents, stragglers, &c., near Alexandria, Maj. W. H. Wood, 17th Infantry, Assistant Provost Marshal General, Army of the Potomac, will repair to Alexandria and take charge of all such officers and men in the various camps of that vicinity as are reported "for duty in the field," superintending their muster and embarkation by corps, under the direction of the corps officer designated for that purpose, and providing the proper escort for the detachment on board the steam boat to Aquia Creek.

II. As the men in those camps are without arms, frequently without proper clothing, and therefore useless with their regiments until supplied, each Corps Commander will appoint, subject to the approval of the Commander of his Grand Division, a suitable officer to take charge of the arming, equipping, clothing, and conducting to Corps Head-Quarters, for distribution to their respective regiments and commands, all officers and men of the Corps who may be turned over to him by Major Wood.

III. The Corps officer charged with this duty must keep himself thoroughly posted as to the calibre and description of all arms, kinds of equipments, clothing, &c., used by the various regiments and commands of his Corps, and on being notified from the office of the Provost Marshal General that a detachment of convalescents, &c., is in readiness for him at Alexandria, will repair to that place with a copy of this order and of the order detailing him for the duty, report to Major Wood and make requisitions for such arms, clothing, &c., as may be necessary to fit out every man of the detachment for immediate service, with forty rounds of ammunition.

IV. As soon as possible after the requisitions are filled, the Corps officer will make the necessary issues to the men (taking such receipts from and making such charges against them as will enable him to transfer the accountability for the property issued, to the commanders of regiments and companies to which the men belong, and furnish the necessary data for the settlement of their account,) and conduct them to the Head-Quarters of his Corps, for distribution to their respective regiments and commands.

V. Capt. H. S. Welton, 19th Infantry, now at Alexandria, will report with his company to Major Wood, and assist him in the execution of this order.

By Command of Major General Burnside:

LEWIS RICHMOND,
Assistant Adjutant General.

Official:

Ass't Adj't Gen'l.

* Erratum

69

DAY OF DELIVERANCE

ON JANUARY 1, 1863, WHEN THE EMANCIPATION Proclamation became law, cannons boomed, church bells rang, and speakers orated at observances throughout the Union and in Union-occupied areas. New Year's Day, previously known among those enslaved as "Heartbreak Day" because large slave auctions were held then, would be known henceforth as a day of deliverance and jubilee. In Union-held Beaufort, South Carolina, on New Year's Day 1863, Colonel Thomas Wentworth Higginson presided over a ceremony where the proclamation was read publicly. After the reading, Higginson related, he waved the flag, and there arose from among the freed slaves on hand an "elderly male voice, into which two women's voices immediately blended, singing . . . 'My country 'tis of thee / Sweet land of Liberty.' . . . I never saw anything so electric; it made all other words cheap . . . the life of the whole day was in those unknown people's song."

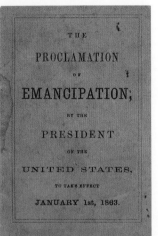

The Emancipation Proclamation was read at similar gatherings as other parts of the South were occupied. Every advance of the Union Army thus became a liberating step. But many held in slavery did not wait to be freed. They forced emancipation by fleeing to Union camps. Many went on to fight as Union soldiers for what Lincoln in his Gettysburg Address called "a new birth of freedom" that transcended racial barriers. As Frederick Douglass declared, "We are all liberated by this Proclamation. . . . The white man is liberated, the black man is liberated." ✛ PG

SPREADING THE WORD *The Emancipation Proclamation, which freed slaves in rebellious states, was printed as a booklet (INSET) to help Union soldiers inform African Americans along the front lines of the proclamation's contents and consequences.*

70

THE LORD IS MY SHEPHERD

NOT LONG AFTER PRESIDENT LINCOLN'S Emancipation Proclamation went into effect on the first day of 1863, artist Eastman Johnson composed the small painting shown opposite. Entitled *The Lord Is My Shepherd*, it portrays a young black man reading the Bible intently. He may well be a former slave, and reading scripture may be an assertion of his newfound freedom. Slaves in the South were not supposed to read or write, and there were laws against teaching them to do so. Achieving literacy was a way for them to declare their independence and their humanity after being denied both by their owners. As a writer for *Harper's Weekly* observed, "The alphabet is an abolitionist. If you would keep a people enslaved, refuse to teach them to read."

The painting's title evokes the comforting words of the Psalms. But the book on this man's lap is not open to Psalms, which are in the middle of the Bible. Rather, he is reading from the front of the Bible, where the book of Exodus offers a compelling message for all those who have endured slavery: "Let my people go." Exodus runs like a river through the stories of African Americans who escaped from bondage. Even those who could not read were steeped in scripture orally. They drew parallels between plantation overseers and Pharaoh, and between those inspired men and women who helped slaves attain freedom—such as Sojourner Truth, Harriet Tubman, and Frederick Douglass—and Moses, who served as a shepherd to his people as he led them out of Egypt to the Promised Land. Many Americans, both enslaved and free, heeded such biblical lessons and felt that Lincoln was fulfilling a moral imperative when he issued the Emancipation Proclamation and opposed a slave system that denied people the right affirmed in this painting: access to the liberating power of the written word. ✛ EJH

BIBLE STUDY *Eastman Johnson's impressive body of work included insightful portraits of African Americans such as the solitary Bible-reader in* The Lord Is My Shepherd.

71

FIGHTING FOR FREEDOM

IN JULY 1862 THE U.S. CONGRESS AUTHORIZED President Lincoln "to employ as many persons of African descent as he may deem necessary and proper for the suppression of this rebellion." Some blacks enlisted in state regiments later that year, but recruitment of men designated officially as U.S. Colored Troops began in 1863 when Lincoln's Emancipation Proclamation took effect, stating that those now "declared to be free" and found to be "of suitable condition, will be received into the armed service of the United States." By war's end, 166 black units had been formed, totaling around 180,000 men. (Another 20,000 or so African Americans served during the Civil War with the U.S. Navy, in which some black sailors were already enrolled when the conflict began.)

Camp William Penn, located about ten miles north of downtown Philadelphia, was the only camp used exclusively to train U.S. Colored Troops. It provided the setting for a patriotic lithograph entitled "Come and Join Us Brothers" (opposite), published in Philadelphia, where the black community strongly supported the volunteers. Members of the St. Thomas African Episcopal Church brought men at Camp William Penn food, clothing, and medical supplies.

Before African American recruits faced the enemy in battle, they had to contend with skepticism and scorn from white Northerners who doubted their capacity to fight. Even the *New York Times*, which backed Lincoln and his war effort, questioned in June 1863 whether "the Negroes were willing to fight at all" and whether "their nature could be kept under such constraints that they would fight in accordance with the laws of civilized warfare." In fact, the most flagrant violations of those unwritten "laws" during

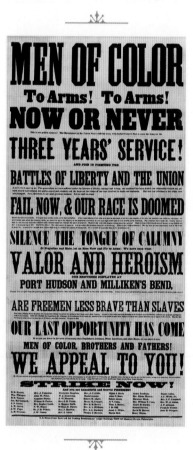

the war were committed by white troops, including Confederates who on several occasions massacred black troops rather than take them prisoner.

African American volunteers faced severe trials off the battlefield as well. They were paid half as much as white troops initially, set to work at the most menial tasks, and received inferior clothing and medical care. The diseases that ravaged their ranks combined with losses in combat to raise the death toll among black troops to an appalling forty thousand before the war ended.

Why would men take such risks to fight for a country that did not yet acknowledge them as citizens? John Randolph, a former slave from Washington, North Carolina, explained that any price he and others might pay in uniform would be worthwhile if "the heroic deeds of colored men on the battlefield would show the world that we are deserving of the rights and title of citizens—a people worthy to be free—worthy to be respected." African American troops proved that they were indeed worthy in fearsome combat at Fort Wagner in South Carolina, Port Hudson in Louisiana, and other battlegrounds. When Colonel Thomas J. Morgan, the white commander of the 14th U.S. Colored Infantry, reminded one of his soldiers that helping the Union secure victory might cost him his life, the man replied firmly: "But my people will be free." ✛ RME

CALL TO ARMS *African American sponsors of the broadside above called on men of "our race" to enlist. A photo of volunteers who responded served as the basis for the lithograph opposite, showing men at Camp William Penn beside their white officer. Some black recruits showed their determination by posing with weapons in hand (OVERLEAF).*

COME AND JOIN US BROTHERS.

PUBLISHED BY THE SUPERVISORY COMMITTEE FOR RECRUITING COLORED REGIMENTS

1210 CHESTNUT ST. PHILADELPHIA.

Tintype of unidentified Union soldier with pistol

Ambrotype of Sergeant Qualls Tibbs, Company E, 27th U.S. Colored Infantry, with rifle

MONEY IN MANY FORMS

PRIOR TO THE CIVIL WAR, THE U.S. TREASURY DID not issue all the nation's money, as it does today. It issued only coins, ranging in value from one cent to twenty dollars. To meet the larger financial needs of a fast-growing nation, hundreds of banks and other businesses issued notes in denominations up to $20,000. The federal government did not guarantee those notes, and they lost value if the issuer defaulted. For everyday transactions, people preferred "hard money": U.S. coins made of gold, silver, or other less-valuable metals. The silver dollar shown here, minted in 1861, was trusted because it had intrinsic value. During the war, anxious Northerners hoarded such coins, and the Union had to come up with other forms of money to keep business going.

Soon after the outbreak of hostilities, war worries and loss of trade with the South caused economic turmoil in the North. By the late summer of 1861, after the disastrous Federal rout at Bull Run, Unionists had to face prospects that were truly nightmarish. What if those stubborn Rebels down South managed to keep up the fight for years—and eventually won the war? What would that mean for the Union's finances and for the money on which its citizens depended? No one knew for sure, but common sense suggested that Northerners should do what people often did when the future looked bleak—cut back. They spent less and squirreled away in safe places assets of lasting value, including U.S. coins. Hoarding those coins seemingly offered people some insurance against hard times. But it only made things worse economically and put the U.S. Treasury in a bind. It could run the U.S. Mint full blast, but it could not stop people from hoarding the new coins along with the old.

As coins grew scarce, Northerners began using U.S. postage stamps as money, even though the stamps got dirty and sticky in the process. In 1862 a resourceful inventor named John Gault patented a device for encasing stamps in a metal frame under a thin sheet of transparent mica. The fact that people were willing to pay extra for stamps that were protected using Gault's process shows how desperate they were for cash of any kind. Enterprising merchants capitalized on that demand by selling encased stamps with advertisements on the back.

In addition to issuing postage stamps that served as money, the government issued notes known as postage currency or fractional currency, with values up to fifty cents. Many of those notes resembled oversize stamps, but they served strictly as substitutes for scarce low-value coins.

In the meantime, Northern businesses of various kinds, from small shops to big banks, compensated for the shortage of coins by issuing their own money, including one-cent copper tokens and notes in small denominations. Like higher-denomination banknotes, those small bills and tokens were not guaranteed by the government. But their low value made them less risky and more convenient for everyday transactions. Together, those private and public alternatives to coins helped sustain the Northern economy until Union forces were well on their way to victory and hoarding subsided. ✛ RD

HARD MONEY *Among the coins hoarded for their intrinsic value during the Civil War was this 1861 silver dollar (*INSET*). The U.S. Mint produced over 77,000 of these 1861 coins, containing 90 percent silver and 10 percent copper.*

STAMPS AS CASH *The three encased U.S. postage stamps at right, with advertisements on the back, substituted for scarce coins during the war. Other substitutes included the five-cent Thomas Jefferson note above—postage currency that looked like a stamp but had no glue and could not be used on mail—and the card below with postage stamps pasted on it, worth five cents and issued by a store in Newport, Rhode Island.*

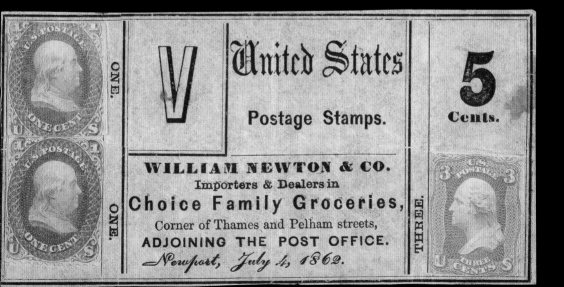

PENNY TOKENS *Wartime tokens like those above were typically worth one cent and often issued by merchants to customers as change. Some tokens featured patriotic emblems or prominent Union figures such as General George McClellan. In 1864 Congress prohibited the issue of these tokens as money, and U.S. coins began circulating more freely as the Union's prospects improved.*

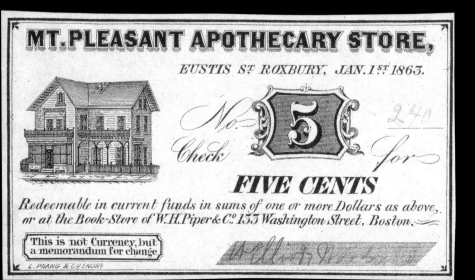

PAPER POCKET CHANGE *Shown at left are notes issued for twenty-five cents by a produce market in Pennsylvania and for five cents by a Massachusetts apothecary, which specified that the paper was not currency and was only a "memorandum for change." By offering to redeem such notes in sums of one dollar or more, businesses encouraged customers to return.*

PRIVATE CURRENCY *Notes issued in small denominations by banks or other businesses (OPPOSITE) were useful as substitutes for scarce coins but could lose value if the public lost faith in the company. The Central Bank of Pennsylvania, for example, ceased operating in 1862 after issuing the five-dollar note shown at top. Notes issued privately in the South like the one at bottom circulated in areas bordering the Confederacy when the war began but rapidly depreciated.*

THE Central Bank of Pennsylvania

No. 2497

Will pay FIVE DOLLARS to Bearer

on demand. Hollidaysburg Feb 14 1857

Cash!   Danforth, Wright & Co. Philada & New York.   Pres!

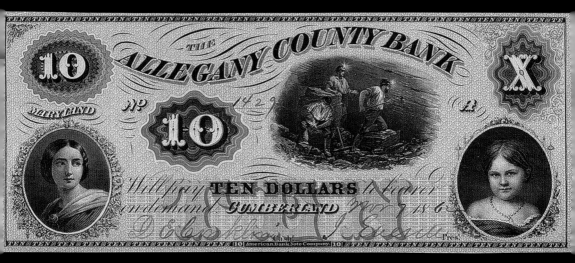

THE ALLEGANY COUNTY BANK

MARYLAND   No.   A

Will pay TEN DOLLARS to bearer

on demand CUMBERLAND   186

Cash!   American Bank Note Company.   Pres!

THE AUGUSTA INSURANCE AND BANKING CO.

Will pay FIFTY Dollars to the

bearer on demand. Augusta 1st May 1860

Pres!   No.   No.   CSA

798   798

STATE OF GEORGIA

Cash!

American Bank Note Company.

73

WINNING WITH GREENBACKS

NEITHER THE UNION NOR THE CONFEDERACY went to war prepared financially for anything more than a brief conflict, paid for with coins and banknotes already in circulation. It soon became clear to the opposing governments, however, that they were in for a long haul and would have to issue paper money to fund their war effort. The Confederate Treasury was quick to do so but ended up issuing too much currency, which contributed to rampant inflation. Before the U.S. Treasury could issue notes, it had to overcome objections from politicians and bankers. Some argued that the Constitution did not give the federal government the right to issue notes. Many thought the Union would be risking ruin if it based its monetary system on anything other than the precious metals in coins.

The first paper money issued by the United States since the Revolutionary War appeared in August 1861—some sixty million dollars' worth of demand notes, so-called because they were payable in coinage on demand. That suited those who wanted gold and silver to remain the nation's monetary standards. But limiting U.S. currency to notes that were redeemable in coin could not meet the vast wartime needs of the Union. In 1862 the U.S. Congress authorized Treasury Secretary Salmon P. Chase (inset) to issue legal tender notes, which could be used legally to pay debts, just as coins could. They were not redeemable in coin, however, and were backed only by the public's faith in the government. Their value fluctuated according to how Northerners thought the war was going. They reached a low point against gold coinage of about thirty-five cents on the dollar in early 1864 before rebounding as the Union neared victory.

The U.S. Treasury issued other kinds of paper during the conflict, including national banknotes. But legal tender notes provided the biggest financial boost to the Union and its war effort. Unlike most privately issued notes, which were printed only on one side, demand notes and legal tender notes were printed on both sides and had only green ink on the back—hence the term "greenback." In other respects, those greenbacks looked much like banknotes and were in fact printed for the U.S. Treasury by the same firms that produced much private currency: the American and National Bank Note Companies.

Northerners would have lost faith in greenbacks if they had been issued indiscriminately to cover all of Washington's wartime expenses. The government avoided that and reduced its debt by imposing the first federal income tax in U.S. history and raising other revenue. Those taxes also helped keep the amount of money in circulation from expanding too rapidly and causing prices to skyrocket as they did in the South, where the inflation rate during the war was more than a hundred times higher than in the North.

Federal notes issued by the Union during the war are scarce today, whereas notes issued by the Confederate government and various Confederate states are fairly common. Why so? Northern paper could be exchanged for coinage or new notes after the war. Southern paper could not, for there was no government left to honor it. That's what happens when you lose a war. ✛ RD

GREENBACK *This ten-dollar demand note, redeemable in coinage, pictures Abraham Lincoln on the front (TOP) and has only green ink on the back (BOTTOM)—a color chosen because it was hard to counterfeit.*

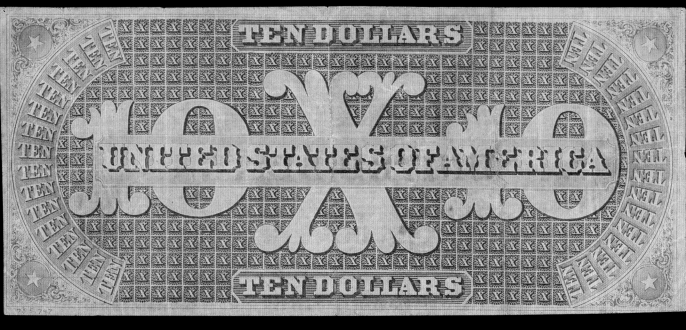

THE GRAY GHOST

IN 1862 THE CONFEDERATE CONGRESS AUTHORIZED THE FORMATION OF bands of partisan rangers. Although paid the same as regular troops and subject to the same regulations, those partisans were licensed to seize enemy arms and munitions, which they would then deliver to Confederate quartermasters. The rangers would be fully compensated for the value of their haul "in such manner as the Secretary of War may prescribe." Among the bands formed to carry out such raids and harass Federal forces was the 43rd Battalion Virginia Cavalry, known as Mosby's Rangers for its celebrated commander, Colonel John Singleton Mosby (1833–1916).

> *I wish I had a hundred men like Mosby.*
>
> **GENERAL ROBERT E. LEE**

In his turbulent youth, Mosby was expelled from the University of Virginia and sentenced to a year in prison for shooting a fellow student. He studied law in jail and was practicing as an attorney in Bristol, Virginia, when his state seceded. He joined up with the Washington Mounted Rifles, which became part of the 1st Virginia Cavalry Regiment, led by the dashing J.E.B. Stuart, who served as Mosby's model.

Organized in 1863, Mosby's Rangers were soon notorious for their daring raids on Union supply depots, after which they seemingly vanished, earning Mosby his nickname, the "Gray Ghost." At Fairfax Court House in March 1863, he stole up on Brigadier General Edwin Stoughton and captured that commander, two captains, thirty other men, and fifty-eight horses. "I can make more generals," President Lincoln reportedly said when informed of the raid, "but I can't make more horses." Although Mosby's partisans profited from their raids, he did not share in the spoils and viewed his forays as a legitimate military tactic, designed to disrupt communications and destroy supplies, thus sapping the enemy's "offensive strength." His men bedeviled Federal forces in the Shenandoah Valley in 1864 and drew the ire of General Philip Sheridan, who vowed to crack down and let Mosby's partisans know "there is a God in Israel." Severely wounded in December 1864, Mosby recovered and went into hiding at war's end with a hefty $5,000 bounty on his head, before General Ulysses Grant officially pardoned him in June 1865. ✠ KG

MOSBY'S RANGERS *Pictured late in the war, a clean-shaven Mosby stands at center with men of the 43rd Battalion Virginia Cavalry. Most of Mosby's Rangers were Virginians—with some Marylanders and a few foreigners mixed in—and all were fine horsemen and crack shots.*

Culpepper C. H.

See other record.

HEADQUARTERS CAVALRY DIVISION,
ARMY OF N. VA., March 12, 1863.

General Orders,
No. —

Captain JOHN S. MOSBY has for a long time attracted the attention of his Generals by his boldness, skill and success, so signally displayed in his numerous forays upon the invaders of his native State.

None know his daring enterprise and dashing heroism, better than those foul invaders, though strangers themselves to such noble traits.

His late brilliant exploit—the capture of Brig. Gen. STOUGHTON, U. S. A., two Captains, thirty other prisoners, together with their arms, equipments and fifty-eight horses—justifies this recognition in General Orders.

This feat, unparalleled in the war, was performed in the midst of the enemy's troops, at Fairfax C. H., without loss or injury.

The gallant band of Capt. MOSBY share the glory, as they did the danger of this enterprise, and are worthy of such a leader.

J. E. B. STUART,
Major General Commanding.

The above is the original order printed on Culpepper & issued by General Stuart to cavalry. He gave me 50
Jno: S. Mosby

HIGH PRAISE *An order from Major General J.E.B. Stuart, dated March 12, 1863, salutes Mosby for his "daring enterprise" and "dashing heroism" and cites his recent raid on Fairfax Court House, where he surprised Brigadier General Edwin Stoughton while he was sleeping. Stoughton mistook him in the dark for a Union soldier and asked if Mosby had been caught. "No," Mosby replied, "but he has caught you."*

GHOSTLY GEAR *Among the "Gray Ghost" relics held at the Smithsonian (BELOW) are his slouch hat, minus the plume, his shell jacket, and a pair of crutches made for him by one of his father's slaves. Mosby was injured in action several times during the war, prompting Robert E. Lee to remark: "The only thing I have to find fault with your conduct, Colonel Mosby, is that you are always getting wounded."*

75

COPING WITH THE BLOCKADE

BY 1863 THE UNION BLOCKADE OF CONFEDERATE ports, proclaimed by President Lincoln days after the fall of Fort Sumter, was taking a heavy toll on the South. In conjunction with Union efforts to seize control of the Mississippi River, as proposed by General Winfield Scott in his so-called Anaconda Plan, the naval blockade was designed to squeeze the Confederacy ever tighter until it collapsed.

The U.S. Navy was hard-pressed to seal off all inlets along the Southern coastline from Virginia to Texas. Confederate blockade-runners—swift steamships with low profiles and shallow drafts—managed to slip through and carry goods to and from New Orleans (until that city was occupied in 1862) and other Southern ports, including Mobile, Savannah, Charleston, and Wilmington, North Carolina. The cargo conveyed by blockade-runners included mail and cotton, which was exported to Europe to help pay for the luxury items and vital war supplies that those ships smuggled back to the South.

Their capacity was limited, however, and many blockade-runners were captured or destroyed by Union warships as the war progressed.

As Southerners lost control of their coast and inland waterways, they faced severe shortages of various items, ranging from lifesaving medicines like quinine to basics such as writing paper and envelopes, without which long-distance business could not be conducted and soldiers could not keep in touch with their kin. Civilians on the home front, many of them women, coped with such shortages by devising substitutes. They fashioned homemade envelopes like the one below, known as adversity covers, using scraps from paper bags, wallpaper, old business receipts and invoices, out-of-date train or ship schedules, advertisements, and maps. Such improvised stationery testifies to the ingenuity of those women who had to make ends meet when their men went off to war, and who faced adversity without flinching as the Union tightened its noose around the Confederacy. ☩ TL

ADVERSITY COVER
This envelope, made from wallpaper, bears a ten-cent Jefferson Davis stamp and was mailed in December 1863 from Georgetown, South Carolina, to Dr. W. C. Truman in Columbia, the state capital. The Union blockade had little impact on such short-distance deliveries within the South but obstructed overseas mail and postal service between Confederate ports.

76

GORDON'S JOURNEY

THE CIVIL WAR WAS FOUGHT BOTH ON THE FIELD of battle and in the court of public opinion. Writers and orators were not alone in making their voices heard. Image makers also contributed. As this carte-de-visite of an escaped slave named Gordon suggests, photography was capable of communicating powerful ideas that undermined the notion that slavery was a benign institution.

The photograph of Gordon showing his scourged back was produced by two itinerant photographers, William D. McPherson and his partner, Mr. Oliver. Gordon had received a severe whipping for undisclosed reasons on a Louisiana plantation in late 1862. By one account, the wounds were inflicted by his overseer, who was discharged by the plantation owner. As Gordon recuperated, he decided to escape and eventually managed to

York journalist wrote that "this Card Photograph should be multiplied by 100,000, and scattered over the States. It tells the story in a way that even Mrs. [Harriet Beecher] Stowe cannot approach, because it tells the story to the eye." Abolitionist leaders such as William Lloyd Garrison and Frederick Douglass referred to it repeatedly in their work.

On July 4, 1863, *Harper's Weekly* reproduced the image as a wood engraving to illustrate an article on Gordon, entitled "A Typical Negro." Two other portraits of him—one "as he entered our lines," and the other "in his uniform as a U.S. soldier"—were also included. Those images and the accompanying article describing his ordeal and the brutal punishments inflicted on other slaves made him a symbol of African American endurance and patriotism.

do so, taking with him onions, which he rubbed on his body to throw off the bloodhounds used by the slave catchers pursuing him. Gordon succeeded in eluding them and reached safety in March 1863 at a Union encampment in Baton Rouge, his clothes torn and his body covered with mud.

Now free, Gordon decided to enlist in the Union Army. President Lincoln had recently granted African Americans the opportunity to serve in segregated units, and Gordon was among the many who enlisted in response. Before being mustered into the army, he received a medical examination in camp that revealed the extensive scars on his back. McPherson and Oliver were there at the time and asked Gordon to pose for a picture revealing the harsh treatment he had recently received.

That portrait provoked an immediate response, and soon copies were circulating widely as cartes-de-visite. One New

According to *Harper's Weekly*, Gordon served as a Union guide in Louisiana and was seized by Confederates, beaten, and left for dead before reviving and returning to camp. There are no further records indicating what became of Gordon. Yet this famous image of him lives on as a searing indictment of slavery and as a tribute to the fortitude of those who resisted and overcame it. ✛ FHG

BEATEN BUT UNBOWED *Slaves were often lashed with small whips similar to the one above. Gordon suffered more drastic beatings, as shown in a carte-de-visite printed at Mathew Brady's Washington studio (OPPOSITE). A doctor at the Union camp Gordon entered wrote that few slaves he had seen endured "worse punishments . . . though nothing in his appearance indicates any unusual viciousness—but on the contrary, he seems intelligent and well-behaved."*

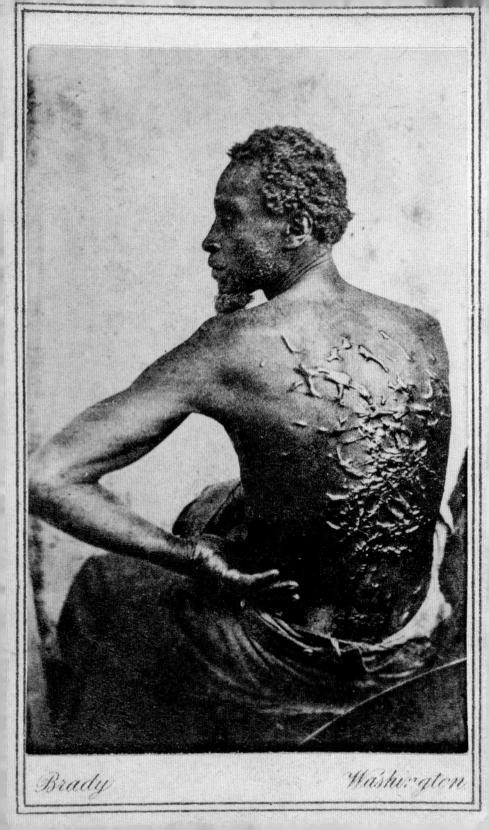

Brady   Washington

SOUTHERN ILLUSTRATED NEWS

"THESE NORTHERN ILLUSTRATED PAPERS ARE all unworthy of respect," declared the *Savannah News* in a January 1861 editorial that dismissed *Frank Leslie's Illustrated Newspaper* as bad and *Harper's Weekly* as "not one whit better." When the war began, Southerners grew even more resentful and envious of popular Northern illustrated weeklies, which ran engravings of the conflict and its leading figures, based on sketches and photographs, that strongly influenced public perceptions and

> *We offer the highest salaries ever paid in this country for good engravers.*
>
> **E. W. AYRES AND W. H. WADE, PUBLISHERS OF THE *SOUTHERN ILLUSTRATED NEWS***

attitudes. Determined to match the ability of the Northern press to boost support for the war effort through pictorial coverage, the Richmond-based publishers E. W. Ayres and W. H. Wade launched the *Southern Illustrated News* in September 1862. Their eight-page weekly faced constant challenges securing adequate supplies of paper and ink as well as access to printing presses. But they spared no expense to offer compelling illustrations, as indicated by an advertisement they ran in July 1863: "Desirous, if possible, of illustrating the 'News' in a style not inferior to the 'London Illustrated News,' we offer the highest salaries ever paid in this country for good engravers."

The publishers' pictorial emphasis was evident in large-scale engravings like that of Lieutenant General Thomas J. "Stonewall" Jackson (1824–1863), which dominates the front page of the August 29, 1863, issue of *Southern Illustrated News* (opposite). Jackson's likeness was based on a photograph of him taken by Daniel T. Cowell shortly before the Battle of Chancellorsville in May 1863, during which Jackson was mortally wounded. This engraved portrait, conveying his resolve and determination, was accompanied by excerpts from John Esten Cooke's biography of the fallen hero, whose legend grew larger even as the fortunes of the Confederacy declined. Cooke extolled Jackson as the embodiment of the South's "faith in God and in itself, its terrible energy, its enthusiasm and daring, its unconquerable will, its contempt of danger and fatigue, its capacity to smite, as with bolts and thunder, the cowardly and cruel foe that would trample under foot its liberty and its religion."

Cooke's account proved extraordinarily popular and helped enshrine Jackson as a Southern idol while offering readers hope that his fighting spirit would live on among the troops and bring them victory. "Jackson's corps will be led forever by the memory of the great chieftain," Cooke declared. In fact, Jackson's death proved an irreparable loss for Army of Northern Virginia and its commander, Robert E. Lee. The Battle of Chancellorsville, where Lee brilliantly outmaneuvered the larger Army of the Potomac, led by Joseph Hooker, was a major Southern victory. But Lee likened the loss of Jackson—felled by friendly fire during a nighttime reconnaissance he conducted after stunning Hooker with an audacious flank attack—to losing his "right arm."

That appraisal proved prophetic as Lee advanced northward into Maryland and Pennsylvania in June and faced his supreme test at Gettysburg without the officer most suited to deliver a decisive blow for him. A few months later, the *Southern Illustrated News* did its best to soothe bitter afterthoughts of that battle by eulogizing Jackson, whose memory was all the more precious to Confederates because he perished at a time of triumph, before the tide turned against them. ✦ ACG

PICTURING A LEGEND *When this edition featuring the late Stonewall Jackson appeared in August 1863, the* Southern Illustrated News *was not yet a year old. But the publishers claimed that their weekly was already read by "more than one hundred thousand respectable and honorable residents of the Southern Confederacy."*

SOUTHERN ILLUSTRATED NEWS

Vol. II.   RICHMOND, SATURDAY, AUGUST 29, 1863.   No. 8.

Recollections of Stonewall Jackson.

Our readers are doubtless aware that we have recently issued from our presses a memoir of this great and good man. The book will be read by thousands, still there will remain many who will never have an opportunity of perusing its pages. For the benefit of such of our readers we make a few extracts from the work. The "Dispatch" of this city has truly remarked, "that the people can never be tired reading even the slightest unveiling of this mysterious man, whom they almost worshipped."

"JACKSON IS DEAD."

"Seldom have words penetrated more deeply to the heart of a great nation. The people of the Confederate States had begun to regard this immortal leader as above the reach of fate. He had passed unhurt through such desperate contests; his calm eyes had surveyed so many hard fought battlefields, from the commencement of the combats to their termination, that a general conviction of the hero's invulnerability had impressed every heart—no one could feel that the light in those eyes of the great soldier would ever be quenched. But that Providence which decrees all things wisely at last sent the fatal bullet; and the South is called upon to mourn the untimely death of one who seemed to his countrymen the chosen standard bearer of liberty. After the battle of Chancellorsville and while the wound of the famous soldier attracted to him the warmest sympathy and drew forth the earnest prayers of many thousands for his recovery, the journals of the land contained many notices of his services and genius, and his death was alluded to as a calamity too frightful to be contemplated. Well has one of these journals in speaking of Lee and Jackson said: 'It is an honor to breathe the air they breathe. Together, they make up a measure of glory which no nation under Heaven ever surpassed. Other great leaders we have, to whom unstinted praise is due and everywhere gladly accorded; but the rays of their fame converge and accumulate but to add to the dazzling splendor that illuminates the names of Lee and Jackson.

"'The central figure of this war is, beyond all question, that of Robert E. Lee. His, the calm, broad military intellect that reduced the chaos after Donelson to form and order. But Jackson is the motive power that executes, with the rapidity of lightning, all that Lee can plan. Lee is the exponent of Southern power of command; Jackson, the expression of its faith in God and in itself, its terrible energy, its enthusiasm and daring, its unconquerable will, its contempt of danger and fatigue, its capacity to smite, as with bolts of thunder, the cowardly and cruel foe that would trample under foot its liberty and its religion.

"'Jackson was no accidental manifestation of the country, could not add one cubit to the stature of his glory.

"'Even should he die, his fiery and unquailing spirit would survive in his men. He has infused into them that which cannot die. The leader who succeeds him, be he whom he may, will be impelled, as by a supernatural impulse, to emulate his matchless deeds. Jackson's men

LIEUT. GEN. T. J. JACKSON.

Entered according to the act of Congress, in the year 1863, by ATERS & WADE, in the Clerk's Office of the District Court of the Confederate States for the Eastern District of Virginia.

the powers of faith and courage. He came not by chance in this day and to this generation. He was born for a purpose. In this conviction, he rests serenely, awaiting the healing of his wounds; willing once more to hear the wild cheers of his men as he rides to the front; or, if that be denied him, content to retire from the field, a maimed, humble, simple Christian man. Civil honor, were it the highest gift of

will demand to be led in "Stonewall Jackson's way." The leader who will not or cannot comply with that demand, must drop the baton quickly. Jackson's corps will be led forever by the memory of its great chieftain.'

"Alas! the termination of his wound was fatal. The great soul has passed away from us: and we are left without his sagacious counsels, his splendid powers of execution; his

unerring judgment, and that intuitive genius for war which made him, in his sphere, the first of living leaders, and ranked him with the greatest who have lived in all tide of time."

HOW HE GOT THE NAME OF "STONEWALL."

'Twas at the first battle of Manassas, when the Southern leaders "saw with irrepressible anguish the exhaustion of the troops; the waning fortunes of the day, and the countless reserves which the enemy hurled incessantly upon their thin and weary lines. Among these was the heroic General Bee, in command of the 4th Alabama and some Mississippians, who were nearly worn out by the terrible ordeal through which they had passed. Bee rode up and down the lines, cheering on the men, and beseeching them, by all they held dear, not to give way, when he met Jackson, and said, in the bitter despair of his heart, "General, they are beating us back!" The face of the stern, silent soldier, betrayed no answering emotion. The keen eye glittered for an instant; the lips opened; and in the curt, peculiar tones of the speaker he said, 'Sir, we will give them the bayonet!' Bee seemed to gather new inspiration from the words; he galloped back to the remnants of his command, and fronting to Jackson, called out to his men: 'There is Jackson standing like a stonewall! Let us determine to die here, and we will conquer. Follow me!' * *

At Manassas, "the country had gained a splendid victory against enormous odds; and although he did not then know it, Jackson had gained a name with which he is forever inseparably identified. When the heroic Bee exclaimed, "There is Jackson standing like a stonewall," he unconsciously employed a term which thenceforth clung to Jackson more closely than his baptismal appellation. From that hot day of battle, the leader of the men of the Valley was known as "Stonewall Jackson,"—his command as the "Stonewall Brigade." Many are ignorant and few recall the fact, that the great soldier was christened "Thomas Jonathan." His veritable christening in the popular heart was on that evening of Manassas when Bee, about to surrender his great soul to his Maker, baptized him, amid blood and fire, "STONEWALL JACKSON!"

PERSONAL APPEARANCE.

The outward appearance of the famous leader was not imposing. The popular idea of a great general is an individual of stiff and stately bearing, clad in splendid costume, all covered with gold lace and decorations, who prances by upon

78

J.E.B. STUART'S PISTOL

WHEN STONEWALL JACKSON WAS MORTALLY wounded at Chancellorsville on May 2, 1863, that fallen Confederate hero was replaced by a living legend—Major General J.E.B. Stuart (1833–1864). A colorful and charismatic Virginian, Stuart had won renown in June 1862 by riding full circle around the Union Army of the Potomac near Richmond in a daring reconnaissance hailed throughout the Confederacy. An officer who accompanied him recalled: "The Southern papers were filled with accounts of the expedition, none accurate and most of them marvelous." Not yet thirty, Stuart became Robert E. Lee's cavalry chief and kept him apprised of enemy movements as battle loomed. Just hours after Jackson fell at Chancellorsville, Stuart took charge of his infantry corps and renewed the attack on General Joseph Hooker. By midday on May 3, Hooker had been knocked out of action and his Federals were retreating.

Stuart's stellar performance at Chancellorsville further enhanced his reputation. There were rumors in camp that as Jackson lay dying, he recommended that Stuart be given permanent command of his corps. "I would rather know that Jackson said that, than have the appointment," Stuart remarked. Lee relied mightily on Stuart as cavalry chief and chose to retain him in that capacity, but some admirers felt he was being slighted. "I always thought it an injustice to Stuart and a loss to the army that he was not from that moment continued in command of Jackson's corps," one officer later remarked. "He had won the right to it." Stuart's chief of staff, Major Heros von Borcke, a Prussian cavalry officer who took leave from his unit to serve the Confederacy, thought that Stuart would surely be recognized as Jackson's successor after Chancellorsville and elevated in rank. In June 1863 Borcke presented him with the .44-caliber Tranter revolver pictured here, held in a case with a plaque on the lid (opposite, top) inscribed to "Lt. Gen. J.E.B. Stuart, C.S.A."

Given time, Stuart might have attained the rank that Borcke anticipated for him and become one of the South's youngest lieutenant generals. But the tide of battle was turning against him, and he had little time left. Union cavalrymen, outmatched by Confederate troopers early in the conflict, were gaining confidence. On June 9 they surprised Stuart's forces at Brandy Station and held their own in that contest. Later that month, Stuart set out on another adventurous circuit around the Army of the Potomac but was prevented from rejoining Lee at Gettysburg until July 2, too late to be of much help there. On May 11, 1864, Stuart was wounded in action at Yellow Tavern, near Richmond, and died the next day. "I can scarcely think of him without weeping," said Lee, who recognized Stuart for what he was—a consummate cavalier, forever seeking glory on horseback. ✢ DDM

CAVALRY CHIEF *Portrayed above with sword in hand in 1863 by photographer George S. Cook, Major General J.E.B. Stuart received this English-made Tranter pistol* (OPPOSITE) *from Major Heros von Borcke not long after the Battle of Chancellorsville.*

I always thought it an injustice to Stuart and a loss to the army that he was not from that moment continued in command of Jackson's corps. He had won the right to it.

GENERAL E. PORTER ALEXANDER, ON J.E.B. STUART AT CHANCELLORSVILLE

REWARDING GRANT'S TRIUMPH AT VICKSBURG

TO WIN THE CIVIL WAR, UNION LEADERS KNEW that they had to regain control of the Mississippi River, thus cutting the Confederacy in half and restoring the free flow of commerce and war material between the Midwest and the Gulf of Mexico. By the spring of 1863, Vicksburg and Port Hudson were the last Confederate strongholds on the Mississippi. Seizing Vicksburg fell to the Army of Tennessee and its hard-driving commander, Ulysses S. Grant. Unable to take Vicksburg from the north or west, where it was shielded by steep cliffs and heavy artillery, Grant circled around to the south and east in a daring move that trapped the city's defenders between his army and Union gunboats on the Mississippi. Grant first tried direct assaults on Vicksburg from the east on May 19 and 22, but both failed. He then reluctantly settled in for a siege, which continued for six weeks. Grant's gunners lobbed over 22,000 rounds into the city, and their foes returned fire. Residents and soldiers on both sides took shelter in hillside caves like those pictured opposite. Finally, on the Fourth of July 1863, the Confederates surrendered. The fall of Vicksburg combined with the Confederate defeat at Gettysburg, where Robert E. Lee began withdrawing his forces that same day, marked the turning point of the war.

President Lincoln recognized Grant's exceptional leadership by appointing him commander of all Union operations west of the Appalachians. For Grant's boosters in Congress, however, that was not enough. Elihu Washburne of Illinois, who represented Grant's district in the House, helped orchestrate a Joint Resolution of Congress on December 17, 1863, thanking Grant and his forces and awarding him a Congressional Gold Medal (below). Lincoln needed no prodding from Congress to continue favoring Grant, who in March 1864 was promoted to lieutenant general—the first U.S. officer elevated to that rank since George Washington—and became general in chief of the Union Army. The Gold Medal did not reach Grant until March 1865 at City Point, outside Petersburg, where he was busy besieging Lee's battered army and made no note of it. The medal was one of many trophies he garnered for his invaluable service, but the only reward he sought was victory and a successful conclusion to this ruinous war. ✣ DKA

FRUITS OF VICTORY *After seizing Vicksburg—where this picture was taken of Union dugouts below the abandoned Shirley House—Ulysses S. Grant was awarded the Congressional Gold Medal (RIGHT). Mingling symbols of war and peace, it pictures him beneath laurel and oak leaves denoting victory and strength. The obverse portrays America as a fruitful maiden with a shield marked "Donelson," Grant's first big triumph; below her are views of Vicksburg and Chattanooga, secured by Grant in late 1863. This medal was donated to the Smithsonian by William Vanderbilt, who received it as a gift after assuming Grant's debts.*

80

PORT HUDSON BURIAL POST

IN MAY 1863, AS ULYSSES GRANT'S ARMY BESIEGED Vicksburg, Union troops under General Nathaniel P. Banks encircled Port Hudson, a strategically vital Louisiana town on the Mississippi River. His force was more than twice the size of the Confederate garrison but suffered losses on the order of ten to one when he assaulted the entrenched defenders. Not until July 9, after the fall of Vicksburg made their position hopeless, did the Confederates yield.

Among the nearly five thousand Union men killed or wounded there was Lieutenant Charles R. Carville. He was only eighteen when he enlisted in the 165th New York Infantry in 1862. Like many others his age, Carville probably felt compelled to serve his country and take part in the great events that would define his generation. His quick rise from private to second lieutenant between May and September 1862 speaks to a potential that would never be fully realized.

On May 27, 1863, Banks attacked the Confederate works in a debacle that left nearly two thousand Federals dead or wounded. Carville fought that day with the "soul and heart of a man and patriot," according to his obituary in a New York paper. The headboard below marked the spot where he was buried—one of ninety-four men in his regiment who gave "their lives in the sacred cause for which they had taken up arms." ✦ RL

81

COLORS OF THE 84TH INFANTRY

AMONG THE UNION SOLDIERS WHO FOUGHT UNDER General Nathaniel P. Banks at Port Hudson were black troops of the newly organized Corps d'Afrique and the Louisiana Native Guards. Men of the 1st Louisiana Native Guards—volunteers from New Orleans who had long been free—resisted pressure from Banks to have white officers assigned to them, as was customary for black units in the Union Army. They retained their own officers, including Captain André Cailloux and Lieutenant John Crowder. Cailloux and Crowder were among the first African American officers to die fighting for the Union, cut down at Port Hudson on May 27 in a desperate attack that cost the Louisiana Native Guards and the Corps d'Afrique more than two hundred casualties.

In June 1863 the Louisiana Native Guards became part of the Corps d'Afrique, and in 1864 soldiers from that corps formed the 84th Infantry, U.S. Colored Troops, which served under Banks in the Red River Campaign that spring. Port Hudson was commemorated on the regiment's colors (opposite), along with later battles in which the 84th took part. A white officer who served as adjutant of the regiment kept the flag. One of his descendants donated it to the Smithsonian, where it resides today, honoring the 84th Infantry and its predecessors, the Louisiana Native Guards and the Corps d'Afrique. ✦ JLJ

IN REMEMBRANCE *Lieutenant Charles Carville's family preserved this carved wooden headboard, erected as his temporary grave marker at Port Hudson by men of the 165th New York. In 1906 his sister, Mrs. E. C. Fiedler, donated it, along with his uniform to the Smithsonian. She wrote that it would be "a satisfaction for me to feel, that these treasured articles, will be in the care of the Government."*

BATTLE HONORS *Inscribed on the flag of the 84th U.S. Colored Infantry are Port Hudson, where the Louisiana Native Guards and the Corps d'Afrique fought before the 84th formed, as well as four battles in which the regiment took part during the Red River Campaign and an engagement in Texas at war's end.*

WOODBLOCK PRINTING

O N JULY 4, 1863, THE *NEW YORK ILLUSTRATED NEWS* published a picture entitled "Camp of the 1st District Negro Volunteers (Colored) on Mason's Island, Opposite Georgetown, D.C.," produced using the engraved woodblock shown here. The original drawing was done by Arthur Lumley, whose eyewitness views of Union camps and campaigns appeared in various publications. During the Civil War, neither sketches by artists like Lumley nor photographs could be reproduced directly in newspapers. They were copied by engravers on woodblocks and then assembled with type in a separate printing form for each page in the paper.

This woodblock is significant not just for the quality of its engraving but for what it portrays—the first African American regiment raised in the nation's capital. Known officially as the 1st U.S. Colored Troops, many in the regiment were former slaves who had sought refuge in Washington, D.C., as contrabands. Now, as freedmen, they volunteered to help defeat the Confederacy and end slavery. Their camp, situated on Mason's Island (now Theodore Roosevelt Island) in the Potomac River, was within the District of Columbia but set safely apart from the city of Washington, where some white residents had attacked black recruits in the streets. Other white Unionists admired the volunteers for their patriotism, which the *New York Illustrated News* highlighted by featuring them on the Fourth of July. "No one can see them," wrote poet Walt Whitman after visiting their camp, "without feeling well pleased with them." Numbering some 700 soldiers when it entered service in Virginia, the regiment lost 185 men before the war was over, including more than 100 who died of disease and 67 who were killed or mortally wounded in battle. ✢ JB

PATRIOT'S CAMPS *This engraved woodblock shows the 1st U.S. Colored Troops on review in 1863, with their tents in the background. Large woodblocks like this one were prepared for engraving by gluing or bolting together pieces of hardwood, such as boxwood or maple, and then planing the surface.*

83

SEARCHING FOR SHOES IN GETTYSBURG

A SEARCH FOR SHOES HAS OFTEN BEEN CITED AS the spark that ignited a blistering three-day battle in the bucolic fields around Gettysburg, Pennsylvania, on July 1, 1863. Procuring shoes was indeed a concern for both sides during the Civil War—and for Robert E. Lee's hard-marching Army of Northern Virginia in particular. But other factors besides a Rebel foray for footwear contributed to the war's costliest battle. Lee and his opponent, George G. Meade, the newly appointed commander of the Army of the Potomac, had only a vague idea of each other's whereabouts, and their forces collided at a place that was not of either general's choosing.

Lee and Meade were little the wiser than Sarah Broadhead, who from her home at the west end of Gettysburg observed Rebels and Yankees approaching and wrote in her diary on the night of June 30, "It begins to look as though we will have a battle soon and we are in great fear." While she was committing her trepidations to paper, A. P. Hill, commander of Lee's newly formed Third Corps, was in Cashtown, eight miles to the west, conferring with division commander Henry Heth and brigade commander James Pettigrew about sending troops into Gettysburg, which reportedly contained a shoe factory. Pettigrew had conducted a reconnaissance there earlier that day and pulled back after observing cavalry on the outskirts of town.

Hill, who had just met with Lee, reckoned that those enemy troopers were inexperienced home guards. Lee had only sketchy intelligence on enemy movements after the cavalry commander who functioned as his "eyes and ears," J.E.B. Stuart set out on a wide sweep around Meade's army and lost touch with headquarters. Lee gathered from scouts that the Army of the Potomac was off to the south, at least a day's march away from Gettysburg. In fact, the Yankees spotted there by Pettigrew on the 30th were veteran cavalrymen of John Buford's brigade, who would be joined the following morning by infantrymen of the redoubtable Iron Brigade. When Meade dispatched them northward, he had no idea that Gettysburg would become an epic battleground. Like Lee, he was simply trying to find the enemy.

For Heth, Gettysburg was an alluring target because of its shoe factory. "If there is no objection, General," he said to Hill that evening, "I will take my division tomorrow and get those shoes." Hill consented, but he was less intent on obtaining shoes than determining if Meade's forces were nearby. As he informed Lee, he was advancing on Gettysburg to "discover what was in my front." A fierce battle erupted there on July 1 because several roads intersected at Gettysburg and brought Heth's troops and other elements of Lee's dispersed army back together at the same time as their foes reached the crossroads from the south in roughly equal strength. When the battle ended on July 3, the hoped-for shoe factory, which did not in fact exist, was all but forgotten. The need for shoes was real, however, and continued to plague soldiers on both sides. "Thousands of the men are barefoot," wrote one Yankee, "but they are bravely struggling on . . . so we may finish the war now." ✣ JGB

LEE'S LIEUTENANT *This portrait of General A. P. Hill, who unwittingly launched the Battle of Gettysburg by sending in Henry Heth's division to "get those shoes," was printed from a glass negative made by Julian Vannerson around 1864. His picture may have been the last taken of Hill before he died in action just before the war ended.*

Thousands of the men are barefoot ...
but they are bravely struggling on ...
so we may finish the war now.

PRIVATE OLIVER W. NORTON, 83RD PENNSYLVANIA INFANTRY,
AFTER THE BATTLE OF GETTYSBURG

UNION SHOES *To keep its troops marching, the Union bought millions*
of brogan-type leather shoes such as this pair from a legion of contractors
utilizing new sewing and pegging machines. These shoes, issued to a U.S.
Army engineer, served as models for those on a statue of General William T.
Sherman near the White House in Washington, D.C.

DEPICTING CAMP LIFE

CANTEENS WERE ESSENTIAL FOR TROOPS WHO wanted to quench their thirst, brew coffee, or cook food. They also symbolized the shared experience of men in uniform. The popular phrase "We drank from the same canteen," repeated often by veterans of the Civil War and other conflicts, hints at the lasting friendships forged by fellow soldiers in perilous times.

Many canteens from the Civil War tell us something about the owner. Soldiers often carved their initials or unit number into wooden canteens. Occasionally, they made similar marks on a metal canteen or embroidered flags or other patriotic emblems on the canteen's fabric covering to signal which side they fought for. The owner of the canteen below, who reportedly fought for the Union at Gettysburg, painted a vivid tableau of camp life on its tin frame. His was an 1862 Union "bull's eye" canteen, so named for the concentric rings on each side. Corrugating the metal in that way made it stronger and allowed the manufacturer to use a thin sheet of tin and produce a lightweight canteen—much lighter than the wooden canteens carried by many Confederate soldiers. For that reason,

Confederates often scavenged these popular canteens from fallen Federals.

The scene painted on this canteen is a snapshot of camp life, preserved as a memento of the war like a letter home or a diary entry. At right, a soldier appears to be on guard duty beside a tent over which flies an American flag. To the left, another soldier sits on a log before a fire. The scene evokes the rituals and chores of camp life: pitching tents, standing guard, gathering firewood, and preparing food. Soldiers accustomed to the orderliness of camp life as depicted here faced a stark contrast when they entered battle at Gettysburg and other chaotic killing grounds. Memories of camp and its monotonous routine could be soothing to men who endured grueling campaigns, which may explain why this unknown soldier-artist chose to depict that theme on an object that meant much to him. ✦ NGE

CAMP CIRCLE *This painted "bull's eye" canteen has a cork stopper and three metal loops soldered to the edges for the carrying strap. The Union soldier who painted the canteen proudly placed the Stars and Stripes near the center of the circular frame shown in detail below, at right.*

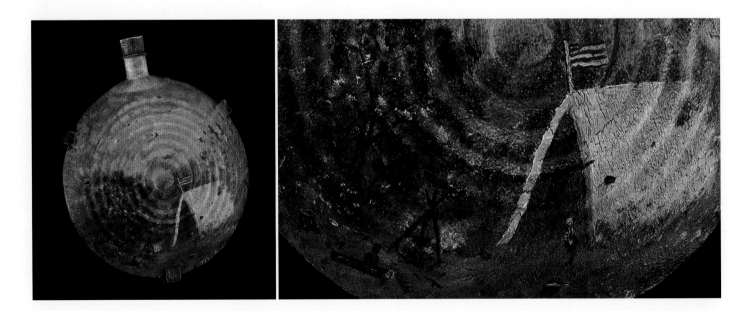

THE SACRIFICE OF STRONG VINCENT

THE DEFENSE OF LITTLE ROUND TOP WAS CRUCIAL to the Union victory at Gettysburg. Colonel Joshua L. Chamberlain of the 20th Maine Infantry received much of the credit for turning back the furious Confederate assault there on July 2, 1863. Chamberlain would not have been in position to do so, however, without Strong Vincent who gave his life defending that hill.

One day before Vincent left Erie, Pennsylvania, and went to war in 1861, he married Elizabeth Carter, who gave him a riding crop as a parting gift. "Surely the right will prevail," he wrote her later. "If I live, we will rejoice over our country's success. If I fall, remember that you have given your husband as a sacrifice to the most righteous cause that ever widowed a woman."

By 1863 Vincent was colonel of the 83rd Pennsylvania Infantry. Shortly before the Battle of Gettysburg, he was placed in command of the brigade to which that regiment belonged. Little Round Top was on the left flank of the Union line, and on July 2, General Daniel Sickles left it undefended just as Robert E. Lee's forces were preparing to attack. Informed of Sickles's blunder, General Gouverneur K. Warren desperately sought troops to defend the hill. Vincent responded by rushing his brigade up Little Round Top. As the Confederates attacked, he placed the 20th Maine on the brigade's left flank—at the very end of the Union line—and told Chamberlain to "hold this ground at all costs." Then Vincent took charge of the brigade's right

I place you here. This is the left of the Union line. . . . You are to hold this ground at all costs.

STRONG VINCENT TO JOSHUA L. CHAMBERLAIN AT LITTLE ROUND TOP, JULY 2, 1863

flank, which was under heavy attack. Mounting a boulder, he flourished his riding crop to rally his men and shouted: "Don't give an inch!" Moments later he fell mortally wounded. One-fourth of the men in his brigade were killed or wounded on Little Round Top, but his sacrifice and theirs was not in vain. Chamberlain repulsed the last Confederate attack there with a bayonet charge. Strong Vincent died on July 7, 1863, probably unaware that he had been promoted to brigadier general.

Fifty years later, his widow donated his sword and scabbard (above) to the Smithsonian. What became of his riding crop is unknown, but it was fitting that he was holding that gift from her when he fell for his "righteous cause." ✛ DDM

SWORD AND SCABBARD *This Model 1850 Staff and Field Officers sword, made by W. H. Horstmann & Sons of Philadelphia, belonged to Strong Vincent, whose widow had brass plaques placed on the scabbard to commemorate her husband's service and sacrifice.*

86

A HARVEST OF DEATH

O N JULY 5, 1863, TWO DAYS AFTER THE BATTLE of Gettysburg ended, photographer Alexander Gardner arrived there with assistants Timothy H. O'Sullivan and James Gibson. All three had once worked for Mathew Brady, but Gardner now had his own studio and had hired Gibson and O'Sullivan away from Brady, who reached Gettysburg belatedly. The first photographers on the scene, Gardner and his cameramen recorded the dreadful carnage on the battlefield, where bloated bodies lay unburied amid what he described as a litter of soldiers' "accoutrements, ammunition, rags, cups and canteens, crackers, haversacks, &c."

Gardner had made a similar photographic record of the dead at Antietam in September 1862 while working for Brady, who displayed the graphic prints in his New York studio to shocked viewers who had never before witnessed the horrors of battle. Brady was often credited for those photographs, and Gardner would often be credited for a picture taken by O'Sullivan that became the iconic image of the grim aftermath at Gettysburg (right), published with the title "A Harvest of Death" in *Gardner's Photographic Sketch Book of the War* (1866).

Gardner deserved much credit, along with Brady and the photographers they employed, for conveying the war's terrible consequences to the public. But no picture could capture the full horrors experienced by those assigned to bury some seven thousand Confederate and Union dead at Gettysburg. The "pestilential stench of decaying humanity," one soldier wrote, covered the battlefield "like a fog, poisoning every breath." Burial parties worked quickly, digging trenches that were only a foot or two deep, and erected few grave markers to identify the victims cut down in the war's deadliest harvest. ✢ JGB

AFTERMATH *Alexander Gardner made this print, held at the Smithsonian American Art Museum, from a glass-plate negative produced by Timothy H. O'Sullivan. Gardner identified the dead here as shoeless Rebels, but analysis of this and other pictures taken by him and his team indicates that they were Federals whose shoes were scavenged.*

87

A HAUNTING RELIC OF GETTYSBURG

AMONG THE MEMENTOS OF THE BATTLE OF Gettysburg is the framed ambrotype shown opposite, found on the field there after the fighting ended. We do not know the name or fate of the soldier to whom this picture belonged. But the portrait may well have been carried into battle by a man who died at Gettysburg and never again saw the wife and child whose image he cherished. If so, this is a relic not just of his loss but of their loss as well. The woman pictured here may have waited anxiously for months without learning of her husband's fate. Thousands of unidentified men were hastily buried at Gettysburg and other Civil War battlefields and listed as missing. Civilians who were duly informed of a soldier's death were rarely able to retrieve his remains for burial nearby. In many homes across the Union and Confederacy, families kept only the memory of the soldier, while distant and often-dismal battlefield burial grounds kept the body.

This unknown woman and child are representative of all those whose husbands, fathers, sons, or brothers were at war and who prayed for news of them and their safe deliverance. When Fanny Carter Scott of Virginia learned on July 6, 1863, that there had been "a fight in Pennsylvania," she feared for her husband and brother who were serving in Robert E. Lee's army and wrote a poignant letter that echoed the thoughts of many people on both sides whose loved ones were in peril: "Where are you, my dear husband what are you doing and what is going on.... I live daily and hourly in dread of a battle."

Historically, the fearful toll that great battles like Gettysburg took on soldiers and grieving civilians placed a burden on war leaders to justify the carnage. In Shakespeare's *Henry V*, a soldier warns King Henry before the Battle of Agincourt that the dead could come back to haunt him: "But if the cause be not good, the king himself hath a heavy reckoning to make, when all those legs and arms and heads, chopped off in battle, shall join together at the latter day and cry all, 'We died at such a place;' some swearing, some crying for a surgeon, some upon their wives left poor behind them ... some upon their children rawly left. I am afeard there are few die well that die in a battle; for how can they charitably dispose of any thing when blood is their argument? Now, if these men do not die well, it will be a black matter for the king that led them to it."

Where are you, my dear husband what are you doing and what is going on. ... I live daily and hourly in dread of a battle.

FANNY SCOTT CARTER TO HER HUSBAND IN ROBERT E. LEE'S ARMY, JULY 6, 1863

For President Lincoln, who was steeped in Shakespeare, the terrible price paid at Gettysburg required that he reassure Unionists that their cause was good and that the sacrifices made by soldiers in the field and their loved ones at home were necessary. He made that case eloquently on November 19, 1863, when he spoke at the dedication of the Gettysburg National Cemetery and recalled the birth in 1776 of a revolutionary new nation, "conceived in Liberty." The future of that nation was at stake, he insisted, and the task of those gathered at Gettysburg for this ceremony was not to dedicate ground already consecrated with the blood of those who had given their lives to preserve the Union: "It is for us the living, rather, to be dedicated here to the unfinished work which they who fought here have thus far so nobly advanced. It is rather for us to be here dedicated to the great task remaining before us—that from these honored dead we take increased devotion to that cause for which they gave the last full measure of devotion." ✣ EWP

LOST IN BATTLE *This ambrotype of a woman and child, found on the battlefield at Gettysburg, is among the Civil War relics at the National Museum of American History.*

88

TREATING THE WOUNDED

NOT EVEN THE MOST EXPERIENCED MILITARY surgeons anticipated the huge numbers of casualties that would be sustained during the Civil War. The Union and Confederate armies entered the conflict ill prepared to treat the wounded. Each side organized field hospitals and an ambulance corps, but after major battles surgeons were overwhelmed with men requiring operations. At Gettysburg, the Union Second Corps alone "lost upward of 3,000 in killed and wounded," a doctor there reported. Lieutenant Frank Haskell witnessed surgeons performing amputations at the Second Corps field hospital. "Their faces and clothes are spattered with blood," he wrote, "and though they look weary and tired, their work goes systematically and steadily on—how much and how long they worked, the piles of legs, arms, feet, hands, fingers . . . partially tell."

The task of treating wounded men in crowded, reeking field hospitals could be exasperating for surgeons. "If there is one thing more disagreeable or more dirty than another," an army doctor remarked, "it is that of dressing sloughing, stinking gun shot wounds." No antiseptics were available then to prevent the spread of infections. But ether and other anesthetics helped surgeons like Lieutenant Colonel William I. Wolfley—a Union physician whose medicine case and instruments are shown at right and on the next two pages—save many lives by operating on wounded men who would otherwise have perished. ✛ JMC

SURGEON'S SUPPLIES *This field medicine case (OPPOSITE), issued to surgeon William Wolfley (INSET), contained bandages, silk ligature, scissors, and drugs such as chloroform and ether (RIGHT). The ether was sold by Dr. Edward Robinson Squibb, a former naval surgeon.*

Their faces and clothes are spattered with blood; and though they look weary and tired, their work goes systematically and steadily on.

LIEUTENANT FRANK HASKELL, DESCRIBING UNION SURGEONS AT GETTYSBURG

STRONGER ETHER
FOR ANAESTHESIA.

HALF POUND or 227 GRAMMES
TO OPEN THE CAN

EDWARD R SQUIBB, M.D.
BROOKLYN, N.Y.

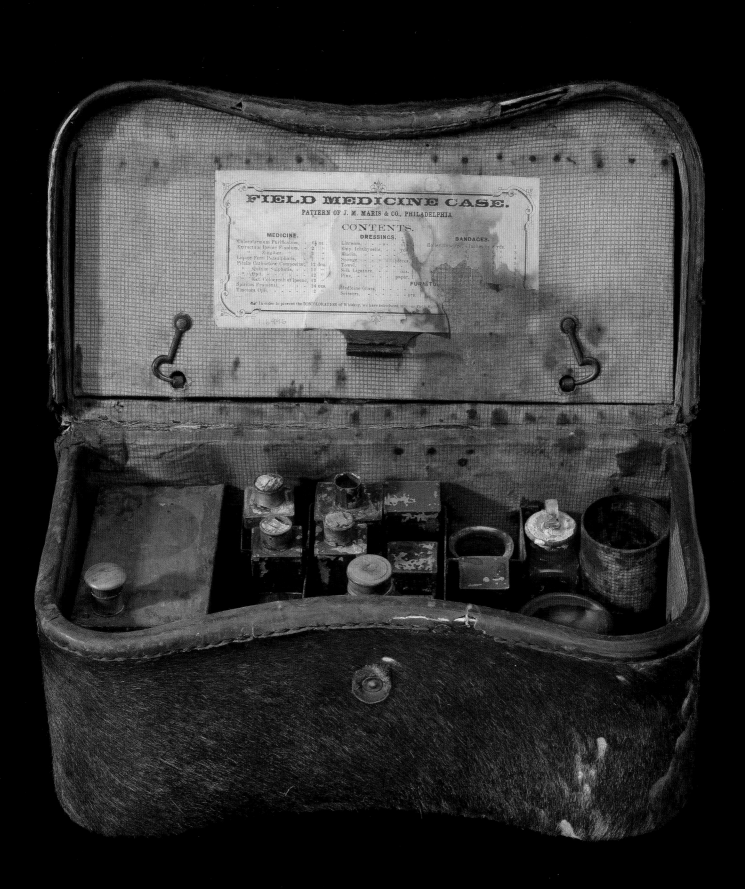

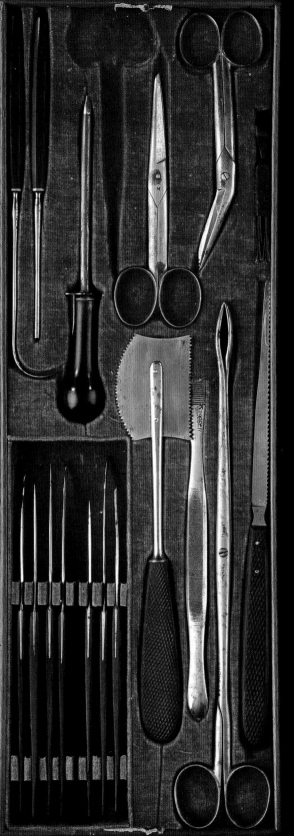

aspect of the joint, carrying them through the tissues composing the anterior and posterior walls of the axilla, to the lower border of each, and dividing their attachments to the humerus; 3d. Push the edges of the wound on either side to expose the joint, and open it, making traction on the bone to put its ligament on the

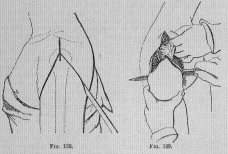

FIG. 138.   FIG. 139.

stretch; 4th. Luxate the bone, pass the knife behind it (Fig. 138), and finish the operation by cutting directly through the tissues in the axilla, which intervene between the extremities of the incisions already made, recollecting that the artery is contained in them, and requires to be compressed by an assistant. The wound which results from this operation is almost perfectly oval in shape."

Modifications.— Guthrie commences his incision just below the acromion, but endangers the exposure of the glenoid cavity, by the subsequent contraction of the muscles and integuments; Guérin dissects the head of

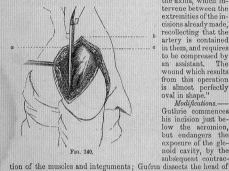

FIG. 140.

SURGICAL TOOLS *The instruments shown here were made of steel, with ebony handles, and used mainly for amputation. The four large Catlin and Liston knives in the box opposite were used to cut through layers of flesh. The large saw was used to complete amputations by cutting through bone. The forceps at lower right in the box on this page could be used to probe wounds for bullets, although many Civil War surgeons used their bare fingers for that purpose. These instruments belonged to Lieutenant Colonel Wolfley, who also possessed a surgical handbook that included illustrations and instructions for amputating an arm at the shoulder (ABOVE).*

BADGE OF HONOR

ON MARCH 10, 1863, PRIVATE ALEXANDER HILL—age 32, height 5'10", complexion brown—enlisted in Company A of the 54th Massachusetts Colored Infantry. On July 18 his regiment lost more than a hundred men in a courageous attack repulsed by Confederates at Fort Wagner, a forbidding bastion on Morris Island that shielded nearby Charleston, South Carolina. Private Hill survived but was shot in the left hand and right hip. Hospitalized briefly, he was wounded again near Charleston in August 1864 while attacking a battery called the Swamp Angel. He suffered a severed Achilles tendon and lost full use of his left hand.

Hill was discharged for physical disability on July 12, 1865. He was denied admission to the U.S. Army Reserve Corps, according to his discharge paper, "because soldiers of his color are not allowed in it." Like other black troops who had served their country, his status as an American went unacknowledged and his contributions unrecognized. The unofficial badge above was his way of affirming that he had served with honor. ✣ PG

PROUD EMBLEM *This pin lists major battles in which Alexander Hill took part and shows an American flag flying over a fort like those he fought to secure for the Union. Such badges were made commercially and purchased after the war by veterans or groups honoring them.*

NEW YORK DRAFT RIOTS

THE SCOPE AND BRUTALITY OF THE CIVIL WAR quickly depleted the military manpower of both the North and South. The Confederacy was first to act. In April 1862 it instituted a draft of able-bodied white males between the ages of eighteen and thirty-five, who were liable to serve for three years. In March 1863 the Union enacted a similar draft of white men between twenty and forty-five.

Both sides hoped that the draft would encourage voluntary enlistment, and it did so. But this was the first time in American history that compulsory military service had been imposed nationally, and many felt that the government was infringing on their individual liberties. Critics charged that the draft laws favored the rich. Both the South and the North permitted draftees to hire a substitute to serve for them. In the North, they could also escape military duty by paying a $300 commutation fee.

Union newspapers backing the Democratic Party condemned the draft as an unconstitutional effort by President Lincoln and Republicans in Congress to make white men fight to free enslaved blacks. Violent attacks on draft officials and African Americans occurred in several Northern cities. But nowhere were the tensions and violence as great as in New York City, where long-standing grievances within poor, mostly Irish neighborhoods turned explosive.

On July 11, 1863, officials in New York City began drafting men by lottery. By Monday, July 13, the crowd's anger erupted and rioters stormed draft offices in the city. For four days, mobs raged out of control, attacking government buildings, prominent Republicans, and abolitionists. The worst assaults were aimed at blacks as rioters burned down the Colored Orphan Asylum, broke into homes, and lynched victims in the streets. Federal troops who had recently seen action at Gettysburg were rushed to the city and finally restored an uneasy peace. The rioting caused more than a hundred deaths and exposed deep fractures within the Union. ✣ HRR

Early in the morning the trouble recommences.... All business in the upper part of the City suspended. Negroes chased everywhere & killed when caught.

WILLIAM STEINWAY, PIANO MANUFACTURER, NEW YORK CITY, JULY 14, 1863

HANGING A NEGRO IN CLARKSON STREET.

LYNCH MOB *This depiction of a lynching during the New York draft riots (ABOVE) appeared on August 1, 1863, in* Harper's Weekly, *which identified the victim as a "negro cartman," attacked by a mob of men and boys who "dragged him to Clarkson Street, and hung him from a branch of one of the trees that shade the sidewalk by St. John's Cemetery.... They danced round their victim, setting fire to his clothes, and burning him almost to a cinder."*

DRAFT WHEEL *Slips of paper that identified Union men eligible for conscription were inserted in this wheel. The large hole at lower right was covered while the wheel was turned, and slips were then drawn to select those drafted. The U.S. War Department transferred the wheel to the Smithsonian in 1919.*

91

THE GENERAL AND THE ACTRESS

I N MID-1863, ACTION UNFOLDED IN TENNESSEE THAT was overshadowed by the news from Vicksburg and Gettysburg but had as much intrigue and suspense as found in any military theater during the war. Among the leading players in that drama were Braxton Bragg (1817–1876), commander of the Army of Tennessee and one of the South's most irascible and unlikable generals, and Pauline Cushman (opposite), a beguiling actress who infiltrated Bragg's camp as a Union spy.

Bragg (inset) was disdained both by his officers and by his men because of his petulant disposition, stern discipline, and proclivity for attacking inopportunely and retreating ignominiously. Defeated at Perryville, Kentucky, in October 1862 after launching a hasty assault with only part of his army, Bragg withdrew to Tennessee, where Union general William Rosecrans repulsed his costly attack at Murfreesboro at year's end in the Battle of Stones River. Bragg then fell back deeper into Tennessee and camped at Shelbyville. He retained command because President Jefferson Davis had admired him ever since they served together in the Mexican War. But he could ill afford to yield any more ground to Rosecrans, who was prodded into action by superiors in Washington, D.C., and descended on Bragg from the north in June 1863.

By her own account, Pauline Cushman's covert role in that campaign began earlier that year when she was a struggling actress in Union-occupied Louisville, Kentucky. Two Confederate parolees offered her a bribe to toast Jefferson Davis during a performance. She consented but only after informing the Federal provost marshal, who encouraged her to pose publicly as a secessionist while serving secretly as a Union agent. After

toasting Davis on stage, she was thrown out of the theater, thereby gaining the trust of Confederates. Pretending that she was seeking a missing brother who had enlisted to fight for the South, she became a camp follower of Bragg's army. Her allure and beauty distracted Confederate officers, enabling her to observe their defenses around Shelbyville and make sketches that she concealed. Soon, however, she was caught in possession of incriminating papers. Bragg had her tried in military court, which sentenced her to hang but delayed the execution when she fell ill. In late June Bragg, outflanked by Rosecrans, hastily decamped, leaving the ailing Cushman behind. The oncoming Yankees rescued her and made her an honorary Union major. Rosecrans introduced her to the public later that year in Cincinnati, Ohio, as a scout, spy, and national heroine.

Braxton Bragg, meanwhile, once again had to retreat. But the forlorn general was handed an opportunity to redeem himself by Rosecrans, a man as moody and impulsive as he was. Overconfident after outmaneuvering Bragg and eager to counter criticism that he was too slow and indecisive, Rosecrans chased after the Army of Tennessee when it abandoned Chattanooga in early September and crossed into Georgia, where Bragg received reinforcements and lay in wait for his foe along a creek called Chickamauga. ✦ JGB

THE GENERAL *This portrait taken by photographer J. D. Edwards around 1861 shows Braxton Bragg as a brigadier general, the rank at which he entered Confederate service. Commenting on Bragg's appearance, one soldier wrote: "The most remarkable feature is the eye, which is dark-gray and as strong and unflinching as a hawk's."*

THE ACTRESS *Pauline Cushman (1833–1893), born Harriet Wood in New Orleans, wears a Federal officer's uniform with the insignia of major in a photograph attributed to Mathew Brady. She may have posed for Brady during her stint in 1864 with P. T. Barnum's American Museum in New York City, where she regaled audiences with tales of her adventures as a spy. When she died destitute at the age of sixty, hundreds of Union veterans of the Grand Army of the Republic attended her funeral in San Francisco.*

92

THE ROCK OF CHICKAMAUGA

VIRGINIA-BORN GEORGE H. THOMAS (1816–1870) was a West Point graduate and the very image of a professional soldier. As a war correspondent remarked, he looked as if he had been "hewn out of a large square block of the best-tempered material men are made of, not scrimped anywhere, and square everywhere—square face, square shoulders, square step." When Fort Sumter fell, Thomas remained loyal to the Union despite the pleadings of

his secession-minded sisters, who turned his picture to the wall. In August 1861 he was posted to Kentucky as a brigadier general and spent the remainder of the war proving himself in the Western Theater. His rise to prominence was as steady and sure as his approach to battle was deliberate and determined.

Serving as a corps commander in the Army of the Cumberland in 1863 under the excitable William Rosecrans, Thomas held the Union left at Chickamauga, in northwest Georgia, when Braxton Bragg's resurgent Confederates poured through a gap in the center of the line on September 20. Unhinged, Rosecrans retreated northward to Chattanooga with most of his forces, leaving Thomas to mount a desperate rearguard defense. His heroic stand averted disaster for the Federals and earned him the title "The Rock of Chickamauga."

Succeeding Rosecrans as commander of the Army of the Cumberland, Thomas served first under Ulysses Grant at Chattanooga—where in November they dealt Bragg a defeat so bitter that Jefferson Davis was compelled to sack him—and then under William T. Sherman as he descended on Atlanta in 1864. Sherman took the city, began his March to the Sea, and left Thomas to reckon with John Bell Hood and the Army of Tennessee at Nashville. Hindered there in December by icy weather, Thomas refused to be rushed into battle by Grant, who was about to relieve him of command when he smashed Hood's army, for which he received a vote of thanks from Congress.

Reared on a slave plantation, Thomas admired the dedication of the black troops who served under him and defended the rights of freedmen as a commander in the occupied South during Reconstruction. At his death in 1870, none of Thomas's Virginia relatives attended his funeral, but President Grant was among hundreds of Union veterans on hand to honor him. ✦ JGB

WESTERN HERO *Portrayed by photographer George Barnard around 1864, George Thomas thrived in the Western Theater as commander of the Army of the Cumberland. After the war, he led the Department of the Cumberland, whose headquarters flag is shown opposite.*

Purchased at Nashville Tenn.
May 1st 1863. Has been with
Co. B, 87th Ind. Vols. at the
following named places:
Salem,
Hoovers Gap, Fairfield, Manchester,
Elk River,
Cumberland Mountain,
Fort McCook,
Chattanooga, Tenn.
Marietta,
Chattahoochee
Rough and Ready
Decatur,
Oxford
Atlanta,
Rome
Kingston
Milledgeville
Sandersville
Thomas Station
Sandtown

93

THE ODYSSEY OF SOLOMON CONN

SOLOMON CONN ENLISTED AS A PRIVATE IN COMPANY B of the 87th Indiana Infantry on July 26, 1862. He was twenty-four years old, the son of a hotel keeper in Minamac, Indiana. His regiment was ordered to Louisville, Kentucky, at the end of August. In January 1863 the 87th Indiana set out on what would prove a long, hard warpath when it joined George Thomas's Fourteenth Corps in the Army of the Cumberland, led by William Rosecrans.

On May 26, 1863, before advancing under Rosecrans against Braxton Bragg's Army of Tennessee, Solomon Conn purchased the violin shown here at a store in Union-occupied Nashville, Tennessee. He may have intended to learn to play the violin, but according to his descendants he never did. Perhaps he shared the instrument with fiddlers in camp, where music and song were favorite pastimes and anyone who owned or could play a violin, banjo, or guitar was much appreciated. Officers sometimes competed to see which unit had the best musicians, and fiddle tunes such as "Arkansas Traveler" and "Soldier's Joy" were as popular among Union troops as among Confederates. Whatever musical use Conn's violin had, it was a prized possession that remained with him throughout the war and served as a ledger of sorts, where he kept account of the many engagements in which the 87th Indiana took part as it marched and fought its way to victory through Tennessee, Georgia, and the Carolinas.

Perhaps no name inscribed on the violin meant more to Conn and his comrades than Chickamauga, where Thomas's corps made the valiant stand against Bragg's Confederates that averted ruin for the Army of the Cumberland. The 87th Indiana lost over two hundred men killed or wounded there, more than half those in the regiment who entered that battle. Chickamauga was the worst trial for men of the 87th but by no means their last. Besieged at Chattanooga, their army—commanded now by General Thomas—broke loose in November by storming Missionary Ridge and sent Bragg packing.

In May 1864 the 87th advanced southward with Thomas's forces and two other armies under the overall command of William T. Sherman and clashed with Confederates in Georgia at Rocky Face Ridge, Resaca, Kennesaw Mountain, and battlefields on the outskirts of Atlanta before seizing that strategic city on September 2. In November 1864 they formed part of Sherman's left wing on his blistering March to the Sea and took Savannah by year's end. From there, they swept northward through the Carolinas under Sherman in early 1865. Reaching Goldsboro by April, they helped subdue Joseph Johnston's Confederate forces and impede Robert E. Lee's battered Army of Northern Virginia, which was cornered at Appomattox and compelled to surrender. On May 24, 1865, the 87th Indiana marched with Sherman's troops in the triumphal Grand Review at Washington, D.C.

Following the war, Solomon Conn returned home with his violin—on which he had recorded the names of more than fifty places where his regiment had campaigned—and went on to raise a family in Indiana and run a livery stable. Upon his death in 1926, the violin became the property of his grandsons. In 1988 they gave "Grandpa's old fiddle" a permanent home by donating it to the Smithsonian. ✛ KG

MUSICAL MEMENTO *Solomon Conn's violin— shown here in front (INSET) and in back with its inscriptions (OPPOSITE)—suffered only minor damage during the Civil War and endures as a unique record of his odyssey with the hard-marching 87th Indiana Infantry.*

94

UNIFORMS AT SCHUYLKILL ARSENAL

IN 1864 MONTGOMERY C. MEIGS (1816–1892), THE Union's quartermaster general, reported that "all difficulties in providing a sufficient supply of clothing and material for our increasing Army have been overcome. The manufacturing power of the country has so expanded as to fully meet the demands." Credit for clothing an army that numbered nearly a million men by war's end belonged not just to the country's manufacturers but to Meigs himself (inset), an administrative dynamo who kept Union forces well supplied with uniforms as well as other things they needed to wage and win the war.

On the eve of the conflict, the small U.S. Army received its clothing from the U.S. Arsenal in Philadelphia, better known as the Schuylkill Arsenal. Its great workshop and warehouses supplied all the furnishings soldiers required, including bedding and blankets as well as socks, shoes, headgear, and uniforms. Cloth, purchased under contract from manufacturers, was received and cut there, then issued to seamstresses and tailors, who returned hand-finished garments to the arsenal for inspection and acceptance. Although the sewing machine had been invented in the 1840s, it was not yet widely used for making uniforms.

Meigs, appointed quartermaster general at Lincoln's urging soon after the Civil War began, established several more depots around the North where Union uniforms were made and expanded production at Schuylkill Arsenal, which employed as many as ten thousand seamstresses during the war. One visitor there observed: "The army sack coats, of which we saw thousands upon thousands, are all made in the establishment by women, as also the great coats." Yet Meigs found that his department could not fully meet the demands of the fast-growing Union Army. He had to contract with private firms to produce uniforms, some of which were made of cheap, perishable fabric dubbed "shoddy." Better cloth made in the North became so expensive that he sent an agent to England in late 1861 to purchase affordable wool fabric, prompting Union manufacturers to step up production and lower prices. By mid-1862 Meigs had surplus uniforms in stock and more than three million yards of cloth stored at the arsenal. Then in July of that year Lincoln called for 300,000 more volunteers, and Meigs had to make additional uniform purchases. This time, he sought competitive bids from manufacturers and avoided shoddy dealers. By 1864 he could report that the army's clothing supplies were ample and of "excellent quality," resulting in "few complaints."

After the Civil War, Meigs preserved uniforms produced at Schuylkill Arsenal—including the examples shown opposite and on the following pages—as part of the historical collection of the Quartermaster Corps. Those outfits were showcased at the spectacular Centennial Exposition of 1876, staged at exhibit halls spread across 450 acres in Philadelphia's Fairmount Park. The War Department maintained that collection at Philadelphia and later on Governor's Island in New York before transferring it to the Smithsonian's U.S. National Museum in 1919. ✣ JLJ

MASTER PLANNER *Pictured above in 1864, Montgomery Meigs helped organize and sustain the Union war effort as the army's quartermaster general. He was also a master builder and engineer who played a major role in the development of Washington, D.C.*

Cavalry Sergeant.

All difficulties in providing a sufficient supply of clothing and material for our increasing Army have been overcome. The manufacturing power of the country has so expanded as to fully meet the demands.

MONTGOMERY C. MEIGS, 1864

CAVALRY JACKET *Modeled by the same man who posed for the hand-colored photographs on the following pages, the Pattern 1855 cavalry jacket (RIGHT) —shown with sergeant's stripes and epaulettes in the picture above—was preserved in the Schuylkill Arsenal collection with a label indicating that the Quartermaster Department paid a minimum of nearly five dollars and a maximum of nearly ten dollars for each jacket.*

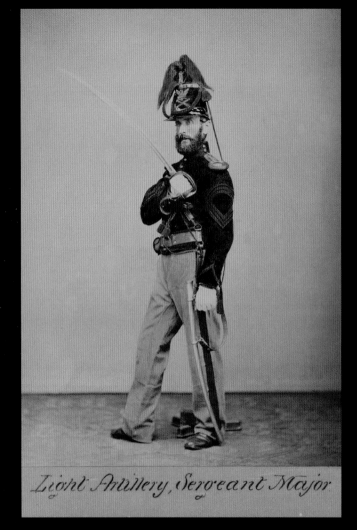

Light Artillery, Sergeant Major

LIGHT ARTILLERY CAP *This Pattern 1864 cap, like several others
in the Schuylkill collection, was manufactured by the firm of
W. C. Dare in Philadelphia according to government specifications.
Made of stiffened felt, it has light artillery insignia, including
the brass crossed cannons and eagle emblem on the brim and the*

CAVALRY MUSICIAN JACKET *This shell jacket was introduced by the U.S. Army in 1854 and was issued to Union cavalry musicians during the Civil War. The bright yellow stripes helped distant cavalry officers and men spot their bugler, who played an important role in battle by sounding orders.*

HOSPITAL STEWARD'S COAT *This coat bears the insignia of a hospital steward— a yellow silk embroidered caduceus on each sleeve. The responsibilities of hospital stewards included maintaining order and discipline, keeping records, dressing minor wounds, assisting surgeons, and serving as*

Hospital Steward.

LONG ARMS

AMONG THE MANY UNION TROOPS ENGAGED AT Chickamauga in September 1863 were mounted infantrymen of Colonel John Wilder's Lightning Brigade. Fighting on foot and armed with Spencer repeating rifles that could fire seven shots without being reloaded, they shattered an assault by two brigades of Confederates. "They fell in heaps," recalled Wilder, who was tempted to order a cease fire "to end the awful sight."

Although fast-firing breech-loaders like the Spencer (overleaf) were available before the war began, military authorities were slow to adopt them. In 1855 the U.S. War Department had settled on rifle muskets as its standard infantry weapons. Those muzzle-loaders shot minié bullets with greater range and accuracy than balls fired from smoothbore muskets, but they were slow to load. Soldiers had to tear open a paper cartridge, pour powder into the barrel, ram home the bullet, and place a percussion cap below the half-cocked hammer before pulling the trigger. Nonetheless, the Union's ordnance chief, General James Ripley, stood by such muzzle-loaders. Concerned that troops with rapid-firing breech-loaders would waste ammunition and cause supply problems, he opposed issuing them to infantry. Ripley resisted adopting the Spencer—which units like Wilder's acquired at their own expense—and equipped foot soldiers with rifle muskets. He did a good job of supplying Union troops with hundreds of thousands of those weapons. Ripley resigned in 1863, leaving it to his successor to begin acquiring fast-firing breech-loaders such as the Spencer repeating carbine, which was issued to cavalry. Like the Spencer rifle, it held self-contained metallic cartridges in its magazine that eliminated the need for percussion caps.

The Confederacy lacked an industrial base but did all it could to supply its forces with long arms. Some were manufactured by armories and contractors in the South, which mostly produced copies of earlier U.S. Army models. Others were imported from England or captured from Union troops, including some newer model breech-loaders. ✛ DDM

CONFEDERATE GUNS

The .69-caliber smoothbore Palmetto Musket (RIGHT, TOP) was made in South Carolina at the Palmetto Armory, which often used surplus or rejected parts from older weapons. The Richmond Armory Rifle Musket (RIGHT, BOTTOM) was made with equipment captured at the Harpers Ferry Armory, where it was used to produce the U.S. Model 1855 Rifle Musket, which accounts for this gun's distinctive "humpback" lock plate. Such muzzle-loaders fired when the hammer struck the percussion cap.

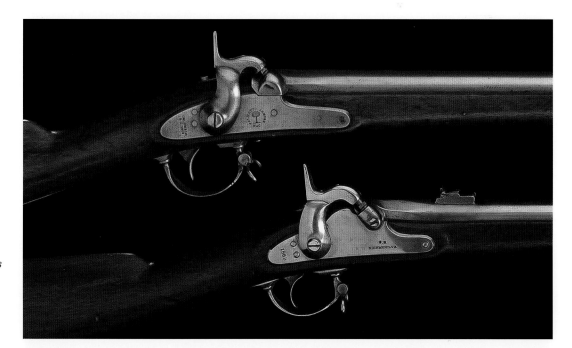

U.S. MODEL 1841 RIFLE *Produced by Eli Whitney Jr., this was known as the "Mississippi Rifle" for its successful use by Jefferson Davis's Mississippi regiment during the Mexican War. It was employed by both sides during the Civil War.*

COLT MODEL 1855 REVOLVING RIFLE *Although deemed too complex for military use, this .56-caliber five-shot rifle was purchased by the commanders of some units. Like Colt's handguns, it had an attached loading lever to ram paper cartridges into each bore of the cylinder (DETAIL).*

EDWIN WESSON MATCH RIFLE *Designed for shooting matches, this was used as a sniper rifle by Edwin J. Stanclift of the 8th Company, 1st Battalion New York Sharpshooters. The telescopic sight on the .45-caliber weapon was made by C. D. Abbey of Chicago.*

SPENCER RIFLE *Unlike most long arms used during the Civil War, the Spencer was equipped with a magazine in the butt stock holding seven .52-caliber brass cartridges. The trigger guard acted as a lever, which when lowered opened the breech and ejected the spent shell (DETAIL). Raising the lever pushed a fresh shell from the magazine into position.*

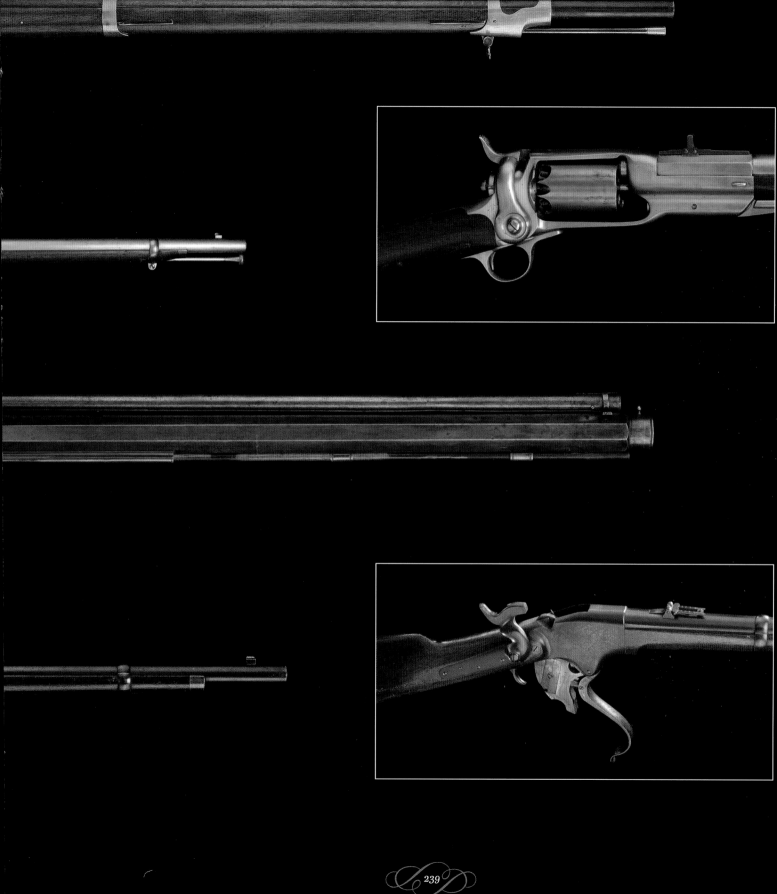

TARPLEY BREECH-LOADING CARBINE *Invented by Jere H. Tarpley and made in 1863 in Greensboro, North Carolina, this .52-caliber carbine fired paper cartridges. It was notorious for leaking scalding hot gas from its breech and only a few hundred were produced.*

MERRILL CARBINE *This .54-caliber, single-shot, breech-loader was patented by James H. Merrill in 1858 and issued to over 15,000 Union cavalrymen. It was loaded by lifting up and pulling back the breech lever (DETAIL). When the lever was closed, the plunger pushed a cartridge into place.*

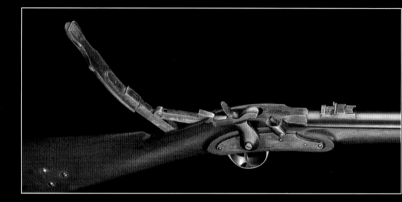

BURNSIDE CARBINE *Designed by General Ambrose Burnside, this .54-caliber breech- loader fired conical metallic or foil cartridges. The Union purchased over 55,000 of them for use by cavalry.*

GALLAGER CARBINE *Nearly 18,000 of these .50-caliber percussion carbines were issued to Union cavalry. Lowering the lever shifted the barrel forward and tilted its muzzle downward, opening the breech for loading a metallic cartridge (DETAIL).*

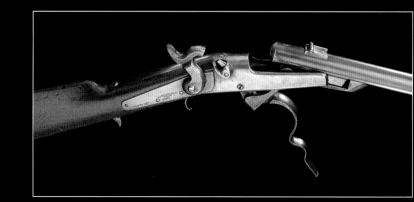

AT HOME IN CAMP

WINTER ENCAMPMENTS OFFERED SOLDIERS the closest thing to home that life in the army could provide. Erected in between campaigns, those semipermanent winter quarters were creative outlets and great sources of pride for soldiers weary of monotonous marches and the carnage of battle. As one Union cavalryman wrote during the construction of a winter camp: "Nearly every man has suddenly become a mason or carpenter, and the hammer, the axe and the trowel are being plied with the utmost vigor, if not with the highest skill. Many of us are astonished at the ingenuity that is displayed.... Our camp is beginning to look beautiful."

Winter quarters could not provide soldiers with all the domestic comforts they left behind when they went to war. But as this photograph by Alexander Gardner reveals, such camps were sometimes graced with the presence of women from home, most of them officers' wives. Letter-writing helped couples separated by war maintain some intimacy, but wives of officers often sought relief from home-front loneliness and anxiety by visiting their spouse in camp when the army allowed it. Among those who did so were Elizabeth "Libbie" Custer and Julia Grant, who frequently stayed with their husbands during lulls between campaigns. Such reunions cheered both homesick officers and dejected wives, who were happy to be "keeping house again," as one captain's wife remarked in her diary. Yet adjusting to camp life was hard, and wives who visited their husbands at length often ended up feeling unwanted and useless. Warfare set soldiers apart from the hallowed domestic sphere wives occupied, and many couples were not truly at home and at one with each other again until the fighting ended. ✛ SMC

VISITING WIVES *Alexander Gardner took this photo at a Union winter camp in Virginia in January 1864 and commented: "Thus secluded, the wives of officers, in their brief visits to the front, find a most pleasant abiding place, from which they return with reluctance to city homes."*

243

AUTOGRAPH LEAVES

SUPPORT FOR THE UNION CAUSE TOOK MANY FORMS and involved people from all walks of life. Some of the nation's leading literary figures contributed to a unique volume entitled *Autograph Leaves of Our Country's Authors* (1864), sold to benefit the Maryland State Fair for U.S. Soldier Relief, commonly known as the Baltimore Sanitary Fair. The book contained lithograph facsimiles of ninety handwritten essays and poems, "generously and carefully furnished" by notable authors, including those pictured opposite. Their signed compositions were assembled by John Pendleton Kennedy, a novelist and former U.S. congressman from Maryland, and Lieutenant Colonel Alexander Bliss, a Union quartermaster general. Also involved in the project was Bliss's stepfather, noted historian George Bancroft (portrayed middle row, far right), who asked President Lincoln to contribute his Gettysburg Address. Lincoln responded by composing his fifth and final draft of that address, reproduced in the author's own hand like the other entries. It appears second in the book, following Francis Scott Key's "Star-Spangled Banner," one of the few manuscripts not contributed by a living writer.

Sales of *Autograph Leaves* at the Baltimore fair helped raise money for the U.S. Sanitary and U.S. Christian Commissions, the two major Northern relief organizations that coordinated volunteer work for the war effort, much of it done by women. The commissions promoted clean and healthy conditions in Union camps, established hospitals and provided nurses, and raised funds for supplies. By the time the Baltimore Sanitary Fair opened on April 18, 1864, such events had become popular wartime attractions. The first fair opened in Chicago in October 1863 with performances, lectures, and exhibits. Cities across the North followed with grand expositions that raised millions of dollars to support the commissions and their work. ✣ HRR

PATRIOTIC PASSAGES
These two pages from Autograph Leaves *feature the final stanzas of "The Star-Spangled Banner," signed by Francis Scott Key, and the beginning of Lincoln's Gettysburg Address. Pictured opposite are some of the book's many contributors, including orator Edward Everett, who spoke at length at Gettysburg before Lincoln delivered his brief address; Julia Ward Howe, author of "The Battle Hymn of the Republic"; and poet Oliver Wendell Holmes Sr.*

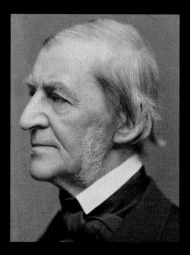

Ralph Waldo Emerson

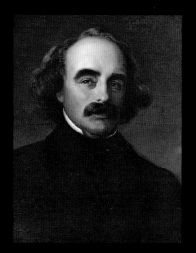

Nathaniel Hawthorne

Harriet Beecher Stowe

Julia Ward Howe

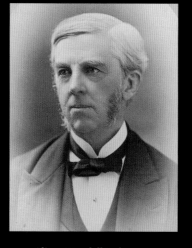

Oliver Wendell Holmes Sr.

George Bancroft

Edward Everett

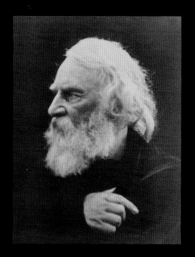

Henry Wadsworth Longfellow

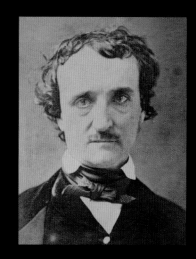

Edgar Allan Poe

98

GRANT VERSUS LEE

IN THE SPRING OF 1864 THE WAR IN VIRGINIA, AND the fate of the Confederate government in Richmond, came down to a contest between the two contrasting figures pictured here—Ulysses S. Grant, a common man risen to high command, slouching and a bit disheveled, never one to stand on ceremony or rest on his laurels; and Robert E. Lee, erect and dignified, impeccably attired, sword at his side, every inch the patrician, honor-bound to serve his state and region.

Three years earlier, the little-known Grant had to plead for a commission, while Lee had the distinction of being offered command of all U.S. forces in the field before he sided with the South. Now Grant was the Union's general in chief and held sizable strategic advantages over Lee in men, weaponry, and supplies. Having won notable victories in the Western Theater, Grant also possessed the confidence of his soldiers and his president.

Lee, too, was esteemed by his troops and his commander in chief, but heavy losses at Gettysburg had left him without the capacity to take the offensive and achieve a decisive victory. His one hope now was to hold his ground and prolong the conflict until Northerners lost patience and turned against the war. That was still possible, but only if Lee could make Grant wilt like his ill-fated predecessors in Virginia did.

Their fateful contest began on May 5 in the densely wooded Wilderness, near Chancellorsville, where Lee had trounced Joseph Hooker a year earlier. Grant's casualties in this battle were as great as Hooker's, but he fought Lee to a draw and pushed on, assuring Abraham Lincoln that "there will be no turning back." The opposing armies clashed again several days later at Spotsylvania, where Grant issued a memorable dispatch: "I propose to fight it out on this line if it takes all summer." Pressed hard, Lee's smaller army bent but did not break. When Grant attacked his entrenched foes on June 3 at Cold Harbor, he took horrific losses to no gain. Shifting course, he crossed the James River east of Richmond and descended on Petersburg. Lee moved quickly to defend that vital junction and prevent his capital from being cut off, but he dreaded being pinned down at Petersburg by Grant's numerous and well-equipped forces. "This army cannot stand a siege," Lee warned, and events in 1865 bore out that prediction.

For many Americans looking back in later years, the Civil War was exemplified by the contrast between these two commanders: who they were, how they fought, and what they represented. Lee would be remembered as the genteel champion of the old South and Grant as the gritty hero of the egalitarian Union, which awarded its highest rank and highest office to a man described by a fellow officer as "a marvel of simplicity, a powerful nature veiled in the plainest possible exterior." ✣ DKA

COMMANDING FIGURE *Portrayed on the cover of* Harper's Weekly *on July 2, 1864, Robert E. Lee was assessed there as follows: "In the present campaign he has displayed great tenacity and skill . . . but in all the elements of strategy Grant has proved more than his equal."*

GRANT IN THE FIELD *Mathew Brady took this photograph of Ulysses Grant in June 1864 at City Point, Virginia, near Petersburg. Brady received permission to visit City Point only after his wife asked Julia Grant for help. The field chair in the photo is similar to the one at right, which Grant gave to Charles Goodsell of the 17th Michigan Infantry after the Battle of the Wilderness. The chair and Grant's field glasses (ABOVE) are held now by the Smithsonian.*

99

WINSLOW HOMER'S WAR DRAWINGS

WINSLOW HOMER (1836–1910) LAUNCHED HIS artistic career in 1861 as a Civil War illustrator for *Harper's Weekly*. He traveled with the Army of the Potomac on several occasions and sometimes portrayed men in battle, but focused more often on the daily lives of men in camp. He learned to work economically to meet deadlines, using the same figure or face in more than one print.

Largely self-taught, Homer trained his hand and eye through the act of drawing. For immediate field jottings, he

drew in graphite on cream paper in small sketchbooks, occasionally using a brush to apply wash or add color, and often blocking out single figures or small groups of figures. Sometimes, he drew in black chalk on beige paper (which has darkened over the years), as in his sketch *Cavalry Soldier on Horseback* (overleaf).

Intent on becoming an artist rather than an illustrator, Homer also made detailed figure studies of the sort done in preparation for paintings, which he began producing before the war ended. The figure study at right, *Soldier Giving Water to a Wounded Companion*, depicts Grant's 1864 Virginia campaign. Homer gave depth to such drawings by using tinted paper that served as the middle ground, to which he applied charcoal or black chalk to portray shadows or recesses and white chalk to provide highlights. ✛ GSD

WARTIME ARTIST *Pictured above in 1863, Winslow Homer drew the sketches shown here and on the following two pages—a sampling of the more than one hundred Civil War drawings by the artist held at the Smithsonian's Cooper-Hewitt National Design Museum.*

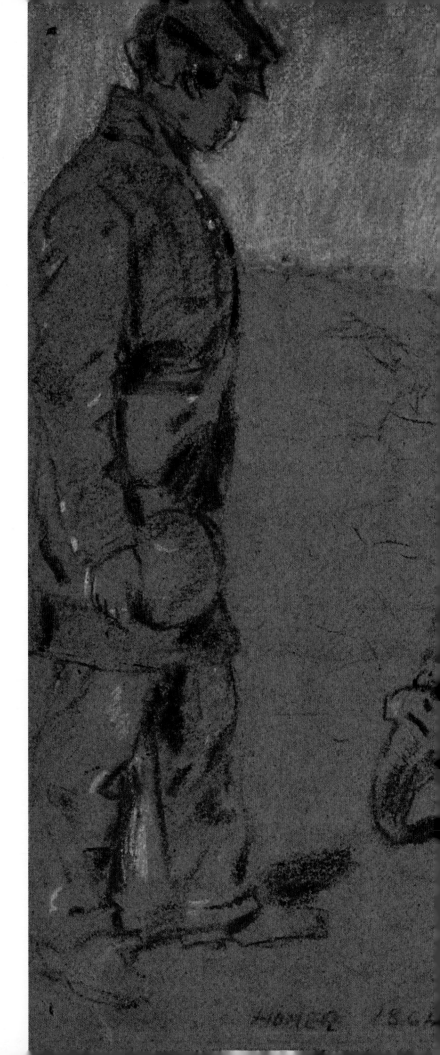

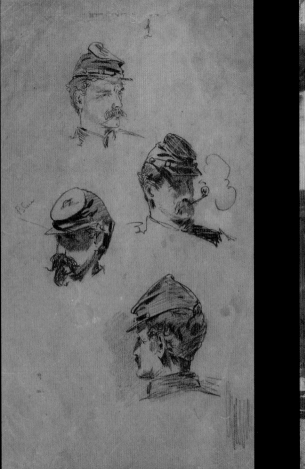

HOMER'S SOLDIERS *Pictured here are five Civil War sketches by Winslow Homer: from left to right,* Four Studies of Soldiers' Heads *(1862–63),* Young Soldier *(1861–64),* Drummer Seen from the Back *(ca. 1864),* Cavalry Soldier on Horseback *(1863), and* Soldier Loading a Rifle *(1863–64).*

100

SHATTERED AT SPOTSYLVANIA

ULYSSES S. GRANT'S OBJECTIVE, WHEN HE CAME east in 1864, was to destroy Robert E. Lee's Army of Northern Virginia, even if that meant heavy casualties for the Union's larger Army of the Potomac. Unlike previous Federal commanders who gave ground when they were hit hard, Grant did not pull back following the costly Battle of the Wilderness but continued south toward Richmond. He knew that Lee would have to risk his army in combat to protect his capital and hoped to catch the Confederates in the open. But Lee was too quick for him and reached Spotsylvania Court House in time for his troops to build four miles of reinforced earthworks before Grant drew near. Their line included a mile-long salient, bending outward in the shape of an inverted U and known as the "Mule Shoe," at the front of which stood a large oak tree.

Grant attacked Lee's stout defenses at Spotsylvania repeatedly. The heaviest assault came on May 12 when Union troops stormed the works at dawn and poured into the Mule Shoe. Lee sent reinforcements, and the two sides fought furiously. It was the war's longest uninterrupted battle at close quarters, raging continuously through a day of driving rain and on into the night. The Union attack faltered after twenty hours of explosive mayhem, which reduced the oak tree to the stump at right, surrounded by piles of bodies. An aide to Grant, Lieutenant Colonel Horace Porter, visited that site, known thereafter as the Bloody Angle, and described the carnage: "Below the mass of fast-decaying corpses, the convulsive twitching of limbs and the writhing of bodies showed that there were wounded men still alive and struggling to extricate themselves from the horrid entombment. Every relief possible was afforded, but in too many cases it came too late." ✣ DDM

BLASTED RELIC *This shattered, bullet-riddled stump was all that remained of an oak tree felled at Spotsylvania in May 1864. Retrieved a year later by a Union general, the stump was sent to the U.S. Army Ordnance Museum and transferred to the Smithsonian in 1888.*

LAID TO REST *In a somber photograph taken by Timothy O'Sullivan, members of a burial detail in Fredericksburg, Virginia, inter men who died at nearby Union field hospitals, where soldiers wounded in the Wilderness and at Spotsylvania were treated.*

The convulsive twitching of limbs and the writhing of bodies showed that there were wounded men still alive.... Every relief possible was afforded, but in too many cases it came too late.

LIEUTENANT COLONEL HORACE PORTER, AT SPOTSYLVANIA

101

SHERMAN MOVES SOUTH

CRITICAL TO THE UNION'S SUCCESS WAS THE remarkable partnership between Ulysses S. Grant and William Tecumseh Sherman (1820–1891). The bond between them was forged under fire in 1862 at Shiloh, where Sherman led a division in Grant's army. Caught off guard there by Confederates on April 6, Union forces were driven back in disarray before rallying and reclaiming the lost ground a day later. Sherman helped Grant avert disaster and displayed remarkable courage at Shiloh, where he was twice wounded and had three horses shot from under him. Thereafter, Grant placed great trust in Sherman, who served him well as a corps commander at Vicksburg and an army commander at Chattanooga.

When Grant went east in 1864 as general in chief to take on Robert E. Lee, he placed Sherman in charge of three Union armies in northern Georgia totaling nearly 100,000 men. His orders from Grant were to break up the opposing Army of Tennessee, commanded now by Joseph Johnston, and "get into the interior of the enemy's country as far as you can, inflicting all the damage you can against their war resources." Sherman proceeded to do just that as he descended on Atlanta and cut a devastating swath across Georgia.

Embarking in May on a campaign timed to coincide with Grant's onslaught in Virginia, the numerically superior Sherman put relentless pressure on Johnston, who fell back slowly toward Atlanta. Dismayed, Jefferson Davis replaced Johnston with the young and aggressive John Bell Hood, who launched several costly and futile attacks around Atlanta before saving what remained of his army by pulling out. On September 2 the city fell to Sherman, who was photographed there in triumph on horseback (opposite). In a highly controversial move, Sherman ordered Atlanta evacuated and then burned everything

he considered of military significance. Nearly one-third of the city went up in flames. Enraged, Hood wrote that his actions surpassed "in studied and ingenious cruelty, all acts ever before brought to my attention in the dark history of war." Sherman offered no apologies. "War is cruelty," he responded, adding that the Confederates who started this war "deserve all the curses and maledictions a people can pour out."

Sherman then launched the campaign for which he is best known. Leaving forces behind under Generals George Thomas and John Schofield to reckon with Hood's battered army, Sherman set out across Georgia to the sea in November with sixty thousand men. When Grant questioned this move, Sherman assured him in writing that "I can make the march and make Georgia howl." As his troops swept eastward, they tore up railroad tracks, burned factories and warehouses, and destroyed food stocks. This was total war on a scale unprecedented in American history, implemented by Sherman in keeping with Grant's policy of stripping the Confederacy of "everything that could be used to support or supply armies," including slaves, thousands of whom sought freedom by following in Sherman's wake. His march was meticulously planned and executed—even foraging expeditions were well organized. On December 21, five weeks after leaving Atlanta, Sherman reached the sea and took Savannah, from which he advanced northward through the Carolinas triumphantly in 1865. ✠ DKA

SHERMAN'S HAT *Wide-brimmed felt hats like the one above, worn by General Sherman on campaign, were useful in any weather. One soldier who served under Sherman recalled him reviewing troops on a foul day: "He had on an old slouch hat, pulled well down over his face to keep the rain off."*

TOKENS OF VICTORY *Portrayed here in 1864 by photographer George Barnard after taking Atlanta, William T. Sherman left to descendants many prized relics of war that were later entrusted to the Smithsonian, including the sword and scabbard below, which he wore during the Battle of Shiloh; and the pin at left, made from buttons cut from his coat.*

102

BIRD'S-EYE VIEW OF ANDERSONVILLE

Andersonville Prison in Georgia was the most notorious compound for soldiers held captive during the Civil War. Built using slave labor in early 1864, it was designed to accommodate no more than 10,000 Union prisoners. By August the population had swelled to 33,000 inmates, many of whom were moved to other camps in late 1864 to prevent General Sherman's troops from liberating them. All told, 45,000 men were held at Andersonville before the war ended. Nearly 13,000 died there of disease, starvation, or other causes.

This bird's-eye view of the camp was based on a drawing by prisoner William D. Broom of the 20th Pennsylvania Cavalry Regiment, who entered service in January 1864, around the time the prison's high wooden stockade was erected. He must have been captured and confined there soon after that, because this view shows hospital wards in the foreground, inside the prison walls. Those wards were moved outside the walls later in the year. Broom accurately depicted details such as the makeshift tents and sheds housing prisoners, the polluted creek bisecting the compound where men bathed and drew drinking water contaminated by nearby latrines, and the infamous dead line at the perimeter of the interior, beyond which anyone approaching the stockade would be shot. Broom may have drawn his sketch while on burial duty at the prison cemetery, located on higher ground outside the wall.

In this lithograph, Broom illustrated the brutal conditions that he witnessed: a chain gang, bodies being carted away, and dogs attacking an escapee (lower left). Published in 1866, the print capitalized on the public's fascination with Andersonville following the military trial, conviction, and execution of the prison's commandant, Henry Wirz. ✥ DSJ

DEATH TRAP *Lithographer William Boel produced this bird's-eye view of Andersonville Prison based on a sketch by survivor William Broom. Key features in the print include the latrines or sinks and armed sentries monitoring the notorious dead line.*

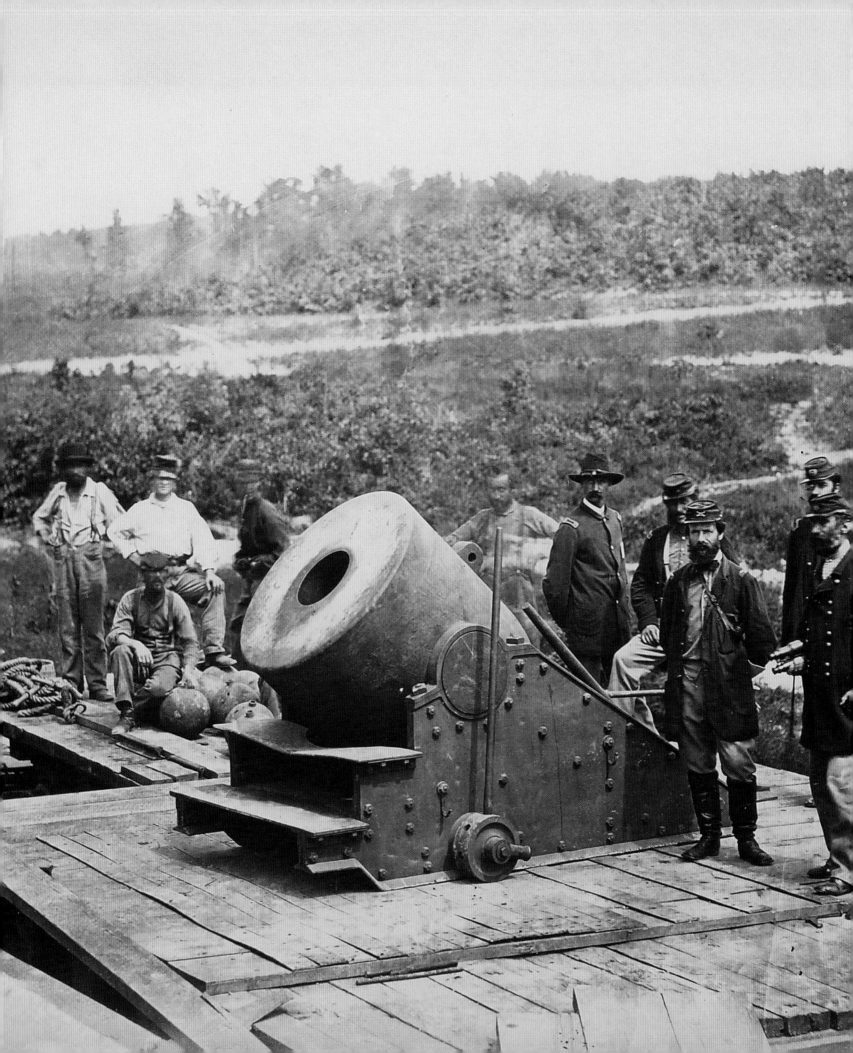

103

THE DICTATOR

WHEN UNION AND CONFEDERATE FORCES DUG IN AT PETERSBURG, Virginia, in June 1864 and began engaging in siege warfare, they gained a new appreciation for mortars. Those guns had not often been major factors earlier in the war, except during assaults on seacoast fortifications, but their high arcing fire made them ideally suited to trench warfare.

Mortars came in many sizes. The biggest of them all was a squat seven-and-a-half-ton Union monster, mounted on a reinforced railroad flatcar stationed on a spur of the City Point & Petersburg Railroad. Officially designated a thirteen-inch seacoast mortar, Model 1861, it was nicknamed "the Dictator." The massive gun was served chiefly by men of Company G, 1st Connecticut Heavy Artillery, led by Colonel Henry L. Abbot, a keen graduate of West Point. Colonel Abbot also had a larger responsibility—commanding the entire Union siege train (including siege artillery, vehicles, and troops) deployed against Richmond, which for the remainder of 1864 and early 1865 chiefly targeted the Confederates at Petersburg shielding Richmond.

The thirteen-inch mortar was the only gun of such dimension in the Union siege train. When fired, "it made the ground quake," one soldier attested. But the Dictator did not fire often. In service for eighty-one days from early July 1864 until it returned to the depot permanently in late September, it hurled only 218 shells at the enemy. Charging the monster with 20 pounds of black powder and loading a 220-pound spherical shell (which had a diameter of slightly less than thirteen inches to fit the barrel) was a time-consuming business. So was aiming the gun. Because of its terrific recoil, which shifted the weapon two feet backward on its mount, and its flatcar twelve feet backward on the rails, it could be fired only in line with the track. Changing aim required moving the flatcar to a new position on the curving railway spur.

With a range of at least two and a half miles, the Dictator could easily shell central Petersburg, but it was used mostly to suppress a menacing Confederate battery in an entrenched position north of town, across the Appomattox River. Shells from the Dictator, fused to explode above the target, sprayed the enemy with case shot, consisting of dozens of iron balls, each weighing nearly a half pound. Colonel Abbot had conducted experiments in 1863 to perfect the technique, which proved well suited to the task of scattering Confederate artillerymen. Traveling at over two hundred feet per second, the case shot could kill or disable any man or horse it struck. ✠ BCH

RENOWNED MORTAR *Colonel Henry Abbot, in black boots, stands next to "the Dictator" in 1864 with Brigadier General Henry J. Hunt (beside Abbot) and men of the 1st Connecticut Heavy Artillery. Photographers found the Dictator irresistible and helped make it famous.*

104

DESIGNATING FLAGS

THE ARMY OF THE POTOMAC THAT FOUGHT IN Virginia in 1864 was a vast force of nearly 120,000 men when Ulysses Grant launched his campaign in May, making it by far the largest army on either side at that time. Managing such an immense body of troops was a challenge, but Grant responded effectively by delegating the implementation of his orders to George Meade, who had led the Army of the Potomac at Gettysburg and remained its commander under Grant. He also benefited from the organizational efforts of Meade's predecessors. George McClellan, the army's founder, was the first Union commander to form corps, which consisted of from two to four divisions and their constituent brigades and regiments. McClellan also devised flags to designate army units. Joseph Hooker refined the way such flags were designed and used after taking command of the Army of the Potomac in 1863. As illustrated here, each corps had a distinctive badge—a diamond for the Third Corps, for example, and a modified Maltese cross for the Fifth Corps. Different colors were used to distinguish one division from another in the same corps, and brigade flags were distinguished from division or corps flags by their triangular shape.

The badges displayed on designating flags derived from badges worn by soldiers on their caps and helped instill a sense of unit pride and cohesion that was hard to maintain within the sprawling army as a whole. Those badges and flags enabled commanders to identify soldiers by unit, and helped soldiers identify the locations of commanders and quartermasters. The flag system adopted by the Army of the Potomac extended to all twenty-five corps of the Union Army and served as the basis for the unit insignia of the modern American military. ✣ NGE

CODED ARMY BANNERS *Some of the flags shown at right and on the following page identified units in the field. Others signaled the locations of chief quartermasters (whose flags displayed the corps number) or corps headquarters (whose flags displayed both the corps number and the corps badge).*

Fourth Brigade, Second Division, Sixth Corps

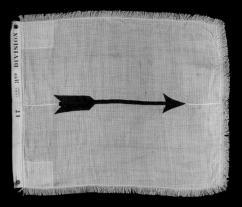

Third Division, Seventeenth Corps

Second Brigade, First Division, Third Corps

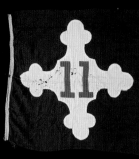

Headquarters, Eleventh Corps

First Brigade, Third Division, Ninth Corps

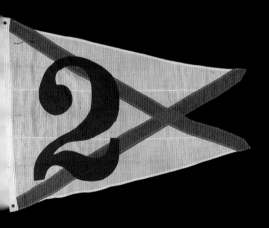

Chief Quartermaster, Second Corps

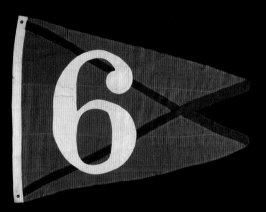

Chief Quartermaster, Sixth Corps

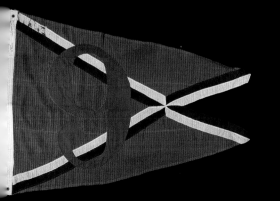

Chief Quartermaster, Ninth Corps

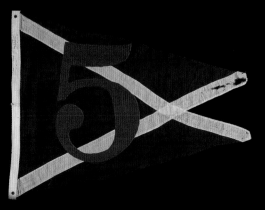

Chief Quartermaster, Fifth Corps

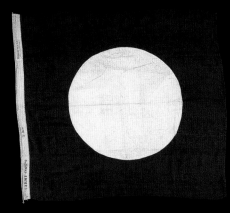

Second Division, First Corps

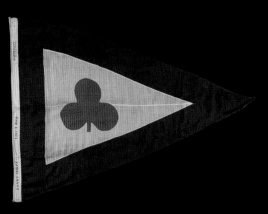

Third Brigade, First Division, Second Corps

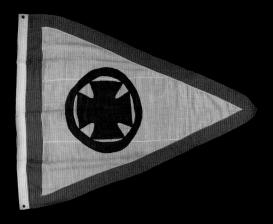

Third Brigade, Third Division, Fifth Corps

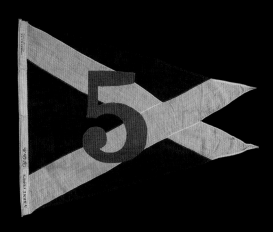

Chief Quartermaster, Fifth Corps

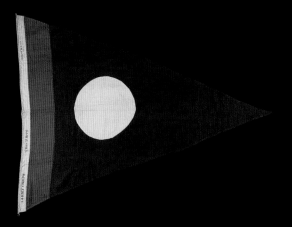

Second Brigade, Second Division, First Corps

First Division, Ninth Corps

105

CIVIL WAR PLANS FOR PLANES

I N THE SUMMER OF 1864 MANY OF THE CONFEDERATE regiments huddled in the trenches around Petersburg welcomed a lecturer, Richard O. "Bird" Davidson, into their camps. He outlined his plan for a winged flying machine that would rain destruction on the enemy, displayed a small model of his craft, and then passed the hat to finance the venture, asking for a donation of one dollar from each enlisted man and five dollars from each officer. It is not clear what happened to the money, but there is no evidence to suggest that the would-be aviator ever left the ground.

On the other side of the lines, Colonel Edward W. Serrell, chief engineer of the Army of the James, demonstrated the principle of the helicopter to General Benjamin Butler and persuaded the commander to release him from duty so that he could travel to Philadelphia and New York to raise funds to build a full-scale technology demonstrator. By war's end, Serrell had completed major elements of his machine and run rotary wing tests, but he abandoned the project when it became clear that no available engine was both light enough and powerful enough to propel his craft into the air.

William Powers, a resident of Mobile, Alabama, and Richmond dentist R. Findley Hunt both developed plans for rotary-wing flying machines intended to deal a crushing blow to the Yankees from the air. Powers was so afraid that Northern spies would steal his plans and turn the device against the Confederacy that he hid his drawings and model away. Hunt, on the other hand, bombarded Jefferson Davis and the Confederate War Department with demands that they fund his scheme. They declined.

During the war, no one came closer to producing a navigable flying machine that might be put to military use than Solomon Andrews. A New Jersey physician and inventor, Andrews constructed an airship called *Aereon* (overleaf), consisting of three eighty-foot-long, cigar-shaped balloons, tied together side by side and equipped with a rudder. Andrews made several flights with the full-scale craft near his home in the spring of 1863. By manipulating the rudder and shifting weight he maneuvered the craft and returned to his takeoff point. In letters to President Lincoln and other officials, he proposed to build an aircraft that could be used against the Confederates. When War Department officials doubted reports of the flying trials, Andrews successfully demonstrated a small model of his craft in the Capitol building and at the Smithsonian Institution. Congress nevertheless chose not to fund development.

Throughout the war years, these and other inventors from both North and South sought to convince their respective governments that navigable flying machines could be developed and used in combat to decide the conflict. Although the invention of the airplane was forty years in the future and none of these would-be aviators had any chance of waging aerial warfare, the dream of military airpower was alive and well on both sides of the lines. ✣ TC

PIONEER'S PORTRAIT *This daguerreotype of inventor Solomon Andrews (1806–1872), made around 1842 before he established his reputation as an aeronaut, is one of the earliest photographs in the collection of the National Portrait Gallery.*

HELICOPTER DESIGNS

Confederate inventor William Powers proposed a helicopter that would be lifted into the air and propelled forward by sets of Archimedean screws (NEAR RIGHT). Colonel Edward Serrell, who took leave from the Union Army to design a steam-powered helicopter, sketched a rotary wing for that machine and other details (FAR RIGHT). Both drawings are held at the National Air and Space Museum.

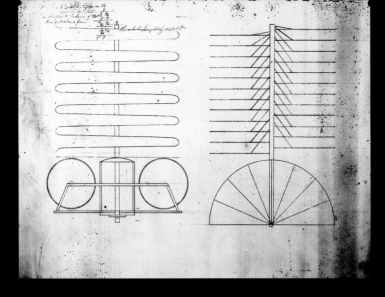

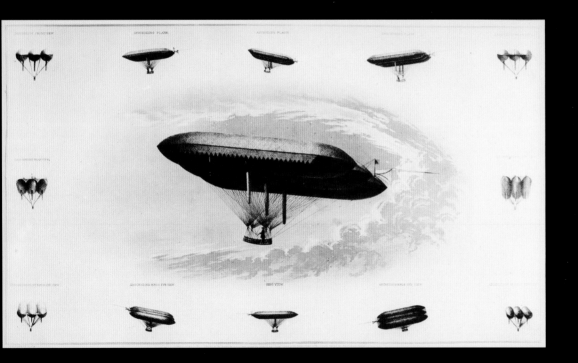

ANDREWS'S AIRSHIP *This print portrays Solomon Andrews's maneuverable airship* Aereon *from various angles. The craft's rudder, shown at right in the large center view, was manipulated by ropes from the platform below, where Andrews stood while in flight.*

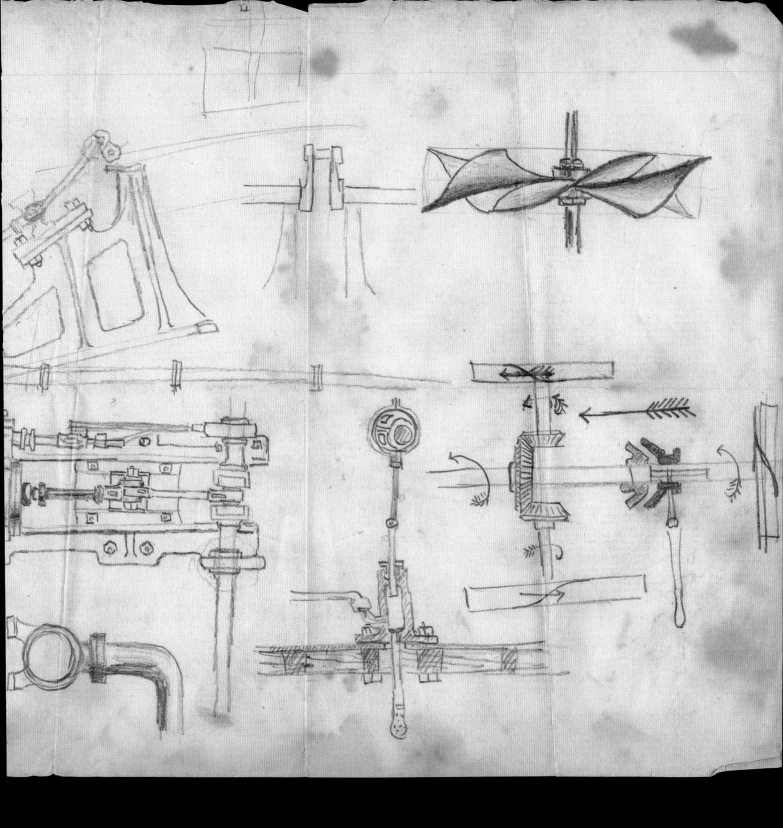

106

ARMING THE NAVIES

IN THE EARLY HOURS OF FEBRUARY 2, 1864, A LOOKOUT aboard the gunboat U.S.S. *Underwriter*, moored in the Neuse River off New Bern, North Carolina, spotted more than a dozen boats with men at oars approaching in the dark and sounded the alarm. The attackers were Confederate seamen led by Commander John Taylor Wood. Using grappling hooks, they boarded the Union steamer with guns and cutlasses in hand and battled crewmen wielding similar weapons. "Now the fighting was furious, and at close quarters," one Confederate recalled. "The cracking of fire arms and the rattle of cutlasses made a deafening din. The enemy gave way slowly." More than fifty Union sailors were killed, wounded, or captured by the victorious Confederates, who made off with their prisoners and left the doomed gunboat in flames.

Such close fighting on deck was uncommon during the Civil War. Most battles at sea were decided by big guns such as the 15-inch Dahlgren, which was installed on Union ironclads and fired a 440-pound shot that could smash armor. Nonetheless, the opposing navies routinely drilled sailors in the use of small arms. On a well-run Union ship, one day a week would be set aside for practice with a variety of weapons used to seize or defend ships, including muskets, rifles, pistols, cutlasses, boarding axes, and boarding pikes. The U.S. Navy, which relied largely on the smoothbore Springfield Model 1842 musket when the war began, ordered thousands of .69-caliber Whitney Model 1861 rifles (overleaf), to which 22-inch-long bayonets were attached for close combat. Such long arms were cumbersome for men in boarding parties who had to clamber up the side

of ships. They favored pistols like the Colt Navy Model 1851 revolver, issued to many Union crewmen, although some had newer model Colts or Remingtons. Cutlasses, swords, and boarding axes (which doubled as tools for tasks like cutting damaged rigging) were time-honored weapons from the age of sail but remained lethal in close fighting. Confederate surgeon Daniel B. Conrad, who treated men wounded in the battle on the U.S.S. *Underwriter*, encountered one unfortunate victim whose "head had been cleft in two" by a cutlass wielded by "some giant of the forecastle."

Although much smaller than the U.S. Navy, the C.S. Navy was fairly well supplied. Shortly before the war began, Jefferson Davis instructed Commander Raphael Semmes "to proceed North and purchase all the arms, ammunition, and other munitions of war ... that he could buy and have delivered." Semmes later prowled the high seas as captain of the commerce raider C.S.S. *Alabama*, which seized more than sixty Union merchant ships before it was sunk in battle by the U.S.S. *Kearsarge* off Cherbourg, France, in June 1864. (Semmes got away and was later promoted to rear admiral.) Like the *Alabama*, which was built in Great Britain, most Confederate naval weapons were of foreign manufacture. Among the revolvers issued to Southern sailors were British-made Kerrs, French-made LeMats, and Union-made Colts. ✛ KG

DRESSED FOR DUTY *Seaman Arnold Reichart, who served on the ironclad U.S.S.* Pittsburg *with the Western Gunboat Flotilla, posed proudly in uniform for this portrait, printed as a carte-de-visite.*

KEARSARGE

NAVY BLUE *Enlisted men in the U.S. Navy during the Civil War wore flat hats like the one above, which belonged to Nathan Ives, who served aboard the U.S.S. Kearsarge when it engaged the C.S.S.* Alabama *in 1864; and jumpers like the one at left, worn by Charles Gillette Pratt of the U.S.S. Rhode Island. Seamen used the battle rattle (BELOW) to sound the alarm aboard ship and to call all hands to battle stations.*

U.S. MODEL 1860 CUTLASS *The Ames Manufacturing Company of Chicopee, Massachusetts, provided the U.S. Navy with this cutlass for use by boarding parties or men defending ships. Based on an earlier French pattern, it has a twenty-six-inch curved blade.*

U.S. MODEL 1852 NAVY OFFICER'S SWORD *Closely resembling U.S. Army officers' swords of the period, this sword was owned by Lieutenant Samuel Howard, who served as pilot aboard the U.S.S.* Monitor *during its historic battle with the C.S.S.* Virginia *at Hampton Roads in March 1862.*

WHITNEY MODEL 1861 RIFLE *The Whitney Arms Company supplied the U.S. Navy with about ten thousand of these .69-caliber rifles, called "Plymouths" because they were recommended by Captain John A. Dahlgren of the U.S.S.* Plymouth, *a naval ordnance expert who developed big Dahlgren guns and other weapons. When the Ordnance Board rejected his recommendation that sailors be armed with a fighting knife, he designed one anyway and called it the Dahlgren bayonet (LEFT).*

CONFEDERATE NAVAL OFFICER'S SWORD *Manufactured by Robert Mole & Sons of Birmingham, England, this sword was taken from a Confederate officer when the commerce raider C.S.S. Florida was seized by the U.S.S. Wachusett off the coast of Brazil in October 1864.*

JOSLYN ARMY MODEL REVOLVER *A five-shot, .44-caliber revolver with a distinctive solid frame and side-mounted hammer, this is one of approximately one hundred such pistols purchased by the U.S. Navy in 1861 from the Joslyn Firearms Company of Stonington, Connecticut.*

107

"GOD HELPS THOSE WHO HELP THEMSELVES"

WHEN RAPHAEL SEMMES TOOK COMMAND OF the commerce raider C.S.S. *Alabama* in 1862, he had the words *"Aide Toi et Dieu T'Aidera"* (God Helps Those Who Help Themselves) inscribed on the ship's wheel. It was an age-old motto, but one that became closely associated with the *Alabama* and its captain, whose exploits were recalled in the South long after the war ended.

> *Aide Toi et Dieu T'Aidera.*
>
> **MOTTO OF THE C.S.S. *ALABAMA***

In 1878 Dr. James H. Kimball, a physician in St. Augustine, Florida, was called upon to treat a woman with yellow fever named Sarah Willax. Her husband was a merchant, and had in his shop, attached to their home, an ironstone vegetable dish (below), sold to him by a former Confederate ship captain. It bore the emblem of the Confederate States Navy (C.S.N.)

above the motto of the *Alabama*. Dr. Kimball admired the dish as he passed through the shop to visit his patient. When she recovered, he received it as payment from Mr. Willax, who was aware of its significance. According to him, the dish was part of a set of china manufactured for the *Alabama* in Europe (it was in fact made in England). The set ended up divided among the captains of other Confederate ships, perhaps because it was not completed until after the *Alabama* was sunk by the U.S.S. *Kearsarge* in 1864. Several pieces of the china came into the possession of Captain Michael Usina of St. Augustine, who had been wounded while fighting as a Confederate infantryman at Manassas but had recovered sufficiently to take command of the blockade-runner *Mary Celestia* at the age of twenty-four. He went on to command other blockade-runners, including the *Atalanta* and the *Armstrong*.

Captain Usina sold the dish to Mr. Willax. It remained in the Kimball family until the death in 1959 of the doctor's son, Samuel E. Kimball, who bequeathed it the Smithsonian. ✣ KG

PRIZED CHINA *The English firm of Bodley & Son produced this ironstone dish intended for use on the C.S.S.* Alabama, *whose motto appears below the crossed-cannons emblem of the Confederate States Navy.*

108

THE OTHER WAR

IN 1864 THE UNION WAS FIGHTING TWO WARS, ONE against Confederates and the other against defiant Sioux. John Feilner fought on both fronts, and lost his life in the service of science for the Smithsonian. A Bavarian immigrant and amateur naturalist, he enlisted in the U.S. Army in 1856 and was posted to California, where he collected bird skins, eggs, and other specimens that he sent to Spencer Fullerton Baird, assistant secretary of the Smithsonian. Impressed, Baird helped Feilner secure an officer's commission as the Civil War loomed. He served with distinction in Virginia in 1862 and was promoted to captain. Baird suggested that he might be of value in the West, where he could again collect for the Smithsonian. Feilner was ordered to report for duty under General Alfred Sully, who was conducting operations against the Sioux.

That conflict began in August 1862 when a band of Dakotas (Eastern Sioux), angered by the government's failure to deliver promised payments they needed to buy food, attacked settlers in Minnesota. Soldiers put down the uprising, and more than three hundred Dakotas were condemned to death by a military tribunal—thirty-eight of whom were executed after President Lincoln commuted most of the sentences. In 1863 and 1864, Sully campaigned against Sioux in the Dakota Territory, where those who had fled Minnesota joined other tribal bands in opposing U.S. forces.

On June 30, 1864, Feilner was collecting specimens on the Little Cheyenne River when three warriors attacked and killed him. In retaliation, troops captured and executed those three and mounted their heads on poles as a warning to others. "It is hard that he should lose his life in this way," General Sully remarked of Captain Feilner. "It was all owing to his enthusiastic desire to collect as many specimens as possible for the Smithsonian Institution." ✛ TC

Capt. Feilner.

Mrs. Feilner

LOST IN SERVICE *Captain John Feilner, whose portrait appears at left beside that of his wife, collected the scientific specimens shown on the following two pages for the Smithsonian before he was killed in 1864. His death was the result of a conflict that originated in Minnesota, where attacks by Sioux left more than a hundred settlers at New Ulm dead or wounded and prompted retaliation by U.S. forces. Among the relics of the New Ulm attacks is this pipe tomahawk.*

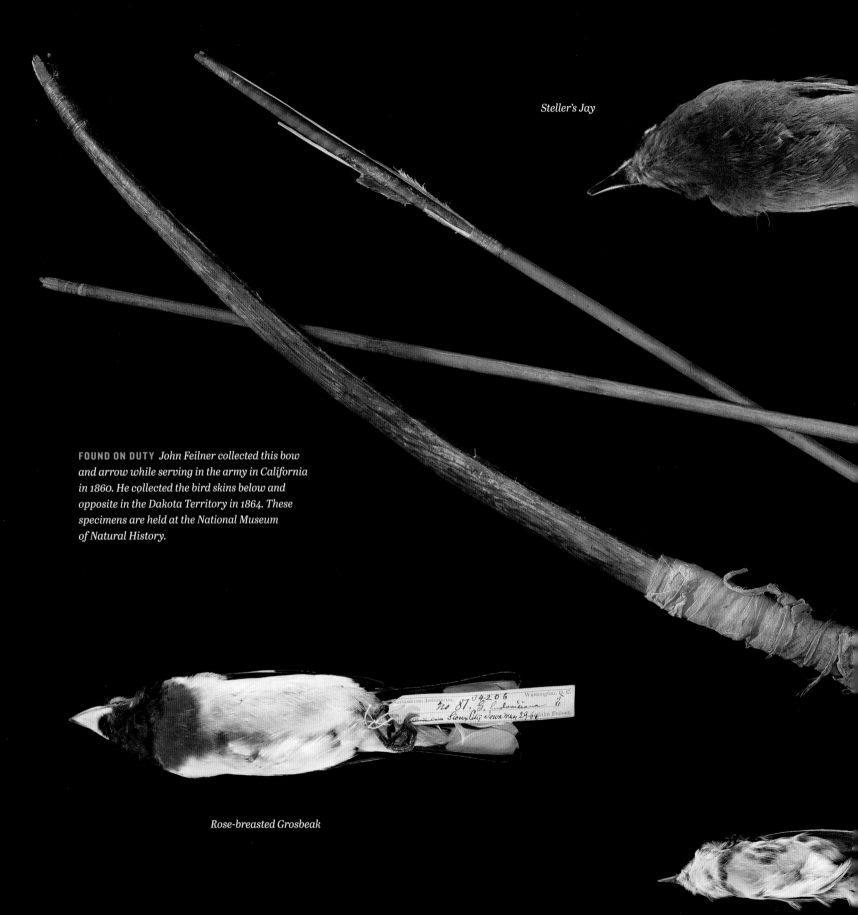

Steller's Jay

FOUND ON DUTY *John Feilner collected this bow and arrow while serving in the army in California in 1860. He collected the bird skins below and opposite in the Dakota Territory in 1864. These specimens are held at the National Museum of Natural History.*

Rose-breasted Grosbeak

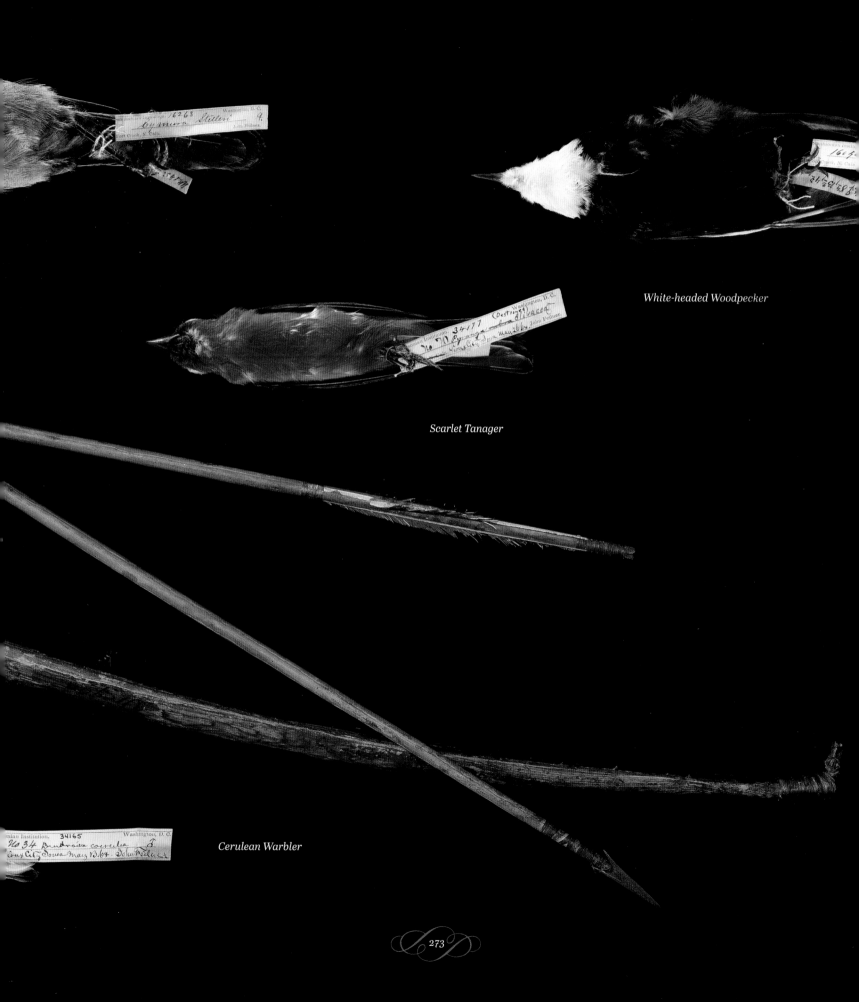

White-headed Woodpecker

Scarlet Tanager

Cerulean Warbler

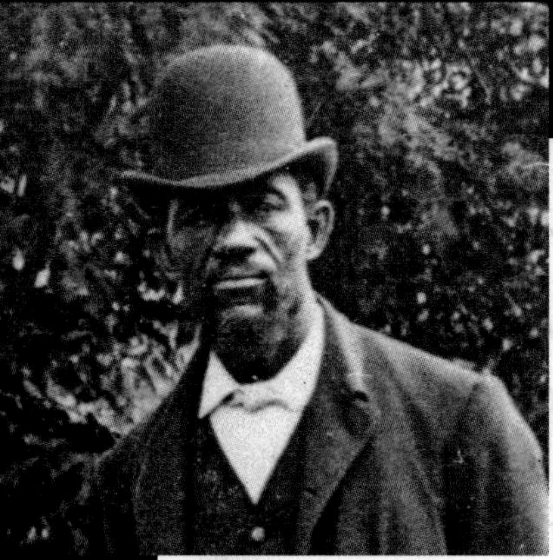

625

Just as I was closing this
Mr Walts came in and Reported for Duty
went out to fight line
could not get a chance.

21

Smithsonian Institution

Washington July 15th 1864

Prof Baird

Dear Sir

Yours dated July 12th have just Arrived and we are all glade to hear from you and famil all here is well – many have been much frightened at the annual visit of the Rebels to their friends at Maryland, but we are told that the jolly Rebs are returning home with lots of Presents ~~an~~ including money from their Joy Entertainers, we are also told here (that among many other funny things they performed) that they knocked. but the door of Washington was not opened unto them. they being a set of high bread gentleme concluded not to come in with no, sure of civil treat-ment, so they marched off. much to thy joy and comfort of a greatly Excited Papalace of this City, but your would really feel Secure were you here just now.

109

THE LETTERS OF SOLOMON BROWN

WASHINGTON, D.C., REMAINED ON HIGH ALERT in 1864. The Rebels were no longer right across the river, as they had been in 1861 when Smithsonian staff high in the Castle could see their flags flying in Alexandria. But they still posed a threat to the capital, as documented here by Solomon G. Brown (ca.1829–1906), an African American clerk at the Smithsonian who wrote this letter to his mentor there, Spencer Fullerton Baird, assistant secretary in charge of the U.S. National Museum. A free man by birth, Brown had his education cut short when his father died, and he was then apprenticed as a clerk. Hired in 1852 as a laborer at the Smithsonian, he advanced to clerk and remained there until he retired fifty-four years later.

While Baird conducted fieldwork each summer in Massachusetts, Brown kept an eye on the museum and informed him regularly in writing of developments in Washington, including the great scare in July 1864 when Confederates led by Jubal Early invaded Maryland and advanced to within six miles of the White House. It was the third invasion of that state in as many years, and Brown remarked that Washingtonians "have been much frightened at the annual visit of the Rebels to their friends at Maryland." He was not impressed with the valor displayed by either side. When Early withdrew after skirmishing with the fortified Federals, Brown wrote that Confederates had knocked, "but the door of Washington was not opened unto them . . . so they marched off." And not until they were gone, he observed, did panic give way to bravado in the city. The many "Brave fighting men that came out from their hiding Places and Paraded through streets in search of arms to meet the Rebels," Brown noted, were soon fighting among themselves in "Saloons, gambling halls and other low places." ✢ PMH

WASHINGTON CORRESPONDENT *Solomon Brown, pictured here late in life, wrote many informative letters to Spencer Baird preserved in the Smithsonian Archives, including this one dated July 15, 1864, describing the recent Confederate advance on the capital.*

110

EQUIPPING THE CAVALRY

BY 1864 THE UNION CAVALRY HAD CAUGHT UP tactically with the Confederate cavalry, which entered the war with better horsemen and bolder commanders who formed large cavalry units acting independently of armies that advanced slowly on foot. Not until 1863 did the Army of the Potomac follow suit and field a cavalry corps capable of competing with that led by Robert E. Lee's accomplished cavalry chief, J.E.B. Stuart. When men of those opposing forces clashed at Kelly's Ford in Virginia in March 1863, one Union trooper remarked, it was the first time that a large body of Northern cavalry "came out spoiling for a fight against the Southern cavalry."

In April 1864 Ulysses Grant made Philip Sheridan his cavalry chief in Virginia. Sheridan vowed to whip Stuart, who was fatally wounded at Yellow Tavern in May. But the ascendancy of Union cavalry involved more than Sheridan's rise and Stuart's fall. Furnishing troopers with arms, equipment, and horses—which broke down on campaigns at an appalling rate—was a costly venture for which the North had greater resources. As the war drew to a close, one Confederate officer observed, some Southern cavalrymen no longer had horses to ride, and those who did relied largely on Union-made gear: "Our breech-loading arms were nearly all captured from the enemy and the same may be said of the best of our saddles and bridles." ✢ KG

OFFICER'S SPUR *One of a pair, the eagle-head strap spur above was worn by Brigadier General David M. Gregg (OVERLEAF), who rose from colonel of the 8th Pennsylvania Cavalry in 1862 to commander of a cavalry division under Ulysses Grant and Philip Sheridan.*

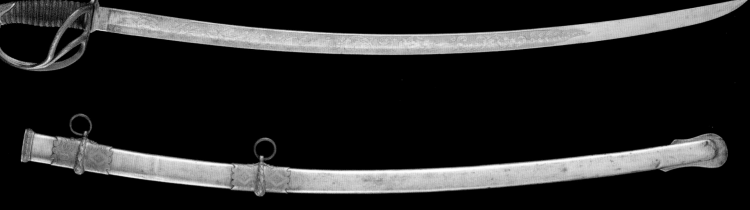

Tiffany Model 1860 Cavalry Officer's saber

Spencer carbine

TOOLS OF HIS TRADE *Brigadier General David Gregg, pictured at right in 1864, graduated from West Point in 1855, two years ahead of Philip Sheridan and one year ahead of J.E.B. Stuart, who was felled at Yellow Tavern by cavalrymen of Gregg's division. The saber at top, decorated by Tiffany & Company, was presented to Gregg by Company E, 6th U.S. Cavalry Regiment, in 1862 when he left that regiment to take charge of the 8th Pennsylvania Cavalry. Unlike sabers, which could be wielded on horseback, breech-loading carbines like the Spencer above were intended for use by dismounted cavalrymen. Federals were better equipped with carbines than their foes. The Union purchased more than 94,000 of these rapid-firing Spencers with a magazine holding seven cartridges; another 120,000 were purchased privately.*

PORTABLE FORGE A Union Army blacksmith prepares a shoe for a waiting horse in an image from Alexander Gardner's Photographic Sketch Book of the War. Forges like this one, transported by wagon, followed cavalry units on the move to keep their mounts well shod.

McClellan saddle

BOOTS AND SADDLE

High boots with high heels like these worn by a Union officer protected the legs of cavalrymen and helped keep their feet in stirrups. The McClellan saddle at right was standard issue for Union cavalry. Light yet sturdy and less expensive to produce than other saddles of the day, it was designed by General George McClellan, who said he was influenced by the saddles of Hussars he observed in Europe.

Cavalry officer's high boots

111

HANDGUNS

ON OCTOBER 3, 1864, LIEUTENANT JOHN R. MEIGS, Major General Philip Sheridan's topographical engineer and the son of Quartermaster General Montgomery Meigs, was riding in the rain with two Union soldiers near Dayton, Virginia, when they overtook three horsemen whose capes covered their uniforms. Meigs called on the men to halt. They were Confederate scouts who drew pistols and fired, killing Meigs. The Confederates captured one of the Union soldiers; the other escaped to tell of the shooting, which Sheridan considered partisan warfare. In retaliation, he had houses in and around Dayton torched.

As this incident demonstrated, handguns could be potent weapons when opponents met at close quarters during the Civil War. Some infantrymen and most officers carried them, and they were often issued to seamen and cavalrymen, who were more likely than foot soldiers to come near enough to their enemies to make handguns useful. Although they remained strictly short-range weapons, those side arms had evolved dramatically in recent years from the cumbersome single-shot muzzle-loaders of old. That era ended in 1848 when Samuel Colt sold a thousand of his innovative .44-caliber revolvers to the U.S. Army, which issued them to dragoons (mounted infantrymen). A few years later, Colt came out with a lighter, .36-caliber revolver. Because the U.S. Navy was an early customer and the cylinder bore an engraved naval battle scene, that model became known as the Colt 1851 Navy Revolver. Thereafter, .44-caliber revolvers were termed "Army" and .36-caliber revolvers were

termed "Navy." Both Colt models were percussion revolvers, which required a percussion cap to be placed at the rear of each bore in the cylinder before the trigger was pulled, bringing the hammer down on the cap and igniting a cartridge filled with gunpowder and a bullet. As was the case with long arms, few revolvers in use during the Civil War fired self-contained metal cartridges that eliminated the need for percussion caps.

Most of the handguns made by Colt and other American gun makers at that time were single-action revolvers, meaning that pulling the trigger performed only one action—firing the gun. Before the trigger was pulled, the hammer had to be cocked manually, which also rotated the cylinder. Some revolvers in production then were double action, meaning that pulling the trigger cocked the hammer and rotated the cylinder as well as firing the gun. Most soldiers were accustomed to the single action, and few purchased or were issued double-action revolvers.

Colt, Remington, and Whitney were the major suppliers of Union handguns, but the government also purchased some from smaller companies and imported others from Europe. The Confederacy imported more revolvers than it produced at home. Unlike Colt, which made hundreds of thousands of revolvers during the war, few Southern contractors turned out as many as a thousand revolvers. ✢ DDM

GUNMAN *Soldiers like this Union sergeant often posed for studio portraits with handguns. Some were their own weapons, but most were provided as props by photographers.*

COLT MODEL 1851 NAVY REVOLVER
This .36-caliber six-shooter was Colt's most popular percussion revolver. Nearly 250,000 were made between 1850 and 1873, and many soldiers and lawmen, as well as outlaws, carried them.

KERR REVOLVER *The five-shot, .44-caliber Kerr was produced in England by the London Armoury Company and exported almost entirely to the Confederacy. A favorite of Southern cavalrymen, it could be fired in either single or double action.*

STARR ARMY REVOLVER *The .44-caliber Starr was the only American revolver produced in both single and double action during the war. This 1863 single-action model was considered an improvement over the double-action model.*

COLT MODEL 1860 ARMY REVOLVER *This .44-caliber six-shooter was one of the most widely used revolvers during the Civil War. Many Confederates carried this or other Colt models—or copies of them made by Southern contractors.*

LEMAT REVOLVER *French physician Jean Alexandre LeMat, an in-law of Confederate General P.G.T. Beauregard, developed the nine-shot .40-caliber LeMat, with a 16-gauge shotgun barrel. Nearly 3,000 were shipped to the South.*

LEFAUCHEUX REVOLVER *The French-made .44-caliber Lefaucheux had metallic cartridges that fired when punctured by pins driven by the hammer. Purchased by the Union, it was also carried by a few Confederate officers.*

SAVAGE NAVY REVOLVER *The .36-caliber six-shot Savage has a lower ring lever to cock the hammer and rotate the cylinder, and a trigger above that to fire the gun. Although hard to aim, some 12,000 were purchased by the Union.*

GRISWOLD & GUNNISON REVOLVER
A Connecticut Yankee who moved to Georgia, Samuel Griswold teamed with Arvin Gunnison in 1862 to produce this close copy of the Colt 1851 Navy Revolver. It was the best revolver made in the South.

REMINGTON 1861 ARMY REVOLVER *Also known as the Old Model Army, this Remington held six shots in a solid frame. Along with its successor, the New Model Army, it helped make Remington second only to Colt in Union revolver sales.*

112

SHERIDAN'S WARHORSE

I N AUGUST 1864 PHILIP SHERIDAN (1831–1888) WAS given command of all Union forces in the Shenandoah Valley. Ulysses Grant gave him orders to secure and strip bare that fertile corridor, which served as Virginia's breadbasket and was used by Confederates to invade the North. After defeating Jubal Early's forces at Winchester and Fisher's Hill in September, Sheridan began burning farms and seizing or destroying livestock. On October 19 Early struck back, surprising Sheridan's troops in camp at Cedar Creek while he was fifteen miles away at Winchester. Informed of the attack, Sheridan hurried to the front on his black Morgan horse, Rienzi, and arrived in time to rally his men and repulse the Confederates. Rienzi was renamed Winchester after the battle and honored in verse along with his owner by Thomas Buchanan Read: "Hurrah! Hurrah for Sheridan! / Hurrah! Hurrah for horse and man!"

Read's poem, and a painting he composed on the same subject (inset), helped make Winchester famous. When the horse died in 1878, Sheridan had him preserved and installed at a military museum on Governor's Island in New York. In June 1922 Winchester was transferred to the Smithsonian to reside at its National Museum in Washington, D.C. Among those who attended a ceremony on Governor's Island to bid Winchester good-bye were elderly Union veterans, some of whom had probably seen him alive and kicking fifty-eight years earlier. ✣ KG

HORSE AND MAN *Philip Sheridan and Winchester posed in New Orleans for this 1871 painting,* Sheridan's Ride, *by Thomas Buchanan Read, who composed a famous poem with the same title.*

WELL-PRESERVED *Pictured above in Washington, D.C., while he was still very much alive, Winchester stood sixteen hands tall. H appears at left in full tack—blanket, saddle, bridle, and martingal as preserved at the National Museum of American History*

113

ELECTION OF 1864

I N THE SUMMER OF 1864, ABRAHAM LINCOLN HAD good reason to doubt his chances for reelection. No president since Andrew Jackson in 1832 had been elected to a second term. Both parties knew the vote would serve as a referendum on Lincoln's handling of the war and his Emancipation Proclamation, which Democrats widely criticized as an abuse of presidential powers. Horrific Union casualties and the unpopular military draft led Lincoln and many in his party to consider victory unlikely. At their convention in Baltimore in

> *This morning, as for some days in the past, it seems exceedingly probable that this Administration will not be reelected.*
>
> **ABRAHAM LINCOLN, AUGUST 23, 1864**

June 1864, Republican delegates gathered under the umbrella of the newly designated National Union Party, which included some War Democrats, who unlike Peace Democrats wanted to continue fighting until the Confederacy yielded and the Union was restored. Nominated on the first ballot, Lincoln left to the delegates the selection of his running mate—War Democrat Andrew Johnson, a former senator and current military governor of Tennessee. The party platform demanded unconditional surrender by the Confederacy and resolved to "forever prohibit the existence of Slavery."

In late August, Democrats met in Chicago. They nominated General George B. McClellan, the former commander of Union forces, for president and chose Congressman George Pendleton of Ohio, a Peace Democrat, as his running mate. Their platform dismissed the war as a "failure" and called for upholding the Constitution, which had been "disregarded in every part," reestablishing states' rights, and ending hostilities "at the earliest practicable moment." In his letter accepting the nomination, McClellan distanced himself from that platform and appealed to War Democrats by stating that restoring the Union in full was the "indispensable condition" for peace.

The great unknown was who would win the soldiers' support—their commander in chief or their popular former general. The outcome rested more on how Union forces fared in the field than on any campaigning done by the two parties. As the election drew near, victories altered the country's mood. Admiral Farragut's triumph in Mobile Bay, followed by General Sherman's capture of Atlanta and General Sheridan's success in the Shenandoah Valley, propelled Lincoln to victory. With a resounding 212-to-21 electoral win and a 400,000 vote majority, secured with the strong support of soldiers, Lincoln declared the election a mandate for unconditional victory and renewed his call for a constitutional amendment to end slavery. ✢ HRR

CAMPAIGN MEMORABILIA
Inexpensive tintypes, made by photographing existing portraits, were used to produce campaign buttons like these for Abraham Lincoln. The broadside opposite, published by H. H. Lloyd and Company, pictures the candidates alongside their party platforms and acceptance letters.

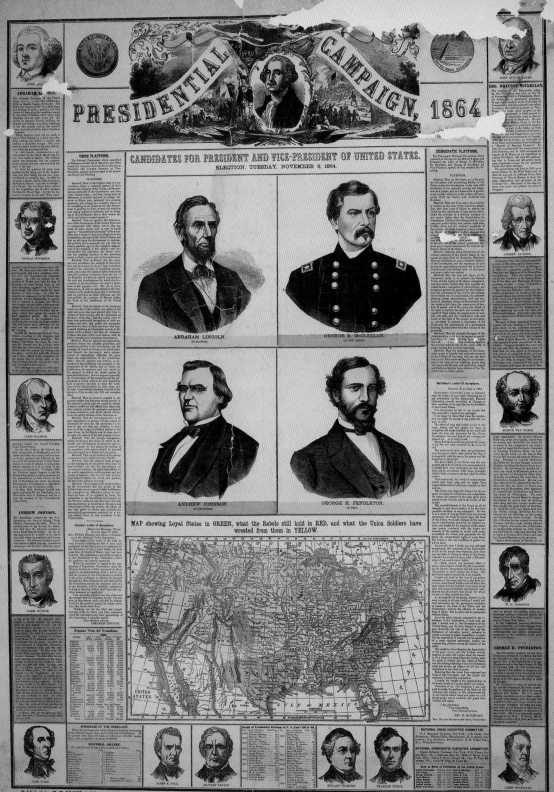

PRESIDENTIAL CAMPAIGN, 1864.

CANDIDATES FOR PRESIDENT AND VICE-PRESIDENT OF UNITED STATES. ELECTION, TUESDAY, NOVEMBER 8, 1864.

ABRAHAM LINCOLN. — GEORGE B. McCLELLAN.

ANDREW JOHNSON. — GEORGE H. PENDLETON.

MAP showing Loyal States in GREEN, what the Rebels still hold in RED, and what the Union Soldiers have wrested from them in YELLOW.

Published by H. H. LLOYD & CO., 21 John Street, New York.   B. B. RUSSELL, 515 Washington Street, Boston.   R. R. LANDON, 82 Lake Street, Chicago.

114

THE MISCEGENATION BALL

THIS PROVOCATIVE CARTOON, PORTRAYING REPUBLICAN SUPPORTERS of Abraham Lincoln engaging in miscegenation—a newly coined term for race mixing—was published in the *New York World*, a Democratic newspaper, on September 23, 1864. Hard-hitting presidential campaigns had long been a staple of American politics, but in this election the stakes were especially high. Lincoln's Democratic foe, George McClellan, opposed the Emancipation Proclamation and thought that the war should be waged only to restore the Union and not to end slavery. Supporters of McClellan accused Lincoln of favoring not just emancipation and abolition but amalgamation of the races—a prospect that most Americans dreaded.

Two journalists at the *New York World*, George Workman and David Croly, fanned such fears by publishing an anonymous pamphlet entitled "Miscegenation: The Theory of the Blending of the Races, Applied to the American White Man and Negro." It appeared to favor emancipation and abolition as steps toward the ultimate goal of achieving a "union of the races." But its real purpose was to frighten readers and turn them against Lincoln. As the authors put it, "When the President proclaimed Emancipation he proclaimed also the mingling of the races."

More effective than pamphlets in pandering to prejudices were cartoons like this one. In "The Miscegenation Ball," racial barriers are breached as whites and blacks dance, cavort, and couple flamboyantly against the backdrop of a large portrait of the president, suggesting that a second term for Lincoln the Great Emancipator would lead to unbridled race mixing. In truth, miscegenation was more common where African Americans were enslaved than where they were free. Long before critics lambasted Lincoln for promoting racial amalgamation, President Thomas Jefferson's intimate connection to his slave Sally Hemings was rumored in the press and alluded to in a political cartoon. Although many whites considered such interracial relationships "unnatural," they were tolerated when owners took slaves as mistresses. Those relationships did not involve marriage, which would legitimize miscegenation and place partners of different races on a more equal footing. During Reconstruction, when those freed from slavery were acknowledged as citizens, laws against interracial marriage were suspended in several Southern states, only to be restored during the Jim Crow era that followed. Not until 1968, more than a century after the Civil War ended, did the U.S. Supreme Court strike down such laws nationally. ✦ JDS

FICTIONAL FROLIC *This political cartoon, the fourth in a series published in the* New York World, *purports to represent a frolic at Lincoln campaign headquarters in Manhattan, where leading Republicans supposedly stayed on after a meeting and joined in a "negro ball."*

Lith. Kimmel & Forster 254 & 256 Canal Street N.Y.

at the Headquarters of the Li New York World Sept. 23ᵈ 1864) No soc the 'Central Lincoln Club' left the *that on the floor during the progr* gathering. There were Republi

POLITICAL CARICATURE. No 4.

UNIVERSAL FREEDOM
ONE CONSTITUTION
ONE DESTINY
ABRAHAM LINCOLN PREST

Entered according to act of Congress in the year 1864 by Bromley & Co New York in the Clerks Office of the Districts Court of the United States for the Southern District of New York.

THE MISCEGENATION BALL

tral Campaign Club, Corner of Broadway and Twenty Third Street New York Sept. 22ᵈ 1864 being a perfect fac simile of the room &c. &c. (From the he formal proceedings and speeches hurried through with, than the room was cleared for a 'negro ball', which then and there took place! Some members of re the mystical and circling rites of languishing glance and mazy dance commenced. But that MANY remained is also true. This fact WE CERTIFY, ll were many of the accredited leaders of the Black Republican party, thus testifying their faith by their works in the hall and headquarters of their political CE-HOLDERS, and prominent men of various degrees, and at least one PRESIDENTIAL ELECTOR ON THE REPUBLICAN TICKET."

AURORA BOREALIS

THE EERIE LIGHT OF THE AURORA BOREALIS WAS long viewed as ominous and apocalyptic. During the Civil War, it was seen as emblematic of that conflict and its carnage. In mid-December 1862 the aurora was visible as far south as Virginia and dazzled opposing forces at Fredericksburg. It flared up "on the side of the enemy," one Confederate wrote, and "turned as red as blood."

Frederic Church's painting *Aurora Borealis*, completed at war's end, was inspired by an expedition launched in 1860 by Dr. Isaac I. Hayes, a noted explorer who wintered in the Arctic, trapped aboard ship in pack ice. His safe return in October 1861 was a rare cause for celebration amid the gloom of war. His schooner, S.S. *United States*, had come through intact, which was more than could be said for the ship of state. "When I left the regions of eternal ice," Hayes declared, "I little dreamed that a powerful rebellion was desolating my country, and that civil war was raging among a people which I left prosperous and happy. . . . God willing, I trust yet to carry the flag of our great Republic, with not a single star erased from its glorious Union, to the extreme northern limits of the earth."

Hayes served as a Union surgeon during the war before returning to exploration. He and Church were fellow members of the American Geographical and Statistical Society, and Church drew on accounts by Hayes, who likened the Arctic auroras he witnessed to "charnel meteors, pulsating with wild inconstancy over some vast illimitable city of the dead." As portrayed by Church, that frigid, unworldly expanse offered a stark contrast to the fertile New Eden evoked in prewar American landscape painting. But he included in his canvas the inspiring sight of the *United States* weathering its icy ordeal, just as the nation it represented endured the fiery conflict signaled by the aurora. ✛ EJH

NORTHERN LIGHTS *Frederic Church, who based this 1865 painting on an Arctic exploration by Dr. Isaac Hayes, was an explorer in his own right who once sketched icebergs off Labrador.*

116

THE FALL OF FORT FISHER

ITH THE POSSIBLE EXCEPTION OF DAVID Farragut, no officer contributed more to Union naval success than his foster brother, Admiral David Dixon Porter (opposite). After teaming with Farragut to take New Orleans, Porter commanded the Mississippi River Squadron and helped Ulysses Grant seize Vicksburg. In late 1864 Porter took charge of the North Atlantic Blockading Squadron and set his sights on Fort Fisher. That stronghold at the mouth of the Cape Fear River protected Wilmington, North Carolina, and shielded blockade-runners destined for that city, one of the last Confederate ports with an opening to the sea and a vital source of supplies for Robert E. Lee's army at Petersburg.

Porter's first attempt to take Fort Fisher, planned jointly with General Benjamin Butler, fizzled in December when they detonated an old Union hulk packed with 215 tons of gunpowder near the fort but failed to breach its walls, formed of densely packed sand that withstood shellfire from Porter's fleet. Butler then launched an assault so feeble that he was removed from command and replaced by General Alfred Terry. In January 1865 Porter and Terry mounted a much stronger attack. Porter's bombardment was so relentless, reported the fort's commander, Colonel William Lamb, that "we could scarcely gather up and bury our dead without fresh casualties." Porter then sent armed seamen ashore to join Terry's troops in fierce fighting that resulted in heavy casualties on both sides before Fort Fisher fell on January 15. This hard-won Union victory led to the capture of Wilmington and left Lee's forces desperately short of supplies. ✛ EWP

OCCUPYING THE PULPIT
Soon after seizing Fort Fisher in January 1865, Union troops stand in the Pulpit Battery (LEFT), which was shielded by mounds of sand and served as the command post of Confederate colonel William Lamb. This picture was taken by Timothy O'Sullivan, who was sent to document the occupation of Fort Fisher by his employer, Alexander Gardner.

FIGHTING ADMIRAL *David Dixon Porter, shown aboard the U.S.S. Malvern (OPPOSITE), directed the naval assault on Fort Fisher from this flagship. He went on to become superintendent of the U.S. Naval Academy after the war and the second full admiral in the navy's history after his foster brother, David Farragut.*

117

THE THIRTEENTH AMENDMENT

FOLLOWING ABRAHAM LINCOLN'S ELECTORAL victory in November 1864, he and fellow Republicans renewed efforts to secure passage of the Thirteenth Amendment, abolishing slavery in the United States. The amendment would complete what Lincoln's Emancipation Proclamation had set in motion on January 1, 1863. That proclamation offered the promise of freedom, but as a wartime measure it was limited in scope and applied only to those held in slavery within the Confederate States. Abolitionists feared that it might not be legally binding when peace was restored. To ensure the end of slavery and make freedom a fact, they had to amend the U.S. Constitution.

Sixty years had passed since the last amendment to the Constitution had been ratified. Few Americans could remember or draw on experience to guide Congress through the arduous process, which required approval by two-thirds of the Senate and the House of Representatives and three-fourths of the states. Republican James Ashley of Ohio had begun the legislative battle in the House on December 14, 1863, when he introduced an amendment to ban slavery in the United States. Senator John Henderson of Missouri, a War Democrat and dedicated Unionist, had joined Ashley and presented similar legislation in the Senate a short time later. The Senate combined those measures to form a joint resolution and passed the amendment in April 1864. But supporters came up short in the House, where Peace Democrats objected that abolishing slavery would alienate Confederates and prolong the conflict.

Lincoln, strengthened in November by his own reelection and by Republican gains in the House, urged Congress to back the amendment before it recessed. "May we not agree that the sooner the better?" he asked. The House responded. On January 31, 1865, the Thirteenth Amendment passed by a margin of three votes. Spectators in the gallery broke out in wild applause, and representatives on the floor celebrated. "Some embraced one another," recalled Congressman George W. Julian, "others wept like children." As a symbolic gesture, Lincoln signed the document before it was sent to the states for ratification. Targeted in April by assassin John Wilkes Booth, he did not live to see the amendment become law. Secretary of State Wil-

liam H. Seward (inset), who had helped win passage of the amendment in the House, was attacked by an accomplice of Booth's on the same night Lincoln was shot. Seward recovered, resumed his duties, and had the honor of announcing to the world on December 18, 1865, that Article Thirteen, abolishing slavery, was now "part of the Constitution of the United States."

Artist and engraver Walter Shirlaw commemorated the Thirteenth Amendment with a decorative print (opposite) in 1868, the year that African American men in the South voted for the first time in national elections. Mirroring the style of the Declaration of Independence, Shirlaw painstakingly reproduced the signatures of those in Congress who backed the amendment and included them at the bottom of his print. For Shirlaw, the Thirteenth Amendment was a new birth of freedom—a newfound declaration of independence—that promised a better America. ✛ NB

HISTORIC PASSAGE *William Seward (1801–1872) helped induce reluctant representatives to pass the Thirteenth Amendment in January 1865. In 1868 Walter Shirlaw celebrated that historic House vote with the print (OPPOSITE) honoring the amendment and its supporters.*

JOINT RESOLUTION OF THE THIRTY EIGHTH CONGRESS
OF THE UNITED STATES OF AMERICA,

PROPOSING AN AMENDMENT TO THE CONSTITUTION OF THE UNITED STATES.

ABOLISHING SLAVERY.

"Resolved by the Senate and House of Representatives of the United States of America in Congress assembled, (two thirds of both houses concurring,) that the following Article be proposed to the Legislatures of the several States as an AMENDMENT to the CONSTITUTION of the UNITED STATES, which, when ratified by three fourths of said Legislatures, shall be valid to all intents & purposes as a part of the said Constitution, namely: ARTICLE XIII.

Section 1. NEITHER SLAVERY NOR INVOLUNTARY SERVITUDE except as a punishment for crime whereof the party shall have been duly convicted SHALL EXIST WITHIN THE UNITED STATES or any place subject to their jurisdiction.

Section 2. Congress shall have power to enforce this Article by appropriate legislation."

Passed in the Senate April 8th 1864.

M Hamlin
Secretary of the Senate.

H. Hamlin
Vice President of the United States & President of the Senate.

Passed the House of Representatives January 31st 1865.

Edw McPherson, Clerk of the House.

Schuyler Colfax
Speaker of the House of Representatives.

Approved Feb. 1st 1865.   A. Lincoln

THOSE WHO VOTED AYE UPON THE PASSAGE OF THE ABOVE JOINT RESOLUTION WERE THE FOLLOWING SENATORS AND REPRESENTATIVES.

118

HELL AND DAMNATION

BY THE SUMMER OF 1864, THE OPPOSING ARMIES of Ulysses S. Grant and Robert E. Lee had dug in at Petersburg for a prolonged bout of siege warfare. The Union line extended in an arc for over thirty miles, facing the Confederate line, which shielded the town as well as vital railways that sustained Lee's army and supplied Richmond. Troops on both sides dug trenches and raised parapets and earthen forts, including one named for Union general John Sedgwick, killed by a sniper at Spotsylvania in May; and another named for Confederate general William Mahone, who repulsed Federals here in the Battle of the Crater on July 30. Union troops entrenched in this infernal landscape dubbed their gloomy Sedgwick redoubt "Fort Hell" (right) and the enemy's nearby Mahone battery "Fort Damnation" (overleaf).

The siege of Petersburg continued into the spring of 1865. A savage war of attrition, it took a heavy toll on both sides but served Grant's purpose by wearing down the smaller Army of Northern Virginia. By March his troops outnumbered Lee's nearly three to one, confirming Grant's calculus that he could prevail through sheer strength of numbers and material. A desperate attack by Lee on March 25 faltered and cost the Confederates several thousand casualties, leaving them critically vulnerable to the onslaught that Grant launched in late March and capped on April 2 when Federals overwhelmed Fort Mahone and other strongholds. "I see no prospect of doing more than holding our position here till night," Lee warned his superiors in Richmond. When he abandoned Petersburg that evening and retreated westward along the Appomattox River with the remnants of his army, Richmond was doomed. Jefferson Davis and his cabinet fled the capital, which fell to the Union on April 3. ✛ DCW

"FORT HELL" *Photographed by Timothy O'Sullivan, Fort Sedgwick was built of earth reinforced with timber and formed a salient jutting toward the Confederate line at Petersburg, a dangerously exposed position that led Union troops to name the place "Fort Hell."*

I see no prospect of doing more than holding our position here till night. I am not certain that I can do that.

ROBERT E. LEE AT PETERSBURG, APRIL 2, 1865

"FORT DAMNATION" *In this hand-colored photograph, Confederates lie dead in a trench at Fort Mahone after Union forces broke through Lee's defenses on April 2 and forced him to abandon Petersburg. Many Union troops died as well in the bloody assault on "Fort Damnation."*

119

SURRENDER AT APPOMATTOX

VIOLENTLY WAVING A WHITE TOWEL AS A FLAG of truce, a lone Confederate horseman galloped up to men of the 118th Pennsylvania Infantry near Appomattox Court House on April 9, 1865, and asked for directions to the headquarters of General Philip Sheridan. The rider was Captain R. M. Sims, who had purchased that towel (inset) in Richmond just days before the Army of Northern Virginia was forced to abandon the Confederate capital. He continued to wave it as he raced deeper into Union lines. Sims carried a message from General John Gordon requesting a truce. He made his way to General George Armstrong Custer, who sent the rider back with the following reply: "We will listen to no terms but that of unconditional surrender." Lieutenant Colonel Edward Whitaker escorted Sims back to the Confederate lines and then asked to use the towel for his own protection as he returned to Union lines.

The Army of Northern Virginia was in its final hours. In the past few days, as Ulysses Grant's army closed in on Robert E. Lee, messengers had carried communiqués back and forth between the two commanders. By April 9, Lee and his men were famished, exhausted, and surrounded. "There is nothing left for me to do but to go and see General Grant," he told his staff that morning, "and I would rather die a thousand deaths." Generals Grant and Lee agreed to meet that afternoon at the home of Wilmer McLean at Appomattox Court House (overleaf).

Lee arrived there first, wearing a crisp gray uniform and dress sword. Grant entered a half hour later, dressed informally in what he called a "soldier's blouse," his boots and pants splattered with mud. Grant's staff officers crowded the room.

The two commanders sat at separate tables and conversed for a while before Lee asked on what terms Grant would "receive the surrender of my army."

Many Unionists considered Confederates traitors who were responsible for the tremendous loss of lives and property. Lee's own army had threatened the nation's capital and had to be driven back in some of the bloodiest battles of the war. But healing the country, rather than vengeance, directed Grant's actions. There would be no mass imprisonments or executions, no parading of defeated enemies through Northern streets. The terms of surrender amounted to a gentlemen's agreement: the Confederate forces would return home after surrendering weapons and agreeing "not to take up arms against the Government of the United States." At Lee's request, Grant allowed Confederates who owned their own horses to keep them so that they could tend their farms and plant spring crops. Once Lee's army had surrendered and disbanded, Grant added, its men were "not to be disturbed by United States authority so long as they observe their paroles and the laws in force where they may reside."

A Union officer copied the terms. Grant then signed the document and passed it to Lee for his signature. Other Southern forces remained in the field, but few would continue fighting when they learned of the outcome at Appomattox. With Lee's surrender, the war effectively came to an end. ✢ HRR

TOKEN OF SURRENDER *Lieutenant Colonel Edward Whitaker cut in two the white towel used by Confederate Colonel R. M. Sims to seek a truce at Appomattox. He kept one half and presented the other to General Custer's wife, Libbie, who later bequeathed it to the Smithsonian.*

TROPHIES OF VICTORY

While meeting at the McLean home (LEFT), Ulysses S. Grant sat beside this table in the leather-padded swivel chair at lower left, and Robert E. Lee sat beside another table in the wicker chair below. Surrender terms drafted by Grant (OPPOSITE) formed the basis for the document signed by the two commanders. Over McLean's objections, Grant's table was taken afterward by General Sheridan, Grant's chair by Colonel Henry Capehart, and Lee's chair by Lieutenant Colonel Whitaker. Through successive donations, those trophies were reunited at the Smithsonian by 1936.

Head Quarters, Armies United States
April 9th 1865.

To Genl R E Lee.
    Comdg Confederate States, Armies
        Genl.
                In accordance with the substance
of my letter of the 8th Inst., I propose to receive the surrender
of the army of Northern Virginia, on the following terms
to wit:
        Paroles of the officers and men to be made in dupli
-cate, one copy to be given to an officer to be designated by Me
the other to be retained by such officer or officers as You may designate.
        The officers to give their individual parole not to take up
Arms against the Government of the U.S. until properly exchanged. and each
Company and regimental commander to sign a like parole for
their commands.
        The arms, Artillery and public property to be stacked, parked
and turned over to the officers appointed by Me to receive them.
        This will not embrace the Side arms of the officers or their
private horses or baggage. This done, each officer and man will be
returned to their homes, not to be molested by the U.S
Authorities as long as they observe their paroles and laws
in force when they reside.
                    Very Respectfully,
        Signed   U S Grant
            Lt Genl Comdg Armies U States

120

APPOMATTOX PAROLE

WHEN ROBERT E. LEE'S ARMY OF NORTHERN Virginia disbanded, Union authorities issued a parole pass like the one below to each of the army's twenty-eight thousand or so men. Major General John Gibbon, commanding the Twenty-Fourth Corps in the Army of the James, was tasked with producing those blank passes, using a portable printing press at his headquarters. Such presses printed a few hundred pages an hour. With several passes on each page, the job could theoretically be completed within twenty-fours, as requested. But Gibbon had too few press operators at headquarters to run his manual press nonstop for an entire day, which required teams working in shifts. So he called for reinforcements. Soon, he wrote, "we obtained all the printers we wanted and the next day the paroles were ready for distribution." Among the thousands who received one of those passes was Private James House of the 14th North Carolina Infantry, reduced by this time to a mere 114 men. As stated on his pass (below), he and his comrades were now free to return home, "and there remain undisturbed." ✣ JB

121

DIGNIFIED IN DEFEAT

SURRENDERING TO ULYSSES GRANT WAS AGONIZING for Robert E. Lee, but he did not show it. Grant wrote that he could not tell what Lee was thinking when they met: "As he was a man of much dignity, with an impassable face, it was impossible to say whether he felt inwardly glad that the end had finally come, or felt sad over the result, and was too manly to show it." That reserve and formality were emblematic of Lee. He was always punctilious and dignified, traits that grew more pronounced with age and responsibility.

After the war, Lee became a near-mythic figure in the South—a living sculpture of Confederate honor, described later by poet Stephen Vincent Benét as "the marble man." Yet that fabled hero of the "Lost Cause," always imagined in uniform, spent his last years quietly as president of Washington College (now Washington and Lee University), seeking "to aid in the restoration of peace and harmony." He put his uniform aside, and this photograph by Mathew Brady (opposite), taken at home in Richmond, Virginia, one week after he surrendered, is the last image of Lee wearing it. ✣ DCW

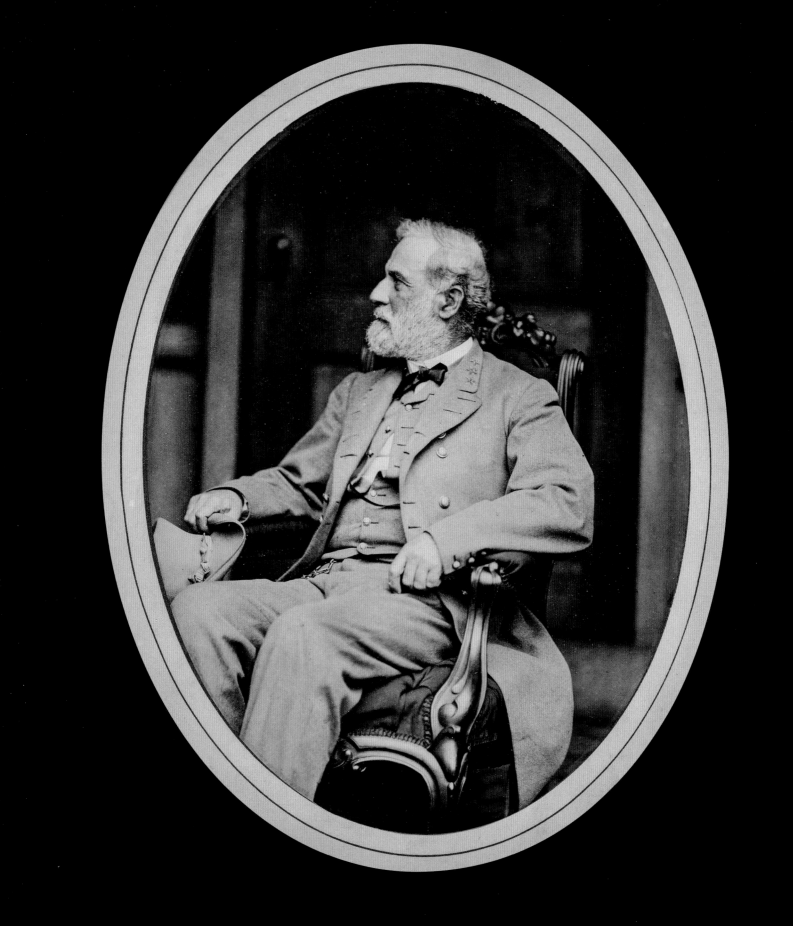

INSIDE THE CONFEDERATE WHITE HOUSE

THE PROMISE OF FREEDOM

ON APRIL 2, 1865, ROBERT E. LEE'S ARMY OF Northern Virginia began its retreat and could no longer defend Richmond. Government officials and others who had the desire and means abandoned the Confederate capital, setting fire to warehouses and other property they left behind. Overnight Union troops occupied the city and converted the executive mansion, known as the White House of the Confederacy, into their headquarters. On April 4, Abraham Lincoln visited the fallen capital. Making his way to Jefferson Davis's former residence, he was greeted as a hero by the formerly enslaved men and women of Richmond. Lincoln sat in Davis's chair as he met with Union officers and local leaders who had remained behind. The symbolism of that day was not lost on anyone. Union officers occupied the house for the remainder of the war. Over time a few of its furnishings, such as this large ceramic punch bowl, were taken to Washington, D.C., as war trophies. ✚ HRR

TAKEN FROM THE MANSION *Once used in the Confederate White House in Richmond, this large earthenware punch bowl with hand-painted Asian motifs became the property of the U.S. War Department and was transferred to the Smithsonian around 1867.*

THE UNIDENTIFIED AFRICAN AMERICAN WOMAN pictured opposite around 1865, wearing an American flag pinned to her dress, did not enjoy in full the freedoms represented by that flag. Even after the adoption in 1868 of the Fourteenth Amendment, which recognized all those born in the United States as American citizens, she would have been disenfranchised because of her gender, and her rights would have been restricted in many other ways because of her race. Despite her experiences, present or future, her squared shoulders, straight back, and direct gaze into the camera suggest she was proud to be part of a nation that rededicated itself to liberty by opposing slavery.

This woman is believed to have served as a washerwoman for Union troops who occupied Richmond, Virginia, in April 1865. Many washerwomen working for the Union Army had emerged from slavery and prized their jobs, even though the work was arduous. Using long sticks, they swirled soldiers' clothing in heavy iron pots full of water, often boiling hot, and supplied their own implements, hauling them from place to place. Military regulations issued in 1861 required washerwomen to carry certificates signed by commanding officers indicating that they were of good character. They were paid up to forty dollars a month directly by the soldiers they worked for. The service they provided was valued because it gave men a sense of dignity. Soldiers were often wet and dirty, wearing sweaty, soiled, and bloodstained clothing. A clean uniform represented civility and order and reminded men of home.

This woman's skills would have been in demand after the war ended, and she could have imagined a rewarding life ahead of her. Whatever the details of her story, this photograph serves as an enduring image of the powerful promise of freedom. ✚ STP

PRIZED PORTRAIT *The woman who posed for this photograph—a handsomely framed and encased ambrotype, featuring a hand-tinted American flag—evidently took pride in having her portrait made, as she did in the U.S. emblem she wore.*

124

GRANT AND HIS GENERALS

COMPLETED IN 1865, THIS GRAND CANVAS BY Norwegian immigrant Ole Peter Hansen Balling, entitled *Grant and His Generals*, is more than a painting. It is a pantheon, enshrining within its heroic ten-by-sixteen-foot frame legendary commanders who secured victory for the Union on various fronts and never came together as a group until the artist united them here. Leading the way at center is General in Chief Ulysses S. Grant on a bay horse, with William T. Sherman at his side on a white horse. Few could have imagined when the war began that the bloody struggle would last as long as it did or claim so many lives. But Grant had always understood that the Union would have to battle relentlessly to prevail. "I can't spare this man," Abraham Lincoln once said of him; "he fights." Grant could have said the same of his right-hand man, Sherman, who knew that there was a heavy price to be paid for victory. "War is cruelty," he remarked. "The crueler it is, the sooner it will be over."

Among the other front-rank generals keeping pace with their chief in this cropped reproduction of Balling's epic painting— which portrays more than two dozens generals—are Winfield Scott Hancock, known as "Hancock the Superb," riding just to Grant's left; and to Sherman's right George Meade, the hero of Gettysburg; George Thomas, the "Rock of Chickamauga"; and Philip Sheridan, conqueror of the Shenandoah Valley. Balling made preliminary sketches of several of the commanders portrayed here when he visited Grant's headquarters at City Point, Virginia, during the siege of Petersburg in late 1864. Others in this painting were sketched by the artist when they returned to Washington, D.C., at war's end. A dedicated Unionist, Balling had a personal stake in the conflict, having enlisted in 1861 and served for two years in a New York regiment. ✛ EWP

UNION VICTORS *Ole Peter Hansen Balling's monumental group portrait,* Grant and His Generals, *was mounted within a specially made, curved frame, and graces a stairwell in what was once the Patent Office Building but is now the National Portrait Gallery.*

125

BURIAL PARTY

THE END OF THE WAR DID NOT BRING AN END TO the grim task of burying its victims. This photograph, taken in April 1865, shows African American soldiers gathering the skeletal remains of troops in an area near Richmond where two bloody contests were waged earlier—the Battle of Gaines's Mill in June 1862 and the Battle of Cold Harbor in June 1864. Both were bitter setbacks for Union forces, who departed hastily, leaving their dead behind.

The duty of burying the dead after a Civil War battle was typically left to the soldiers themselves. When military necessity required them to move on prior to the job's completion, local residents often took up the task. For those who assisted the burial here, attending to the Confederate dead took priority. Many Union troops who fell in battle at this site went unburied or were laid in graves too shallow to cover their remains permanently. At the end of the war, the field remained strewn with skeletons. The scale of the destruction, and local animus toward the Union, meant that burial parties like the one shown at left still had much work to do. Remains collected around Richmond by such burial parties were later interred at Cold Harbor National Cemetery, established in 1866.

John Reekie, a former assistant to Mathew Brady who went to work for Alexander Gardner, took this photograph days after Robert E. Lee surrendered at Appomattox. Reekie and Gardner had rushed from Washington after the surrender to secure some of the first images of the postwar South. In the foreground of Reekie's haunting photograph, a man stares at the camera while seated beside a stretcher laden with skulls and bones, including an outstretched leg with a shoe still attached. A canteen lies on the ground, a sad relic of a soldier whose remains may be scattered here. Peace now reigned, but the job of attending to the fallen was far from over. ✚ FHG

LOST IN A BATTLE *A burial party at war's end gathers remains of men killed in action near Richmond. Some 1,300 unknown soldiers were interred at Cold Harbor National Cemetery.*

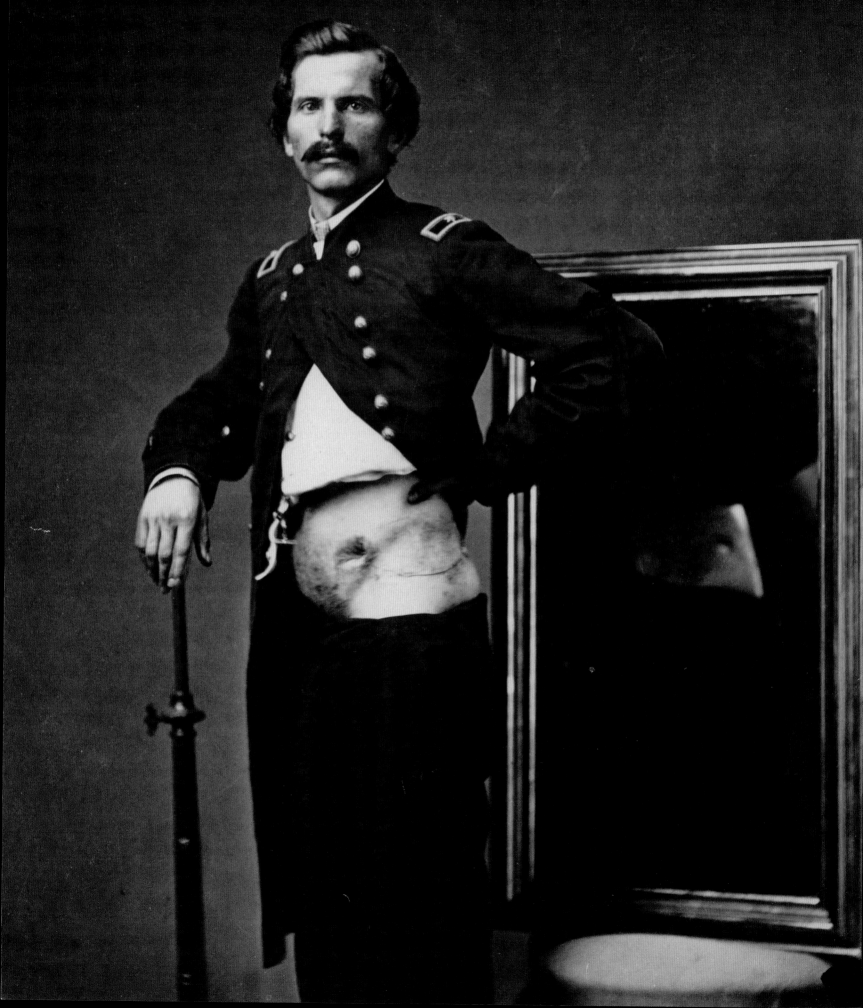

126

DOCUMENTING THE WOUNDED

ONE OF THE GREAT SCIENTIFIC LEGACIES OF the Civil War was the work of the Army Medical Museum, founded in 1862 by Surgeon General William Hammond in response to the overwhelming tasks faced by the Union Army Medical Corps, which was ill equipped to handle the carnage on the battlefield and the epidemics in soldiers' camps. The museum became the nation's first federal medical research facility and compiled documentary evidence on war wounds and diseases that led to advances in treatment during and after the conflict. By 1863 the museum was collecting case histories, photographs, and anatomical specimens from many army hospitals and surgeons. In 1865 William Bell of Philadelphia became head of the museum's photography department and began systematically documenting on camera the medical experiences, experiments, and travails of military physicians and the men they treated.

Bell's work for the Army Medical Museum reflects his background both as a portrait photographer and as a Civil War veteran. In images like that of Henry A. Barnum, the wounded officer shown opposite, there is a sharp juxtaposition between the formal elegance of the composition and the brutal nature of the man's wound, and between clinical detachment and emotional exposure. Bell deliberately posed such wounded survivors in such a way as to reveal distinctive features—in this case, Barnum's scars where the bullet entered and exited (as reflected in the mirror). By portraying his subjects in uniform, Bell left them some dignity, but the haunted and heartbreaking expressions he captured on their faces were often those of despair, relief, or humiliation. These

portraits served as important visual medical references for students and surgeons. Yet they were also poignant reminders of the subject's individuality and stand as photographic works of art transcending the clinical images found in the typical medical textbook.

Bell also photographed skeletal remains held at the museum, including shattered skulls and broken bones, but those too were often personalized through the descriptions accompanying them, which named the victim when his identity was known. For example, the shattered bone pictured on this page was labeled "Lieutenant Goodwin, Deceased, Ununited Gunshot Fracture of the Upper Third of the Right Femur." Naming the deceased helped transform an anatomical study into an act of remembrance at a time when the fate of many soldiers who fell in battle during the Civil War remained unknown.

Beginning in 1870, the museum published its collections in seven volumes entitled *Photographic Catalogue of the Surgical Section of the Army Medical Museum*. Each volume detailed case histories and documented wounds, treatments, and the results, providing medical students and surgeons with a great fund of knowledge. The vital research begun by the Army Medical Museum continues at the institution known today as the National Museum of Health and Medicine. ✣ SMC

WAR WOUNDS *Among the works by William Bell held at the Smithsonian American Art Museum are his photographs of Brigadier General Henry A. Barnum (OPPOSITE)—who returned to action after being shot through the abdomen in 1862 and was awarded the Medal of Honor— and the shattered femur of the late Lieutenant Goodwin (INSET).*

127

THE CRACKED NEGATIVE

THE LAST FORMAL PHOTOGRAPHIC PORTRAIT of Abraham Lincoln was taken in February 1865, a time of promise and renewal for the president. Buoyed by his reelection, recent Union Army advances, and passage of the Thirteenth Amendment, he could begin to contemplate the war's end. The next four years would be about bringing the nation back together. As he well knew, that would be no small task, but far less horrific than war.

On February 5, one week before his fifty-sixth birthday, Lincoln and his son Tad entered the Pennsylvania Avenue studio of Alexander Gardner, who had portrayed Lincoln on at least four previous occasions. There father and son sat for several photographs. With the inauguration a month away, Lincoln wanted new portraits that might be used to usher in his second term.

As Gardner was completing the development of the glass-plate negative for this portrait—the largest made on that occasion—a crack suddenly materialized in the negative. Before discarding it, Gardner produced this one print (opposite), the crack clearly visible running through the top of Lincoln's head.

In Gardner's portrait, produced just two months before the assassination of the president, one sees the physical toll that four years of war had taken on Lincoln. Yet he wears a slight smile and a look of quiet confidence, suggestive of his sense of hope at this moment. ✣ FHG

LAST LOOK *This photograph by Alexander Gardner, held at the National Portrait Gallery, captures Abraham Lincoln in his last months. Late in Lincoln's presidency, Horace Greeley observed that his face looked "care-ploughed, tempest-tossed, and weatherbeaten."*

128

A FINAL CUP OF COFFEE

ON THE NIGHT OF APRIL 14, 1865, A WHITE HOUSE servant watched as Abraham Lincoln finished his after-dinner coffee and placed the cup on an open window sill. This Good Friday had been a long day for the president. That morning at breakfast his eldest son, Robert Todd, who had been present at Appomattox, recounted for his father the details of General Robert E. Lee's surrender. There were visitors for Lincoln to greet and a cabinet meeting to attend. At three that afternoon, he invited Mary to join him on a carriage ride around town. She later recalled that outing: "During the drive he was so gay, that I said to him, laughingly, 'Dear husband, you almost startled me by your great cheerfulness.'" To which he replied, "And well I may feel so, Mary, I consider this day the war has come to a close." Referring to their beloved son, who had died in 1862, Lincoln added: "We must both be more cheerful in the future—between the war and the loss of our darling Willie—we have both been very miserable." That night after dinner, the presidential party left for Ford's Theatre.

When news of the assassination reached the White House, the servant noticed that Lincoln's coffee cup was still on the window sill. Rather than return it to the kitchen, he kept it as a relic of that tragic night. The cup later came into the possession of Captain D. W. Taylor, who presented it in 1887 to Robert Todd Lincoln, the president's last surviving child. ✣ HRR

LEFT TO POSTERITY *Among the treasured items associated with Lincoln's final moments is this presidential coffee cup (INSET). The cup remained with his descendants until his great-grandson Lincoln Isham donated it to the Smithsonian in 1958.*

129

A NIGHT WITH LAURA KEENE

THE WAR WAS FINALLY COMING TO AN END. IT WAS time for the president to celebrate victory. The deep lines etched into Abraham Lincoln's face documented the strain of wartime pressures, sleepless nights, and personal tragedies. His great resolve had sustained him through the conflict, and he looked now to a brighter future. On that fateful Friday, April 14, 1865, he and his wife decided to spend a relaxing evening at the theater.

The Lincolns and their two guests, Clara Harris and her fiancé, Major Henry Rathbone, arrived late at Ford's Theatre for a production of *Our American Cousin*, starring actress Laura Keene (opposite). As they entered, the performers on stage paused, the crowd cheered wildly, and the orchestra played "Hail to the Chief." Lincoln then set his silk hat down in the presidential box, and the play resumed.

Around 10:15 p.m., Confederate sympathizer John Wilkes Booth—a well-known actor who had easy access to Ford's Theatre—entered Lincoln's box, pointed a derringer at the back of his head, and fired. Booth then pulled out a knife, slashed Rathbone, and jumped down onto the stage, shouting *"Sic semper tyrannis!"* (Thus always to tyrants!). Despite breaking his leg when he jumped, Booth exited backstage, mounted a waiting horse, and got away.

The theater erupted into chaos. Laura Keene pleaded unsuccessfully with the audience to remain calm. Another cast member, Helen Truman (listed on the playbill opposite as Miss Trueman), stated afterward: "The shouts, groans, curses, smashing of seats, screams of women, shuffling of feet and cries of terror created a pandemonium that . . . through all the ages will stand out in my memory as the hell of hells." Amid the confusion, someone called to bring the president water. Keene ran to her dressing room, grabbed a pitcher of water, and made her way to the presidential box, where Dr. Charles Leale, an army surgeon on hand, allowed her to cradle Lincoln's head in her lap. Drops of blood stained her dress and cuff.

The next day, as news of the president's death gripped the city, Keene met with her husband's nephew at a nearby hotel and presented him with a bloodstained cuff from her dress. Preserved by family members, this memento of Keene's historic role on that tragic night was bequeathed to the Smithsonian in 1962. ✣ HRR

BLOODIED CUFF *Worn by Laura Keene on the night Abraham Lincoln was shot, this cuff was stained with his blood after she asked Dr. Charles Leale if she could hold the president. "I granted this request," he recalled, "and she sat on the floor of the box and held his head in her lap."*

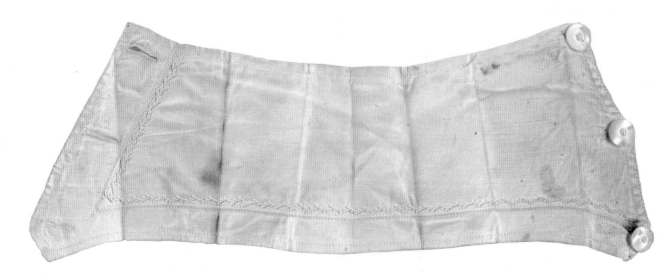

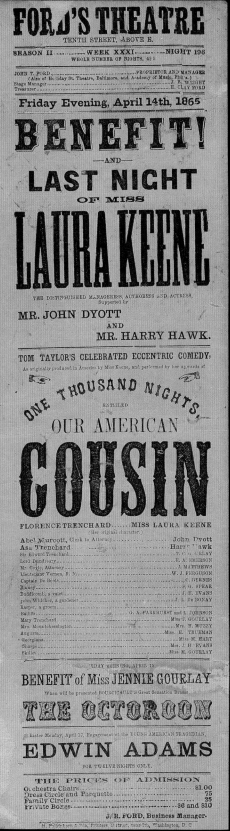

LEADING LADY *Pictured above, Laura Keene (1826–1873), a British actress, would be forever associated with Abraham Lincoln's assassination. She had come to America in 1852 and soon established her own company that she managed. Her production of* Our American Cousin, *in which she played a leading role and received top billing (LEFT), was staged at Ford's Theatre the night John Wilkes Booth made his attack. Keene continued to manage her company and perform until contracting tuberculosis. She died in 1873 at the age of 47.*

130

DEATH BED OF THE PRESIDENT

MANY AMERICANS VISUALIZED ABRAHAM Lincoln's last moments as pictured in the iconic Currier & Ives print below, which conferred an aura of sainthood on the martyred president, lying on bloodless sheets, with wife Mary and son Tad at his side. In fact, neither Mary nor Tad was present when Lincoln died in a small room across from Ford's Theatre at 7:22 a.m. on April 15, 1865. Later prints crowded many notable figures into the room who were not all there at the same time.

Mary Anna Henry (opposite, inset), the daughter of Smithsonian Secretary Joseph Henry, whose family socialized with the Lincolns, provided a more accurate portrayal of the president's death. She kept a vivid diary throughout the war years and told of being awakened on April 15 with news that Lincoln had been shot but was still alive. Soon, however, tolling church bells signaled that he was dead. She wrote in her diary: "Deeply must the country mourn this death for although uncouth & ungainly he was true hearted, magnanimous and kind." A few days later, Mary Henry visited her minister, Reverend Phineas D. Gurley, who was close to the Lincolns. He was with the president at the end, and she faithfully recorded his account in her diary. Summoned at four in the morning on the 15th, Gurley found Lincoln "lying insensible upon a bed with the life blood dripping from the wound in his head." He later went to comfort Mary Lincoln and returned to the president's side just before he died. Lincoln, he related, was "slowly drawing his breath at long intervals lying as before perfectly motionless. A faint hardly perceptable motion in his throat and all was over. So still was the room that the ticking of the President's watch was distinctly heard." ✣ PMH

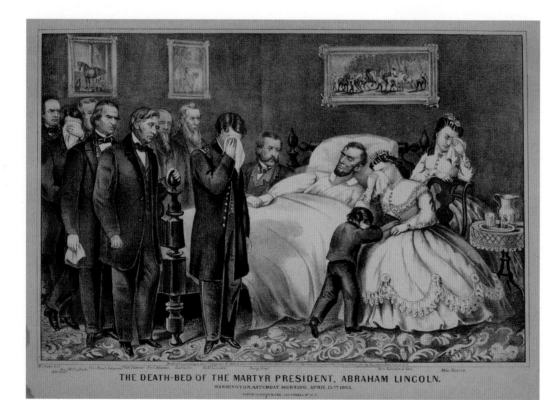

THE DEATH-BED OF THE MARTYR PRESIDENT, ABRAHAM LINCOLN.
WASHINGTON, SATURDAY MORNING, APRIL 15TH 1865.

MOURNFUL VIGIL *Images of Abraham Lincoln's last moments, like this popular 1865 Currier & Ives print (LEFT), idealized his death, which occurred on a bloodstained bed too small for him. Robert Lincoln (standing at center in uniform) was present when he died, but Mary and Tad Lincoln were in another room, as was Clara Harris (seated behind Mary).*

DILIGENT DIARIST *Pictured opposite (INSET) around 1855, Mary Henry kept a detailed diary from 1858 to 1868, encompassing the bitter war years. In this entry on April 15, 1865 (OPPOSITE), she relates learning of Lincoln's death: "When the morning paper was issued he was still alive ... but now the tolling bells tell us he has ceased to breathe."*

1865

were rewarded by a speech from the
Sec and another from some one whom
we did not recognize. After cheers
for the Union, the President, the
Army, the Navy and & for the brave
dead and wounded the patriots
moved off to the inspiriting air of
"Rally round the Flag Boys".

15th. We were awakened this morning
by an announcement which almost
made our hearts stand still with
consternation. The President was
shot last night in the Theater.
When the morning paper was issued he was still alive although
little or no hopes were entertained
of his recovery but now the tolling
bells tell us he has ceased to breath.
He is dead Mr. De Bust has just
told Hannah he died at 1/2 7 O'clock.
Deeply must the country mourn
this death for although uncouth &
ungainly he was true hearted magnanimous and kind and in the
present crisis ready to follow the
such a course with the defeated

131

ABRAHAM LINCOLN'S TOP HAT

SOON AFTER JOHN WILKES BOOTH SHOT PRESIDENT Lincoln at Ford's Theatre on the night of April 14, 1865, the War Department recovered his hat and his chair from the presidential box. Once the trial of Booth's co-conspirators had concluded, the two items were no longer held as evidence, and they were transferred to the Interior Department, which stored them with other national relics at the U.S. Patent Office. The hat was briefly exhibited there in the public gallery. Then in 1867, with Mary Lincoln's permission, the Patent Office presented the hat to the Smithsonian along with the chair. Secretary Joseph Henry, who had served during the war as a scientific advisor to Lincoln, ordered the two items crated and placed in storage in the basement of the Castle. He cautioned the staff "not to mention the matter to any one, on account of there being so much excitement at the time." Although Henry did not explain his decision further, it appears that he shared the belief that displaying items so closely associated with Lincoln's assassination was offensive, and that pandering to curiosity seekers would disrupt the more important scientific work of the Institution.

The Smithsonian would eventually return the chair to descendants of the owners of Ford's Theatre. The hat remained in storage for twenty-six years, unseen by the public, until it was loaned to a Washington, D.C., gallery in 1893, after which the Smithsonian regularly placed it on display. Of all of Lincoln's personal items in its collections, the hat has become the iconic emblem of the martyred sixteenth president.

At six feet four inches tall, Lincoln towered over most of his contemporaries. He chose to stand out even more by regularly wearing top hats. Lincoln acquired this silk hat from J. Y.

Davis, a Washington hat maker, whose label appears inside the crown. The hat, which measures approximately a modern size 7 ⅛, is trimmed with two bands: a thin ⅜-inch ribbon with a small metal buckle, just above the brim; and a 3-inch grosgrain mourning band, discolored over time. The stitching on that band indicates that it was added after Lincoln purchased the hat to signal his ongoing mourning for his son Willie, who died of typhoid fever on February 20, 1862. In a very public way, Lincoln was linking his own loss with the losses suffered by so many Americans during the war.

Lincoln used his hat as an actor employed a theatrical prop. He famously stored papers inside its crown, removed it humbly when speaking publicly, and threw it down in front of generals to emphasize his anger. On April 4, 1865, Lincoln toured the fallen Confederate capital of Richmond, Virginia. A writer for the *Atlantic Monthly* reported that Lincoln was approached by an elderly black man who removed his hat in tribute and bowed before the president. Lincoln, in turn, "removed his own hat, and bowed in silence; but it was a bow which upset the forms, laws, customs, and ceremonies of centuries. It was a death-shock to chivalry, and a mortal wound to caste."

Because the top hat was so much a part of Abraham Lincoln's persona, and because Lincoln is so much a part of this nation, the hat, which the Smithsonian first hid away, is now one of its greatest treasures. ✣ HRR

STANDING TALL *Meeting in October 1862 with General John McClernand (RIGHT) and Allan Pinkerton (LEFT), intelligence chief for the Army of the Potomac, Abraham Lincoln wears a top hat like the one he later wore the night he was slain (OPPOSITE).*

SURRAT.   BOOTH.   HAROLD.

War Department, Washington, April 20, 1865,

👉 # $100,000 REWARD!

THE MURDERER

Of our late beloved President, Abraham Lincoln,

IS STILL AT LARGE.

$50,000 REWARD

Will be paid by this Department for his apprehension, in addition to any reward offered by Municipal Authorities or State Executives.

$25,000 REWARD

Will be paid for the apprehension of JOHN H. SURRATT, one of Booth's Accomplices.

$25,000 REWARD

Will be paid for the apprehension of David C. Harold, another of Booth's accomplices.

LIBERAL REWARDS will be paid for any information that shall conduce to the arrest of either of the above-named criminals, or their accomplices.

All persons harboring or secreting the said persons, or either of them, or aiding or assisting their concealment or escape, will be treated as accomplices in the murder of the President and the attempted assassination of the Secretary of State, and shall be subject to trial before a Military Commission and the punishment of DEATH.

Let the stain of innocent blood be removed from the land by the arrest and punishment of the murderers.

All good citizens are exhorted to aid public justice on this occasion. Every man should consider his own conscience charged with this solemn duty, and rest neither night nor day until it be accomplished.

EDWIN M. STANTON, Secretary of War.

DESCRIPTIONS.—BOOTH is Five Feet 7 or 8 inches high, slender build, high forehead, black hair, black eyes, and wears a heavy black moustache.

JOHN H. SURRAT is about 5 feet, 9 inches. Hair rather thin and dark; eyes rather light; no beard. Would weigh 145 or 150 pounds. Complexion rather pale and clear, with color in his cheeks. Wore light clothes of fine quality. Shoulders square; cheek bones rather prominent; chin narrow; ears projecting at the top; forehead rather low and square, but broad. Parts his hair on the right side; neck rather long. His lips are firmly set. A slim man.

DAVID C. HAROLD is five feet six inches high, hair dark, eyes dark, eyebrows rather heavy, full face, nose short, hand short and fleshy, feet small, instep high, round bodied, naturally quick and active, slightly closes his eyes when looking at a person.

NOTICE.—In addition to the above, State and other authorities have offered rewards amounting to almost one hundred thousand dollars, making an aggregate of about TWO HUNDRED THOUSAND DOLLARS.

132

WANTED FOR MURDER

PUBLISHED FIVE DAYS AFTER ABRAHAM LINCOLN'S death, this broadside reflected popular outrage at the first successful attempt on the life of a U.S. president and the larger conspiracy surrounding the assassination. John Wilkes Booth and his accomplices had planned to decapitate the federal government by murdering not only President Lincoln but also Vice President Andrew Johnson and Secretary of State William Seward, all in one night. The attempt on Johnson was aborted. Seward was attacked at home along with his son Frederick and others, but they survived. Secretary of War Edwin Stanton took charge of the investigation and authorized the huge rewards offered here for the apprehension of Booth and two of his co-conspirators: John H. Surratt, a Confederate agent who had schemed with Booth and others to kidnap Lincoln before the assassination plot was hatched; and David E. Herold, who aided the attack on Seward and then escaped with Booth.

Pasted onto this hastily assembled wanted poster are photographic prints of the three fugitives. Booth, a popular actor famous for his handsome face, appears in a carte-de-visite designed for his admirers. Surratt and Herold were not well known to the public or to authorities, as indicated by the fact that a "t" is missing from Surratt's name under his portrait and in the description of him at bottom and Herold's name is misspelled throughout.

Surratt fled abroad, and when he was later brought back to the United States to stand trial, a divided jury failed to convict him. Booth and Herold sought safety among Confederate sympathizers, first in Maryland and then in Virginia, but they were vigorously pursued. The South had been defeated, and there was no lasting refuge for the assassin or his accomplice. ⊹ ACG

A BROAD CONSPIRACY *When the War Department issued this poster on April 20, 1865, the investigation into the plot to kill Abraham Lincoln and others in his administration was ongoing. Several more conspirators would be identified and apprehended in the days to come.*

133

THE RICHMOND HOARD

IN MID-APRIL OF 1865, UNION SOLDIERS GUARDING several covered wagons headed north from Richmond, Virginia, to Washington, D.C. Their cargo consisted of hundreds of thousands of Confederate notes, rendered worthless by the South's defeat but still of interest to Union officials. The huge hoard, consisting of notes called in by the Confederate government and exchanged for its final issues of 1864–65, went first to the U.S. War Department, then to the U.S. Treasury, and later to the National Archives. Finally, after more than a century in storage, it arrived in a large truck at the National Museum of American History in February 1998.

Examining stacks of those old notes, Smithsonian staff found that many were pinned, sewn, or glued together. Old scraps of paper, were often used to patch them back together. Why did Southerners go to the trouble of repairing currency that by 1864 was barely worth the paper it was printed on? One simple reason was that they could still use large sums of the currency to make small purchases. But there was another, deeper reason for saving those notes, having to do with the very nature and meaning of money, which proclaims a nation's existence and aspirations. As long as Southerners had any hope for their country, they continued to patch together their currency and pray that the faltering Confederacy would somehow emerge from its ordeal sovereign and solvent. ⊹ RD

Notes from the Richmond Hoard

134

DEATH TO THE CONSPIRATORS

JOHN WILKES BOOTH EVADED CAPTURE FOR TWELVE days. On April 26 pursuing Union cavalrymen surrounded him and co-conspirator David Herold in a barn near Port Royal, Virginia. Herold surrendered, but Booth refused to come out. Shot through the neck, he died that evening.

In addition to Booth, Herold, and the elusive John Surratt, seven others were accused of plotting against President Lincoln, Vice President Johnson, and Secretary of State Seward. Those suspects were Lewis Powell, also known as Lewis Payne (left), who attacked Seward; George Atzerodt, who was assigned to kill the vice president but backed down; Mary Surratt, the mother of John Surratt and proprietor of a Washington boardinghouse where the conspirators met; Dr. Samuel Mudd, who treated Booth's broken leg and allowed Booth and Herold to spend the night at his Maryland home; Michael O'Laughlin, who was linked to an earlier plot to kidnap Lincoln; Samuel Arnold, who was implicated in that same plot; and Edman Spangler, who worked at Ford's Theatre and arranged for another employee there to wait with the horse on which Booth escaped.

A military commission under the close direction of Secretary of War Stanton presided over the trial, which lasted two months. The outpouring of grief expressed during the national mourning for Lincoln fueled the demand for vengeance and hatred of the prisoners, whose treatment was torturous. Many people agreed with Stanton, who wrote: "The stain of innocent blood must be removed from the land."

Several of the men accused of conspiring with Booth were confined to their cells in shackles (opposite), and Stanton had eight canvas hoods made that covered the prisoners' eyes (overleaf) and were to be worn at all times except in court. Only Mary Surratt was spared wearing a hood as Stanton sought to avoid the possibility of public sympathy being directed toward the one female conspirator.

On June 20 the military commission found all eight suspects guilty. Lewis Powell, David Herold, George Atzerodt, and Mary Surratt were sentenced to death and hanged on July 7, 1865. The remaining four defendants were imprisoned at Fort Jefferson in Florida. ✢ HRR

Conspirator Payne

SEWARD'S ASSAILANT *Pictured with his hands shackled, Lewis Powell is identified here by his alias, Payne. He entered Seward's home on the night of April 14, slashing at anyone standing in his way, and stabbed the secretary of state in the chest and face. Powell then fled on a horse held by David Herold and was later arrested at Mary Surratt's house.*

LOCKED AWAY *Among the relics of the imprisonment of the eight accused conspirators, held at Washington's Old Penitentiary, are the cell key and shackles shown above and the hoods pictured on the following two* *pages. The hoods were designed to be cinched around the prisoner's neck with a rope. In 1903 the War Department transferred these and other materials related to the conspiracy to the Smithsonian.*

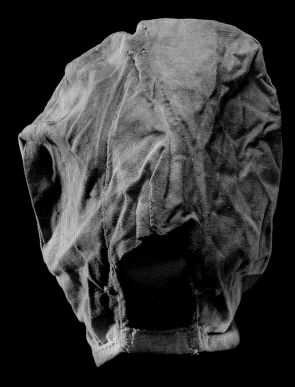
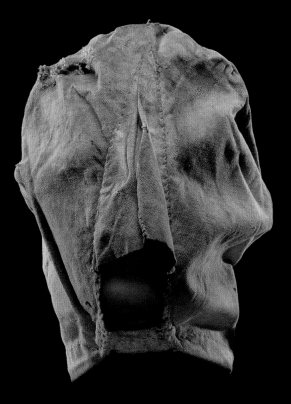
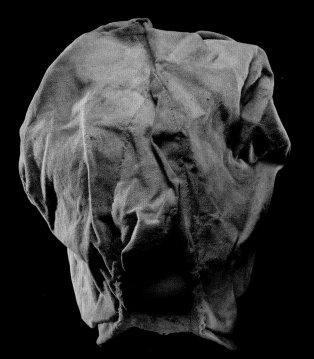

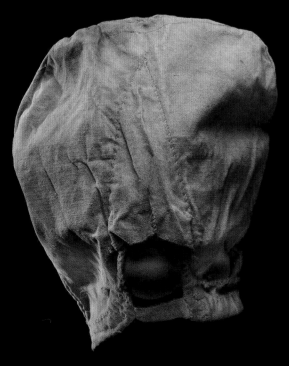

135

A FUNERAL PROCESSION 1,700 MILES LONG

IN DEATH, ABRAHAM LINCOLN ACHIEVED A DEGREE OF adoration and reverence that eluded him in life. Following his assassination, he was transformed into a martyr for the cause of national unity and equality, and a hero to multitudes who responded to his death with an unprecedented outpouring of grief. The millions of Americans who attended Easter services just two days after Lincoln was fatally wounded saw his sacrifice as atonement for the sins of a nation torn apart by war.

In Washington, D.C., his body lay in state, first in the East Room of the White House and then in the rotunda of the Capitol. The city became overcrowded with mourners, who witnessed the grand funeral procession from the executive mansion to the Capitol and filed past the coffin in both locations. On April 19 an estimated twenty-five million Americans attended memorial services for Lincoln in Washington and around the country.

Mary Lincoln insisted that her husband be buried in Oak Ridge Cemetery, outside their home town of Springfield, Illinois. A special nine-car funeral train left Washington on April 21, taking the fallen leader back west, along with an honor guard, close friends, dignitaries, and the remains of their son Willie, who was to be reburied alongside his father. Placed under military authority, the engineers were ordered never to exceed twenty miles an hour. The train slowly made its way up to New York and then westward to Illinois, roughly retracing the original route to Washington that Lincoln had taken little more than four years ago.

Newspapers publicized the train's schedule so that day and night citizens waiting along the tracks could pay their last respects as it passed. In ten cities, with their buildings draped in black bunting, Lincoln's casket was removed from the train for elaborate memorial services and public viewings. Hundreds of thousands of mourners, including city leaders, wounded soldiers, and African Americans, some of them recently freed, filed past the open casket.

On May 3, 1865, the funeral train reached its final destination. The following day, Lincoln's body was placed in its tomb at Oak Ridge Cemetery. In a graveside sermon there, Methodist bishop Matthew Simpson declared: "More people have gazed on the face of the departed than ever looked upon the face of any other departed man. More have looked upon the procession for 1,600 miles or more—by night and by day—by sunlight, dawn, twilight and by torchlight than ever before watched the progress of a procession." Simpson concluded by addressing Lincoln in spirit: "We crown thee as our martyr—and humanity enthrones thee as her triumphant son. Hero, Martyr, Friend, Farewell."

In those twenty days that elapsed from his assassination to his burial, Lincoln became a mythic figure. The funeral train did not just bring his body home; for millions of Americans, it carried him to immortality. In the years that followed, the items closely associated with his national mourning became treasured heirlooms, whether it was a commemorative ribbon (inset) or the sword (overleaf) worn by one of the honor guards. ✣ HRR

MOURNING THEIR LOSS *Printers produced a wide array of badges and ribbons proclaiming America's loss to meet the demand for symbols of grief among those participating in the national mourning that followed Abraham Lincoln's assassination.*

FUNERAL TRAIN This thirty-six-star U.S. flag was one of two that flew from the locomotive of the Lincoln funeral train as it proceeded westward from Albany to Utica, New York. Shown below with a portrait of the slain president displayed between its two flags, the locomotive hauled nine cars, carrying three hundred guests and the caskets of Abraham Lincoln and his son Willie back to Springfield. In small towns where the train did not stop, people gathered by the hundreds, holding bouquets or torches, to bid Lincoln farewell as his funeral car passed slowly by.

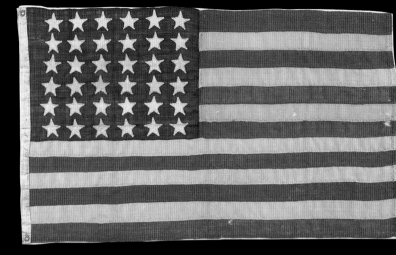

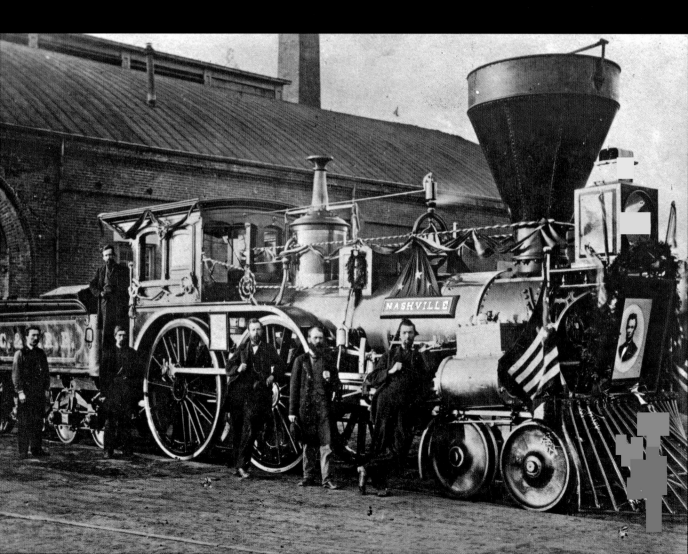

PUBLISHED BY CURRIER & IVES

Entered according to Act of Congress, A.D.1865 by Currier & Ives, in the Clerk's Office of the District Court of the United States, for the Southern District of N.

THE FUNERAL OF PRESIDENT LINCOLN, NEW YORK,

PASSING UNION SQUARE.

The magnificient Funeral Car was drawn by 16 gray horses richly caparisoned with ostrich plumes and cloth of

877.

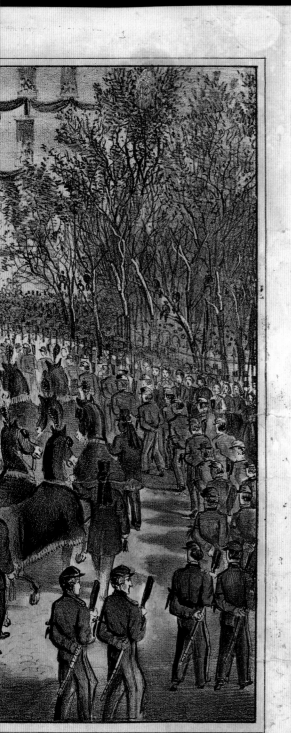

RIL 25.TH 1865.

trimmed with silver bullion.

152 NASSAU ST NEW YORK

PROCESSION IN NEW YORK *In this 1865 Currier & Ives print (LEFT), soldiers in blue escort the hearse carrying Abraham Lincoln's body to City Hall in New York, where it lay in state. One witness described the city as it appeared during the massive funeral procession: "Every house, from pavement to roof, all the way from the Battery to Central Park, was draped in black."*

HONOR GUARD'S SWORD *Dr. Charles Leale, the U.S. Army medical staff officer who was the first doctor to reach the dying president at Ford's Theatre, wore this sword (RIGHT) while serving in the honor guard when Lincoln's body lay in state at the White House and the Capitol.*

FUNERAL PALL *This black silk cloth (BELOW) draped Lincoln's coffin while his body lay in state in Cleveland, Ohio. The same cloth later covered the coffin of James A. Garfield, who in 1881 became the second U.S. president to be assassinated.*

136

THE FATE OF MARY LINCOLN

ON THEIR LAST DAY TOGETHER, ABRAHAM AND Mary Lincoln spoke of a retirement filled with travel and the happiness that had eluded them in the White House. Instead, his widow lived the next sixteen years mostly alone, restlessly visiting spas and living in hotels across America and Europe as she attempted to ease her ailing body and escape painful memories.

Negative publicity followed her. Mary's efforts to secure a government widow's pension and raise money to pay off debts drew ridicule from the press and political enemies. Elizabeth Keckly, Mary's dressmaker and confidante, unintentionally painted an unflattering picture of her in print. The president's former law partner, William Herndon, toured the country claiming that Lincoln's true love was Ann Rutledge, of New Salem, Illinois, who died seven years before he wed Mary Todd.

She could not comfort herself with family. Her son Tad died in 1871 at age eighteen. Concerned and embarrassed by her financial schemes, shopping sprees, and attempts to communicate with her deceased husband and sons through spiritualism, her firstborn and sole surviving son, Robert, committed her to a mental sanatorium. She contrived her own release after a few months and did not speak to Robert for the next five years.

Mary Lincoln mourned her husband for the rest of her life. In 1882, sick and nearly blind, the sixty-four-year-old widow died at her sister Elizabeth's house where, almost forty years earlier, she had married Abraham Lincoln. Among her valued possessions was an onyx-and-gold mourning watch (below) that Robert Lincoln inherited along with the trunks of mementos. His grandson donated the watch, a testament to grief and shattered hopes, to the Smithsonian in 1958. ✛ LKG

Time, does not soften it, nor can I ever be reconciled to my loss, until the grave closes over the remembrance, and I am again reunited to him— the worshipped one.

MARY LINCOLN, AUGUST 25, 1865

INCONSOLABLE WIDOW *Mary Lincoln wore mourning for family and friends several times as first lady. This photograph by Mathew Brady, published in 1865, was taken in 1863 while she was still lamenting the death of her son Willie the year before. After her husband's death, she lightened her deep mourning only once, for Tad's birthday, when she wore a black silk dress instead of "widow's weeds," which her onyx-and-gold mourning watch (LEFT) was designed to accompany.*

BRINGING IMAGES OF WAR HOME

ALREADY A DYNAMIC VISUAL COMPONENT OF American life when the Civil War began, photography provided the public with captivating three-dimensional views of the conflict to experience at home. Those stereoviews were produced using cameras with two lenses, through which the photographer took two pictures. When viewed side-by-side on a stereoscope, these pictures were perceived as one three-dimensional image. Stereoscopes came in a variety of styles and were handsomely designed to blend in with Victorian parlor décor. Some were handheld devices, some were freestanding like the one at right, others were housed in handsome tabletop cabinets.

Many early stereoviews were pictures from around the world intended for armchair travelers. Informative and entertaining, they took on a more serious and somber tone during and immediately after the Civil War when curiosity about the conflict remained intense. Photographers produced images in series, often with explanatory text, including a set by Alexander Gardner showing how the Union buried its dead. Such images brought the war's destructive impact home to the public, but other stereoviews made the conflict seem heroic, such as three-dimensional views of generals on their steeds. Some celebrated the Union victory by depicting Fort Moultrie or Fort Sumter (overleaf) after they were recaptured from Confederates in Charleston, South Carolina, in early 1865—or by portraying free African Americans standing outside their church in Richmond at war's end.

Many stereoviews were sold late in the war, as indicated by the U.S. revenue stamps on their back. These stamps were required for photographs purchased beginning mid-1864. The stereoscope made such images a shared viewing experience and a topic of conversation for family members and friends, much like watching the news today. They allowed people to visually experience the history of their times in a way unsurpassed until motion pictures and newsreels were introduced. ⊹ STP

IN-DEPTH VIEW *This freestanding viewer holds a stereoview by photographer John P. Soule portraying the ruins of Fort Moultrie. Soule maximized the three-dimensional experience by showing a soldier standing guard by a tunnel through which one's eyes would travel to the rubble beyond.*

Interior of Fort Sumter at war's end in 1865

House near York River, commandeered as headquarters of Union General Fitz-John Porter, 1862

2510.   Fort Sumner, near Fair Oaks, Va., 1862.

[FOR DESCRIPTION OF THIS VIEW SEE THE OTHER SIDE OF THIS CARD.]

Union troops preparing for battle near Fair Oaks, Virginia, 1862

The monitor-class ironclad U.S.S. Canonicus *(LEFT), taking on coal in the James River, 1864*

138

GARDNER'S PHOTOGRAPHIC SKETCHBOOK

IN 1866 ALEXANDER GARDNER (1821–1882), ONE OF THE first to capture on camera the harsh reality of modern combat, published *Gardner's Photographic Sketch Book of the War*, a two-volume, leather-bound collection of a hundred photographs from the recently concluded conflict. He gave each photograph a title and included an extended written description of its subject. In these two volumes, among the earliest photographically illustrated books in America, Gardner (inset) aimed to bring front-line photographs of the war to public attention. Furthermore, by carefully selecting the images and placing them in sequence from the conflict's earliest months to its conclusion, he revealed the documentary power of photography and demonstrated that such images were not just static likenesses but were capable of conveying narratives and recording history.

Having immigrated to America from Scotland in the mid-1850s, Gardner became a distinguished portraitist and a leading contributor of photographic views to the illustrated press. Initially he worked as an assistant to Mathew Brady in New York before moving to Washington, D.C., in 1858 to run Brady's new studio there. Gardner's first views of the war were made under the auspices of Brady, who sent him to document the aftermath of the Battle of Antietam in 1862. When photographs taken there were first displayed at Brady's New York studio that fall, the *New York Times* wrote: "Mr. Brady has done something to bring home to us the terrible reality and earnestness of war. If he has not brought bodies and laid them in our dooryard and along the streets, he has done something very like it."

Gardner soon left Brady and in 1863 opened his own Washington studio. He brought with him several of Brady's former assistants, including most notably Timothy O'Sullivan, who took a number of the pictures in Gardner's book. Although he affixed his name to the book's title, Gardner was just one of its eleven contributing photographers, and only eleven of the hundred images are credited to him. Yet it was he who conceived and financed the collaborative project. Gardner and his assistants created more than a hundred copies of the two-volume work, a laborious task in the days before photomechanical reproduction. Each image was printed separately and hand-tipped into the albums. Priced at $150, the volumes were well beyond the means of most families and were evidently meant for libraries and other institutions.

It is unclear whether Gardner's book was a financial or critical success in its day. It is apparent in retrospect, however, that the book reimagined the creative possibilities of photography and helped reshape how the larger public understood the nature of war. ✢ FHG

PICTURING WAR *Pictured in 1863, Alexander Gardner was arguably America's first modern photographer, in the same way that the Civil War was the first modern war. Artist Alfred Waud designed the title page of Gardner's masterwork (OPPOSITE), which included the photographs on the next two pages, shown with the titles he assigned them.*

Gardner's

Photographic

Sketch Book

of the War.

PHILP & SOLOMONS, Publishers — Washington, D.C.

VOL. II.

A. R. WARD, DEL.

ALEX. GARDNER, Photographer,   Entered according to act of Congress, in the year 1865, by A. Gardner, in the Clerk's Office of the District Court of the District of Columbia,   511 Seventh Street, Washington.

HOME OF A REBEL SHARPSHOOTER, GETTYSBURG.

No. 41.   July, 1863.

KILLED IN ACTION *Alexander Gardner arrived at Gettysburg two days after the battle's completion and created a series of views of the battlefield and those who had fallen there. Although photographic technology did not allow him to capture soldiers in action, Gardner and others hurried to major battlefields when the fighting ended to document the aftermath.*

Negative by DAVID KNOX. Entered according to act of Congress, in the year 1865, by A. Gardner, in the Clerk's Office of the District Court of the District of Columbia. Positive by A. GARDNER, 511 7th St., Washington.

A FANCY GROUP, IN FRONT OF PETERSBURG.

No. 76. August, 1864.

SOLDIERS' PASTIME *Games and other amusements were common in Union camps during the war. Gardner's assistant David Knox covered the 1864 Petersburg Campaign and photographed this cockfight during an interval in the fighting. Two African American men, identified by Gardner as contrabands, handle the birds while various soldiers look on.*

139

THE MEDAL OF HONOR

ONE LASTING CONTRIBUTION OF THE CIVIL WAR to America's military heritage was the Medal of Honor, which originated early in the conflict when the nation had no such award for valor. The Certificate of Merit, presented during the Mexican War, had been discontinued. First approved for the U.S. Navy in late 1861, Medals of Honor were authorized for the army as well in July 1862, when Congress designated them for "such non-commissioned officers and privates as shall most distinguish themselves by their gallantry in action, and other soldier-like qualities." Later, commissioned officers became eligible for the award.

The first Medals of Honor went to six Union soldiers who volunteered for a daring raid behind Confederate lines in 1862 and commandeered a locomotive called "The General." The first action for which a Medal of Honor was ever granted occurred earlier, however, when Corporal Francis E. Brownell killed the man who murdered Colonel Elmer E. Ellsworth in Alexandria, Virginia, on May 24, 1861. Brownell did not receive his medal (inset) until 1877, and some other veterans waited even longer for their awards. Sergeant William Carney of the 54th Massachusetts Infantry, wounded while rescuing his regiment's flag at Fort Wagner in July 1863, was the first African American to perform a deed recognized with a Medal of Honor, but he was not granted it until 1900. Carney was one of many Civil War soldiers awarded the medal for guarding their flag in battle. ✣ JLJ

LONG-SOUGHT HONOR *After the war, Francis E. Brownell twice put his name forward before receiving this Medal of Honor in 1877 "for gallantry in shooting the murderer of Col. Ellsworth." All recipients at the time who had served in the army received a medal like this one.*

140

PRESENTATION SWORDS

PRESENTATION SWORDS WERE among the most conspicuous honors awarded to Civil War officers. These nineteenth-century relics drew on a long-standing European tradition. For centuries kings had been invested, commoners had been knighted, and soldiers had been rewarded with presentation swords. In 1786 the Continental Congress sent one of George Washington's aides to Paris to purchase ten swords for officers who had served with distinction during the American Revolution. In later conflicts, the U.S. Congress and various states, municipalities, and organizations presented swords to military heroes. The heyday of presentation swords was the Civil War.

Not all such swords in the Smithsonian collection are as ornate as those depicted here. Some came in regulation patterns with few embellishments and were given to popular officers by soldiers serving under them. The more ostentatious and expensive swords were usually given by states or municipalities to a favorite son, or by wealthy donors to officers they esteemed, and were often ordered from well-known silversmiths or jewelers like Tiffany & Company.

Dealers also donated swords to charitable functions. At fairs held to benefit the U.S. Sanitary Commission, visitors "voted" with a dollar for their favorite officer, and the winner received a presentation sword. New York City newspapers covered one such contest between Generals McClellan and Grant as closely as a prize fight or national election. ✣ DDM

SHERIDAN SWORD *General Philip Sheridan received the sword at right from "A Few Friends in New York," possibly the Union League Club. The hilt, shown in detail beside the scabbard (OPPOSITE), depicts Liberty slaying the serpent of rebellion.*

I must tell you about our division Commander having a sword presented to him. It is the most beautiful thing I ever saw.

LETTER FROM A SOLDIER IN SHERIDAN'S DIVISION

KILPATRICK SWORD
General Hugh Judson Kilpatrick received this sword around 1865 from the officers of his 3rd Cavalry Division. The counterguard portrays Kilpatrick astride a charging horse, and the blade is inscribed with battles he fought.

WILKES SWORD
Captain Charles Wilkes arrested Confederate commissioners James Mason and John Slidell on board the British mail ship Trent in 1861. The British government was furious, but the city of Boston presented Wilkes with this sword in 1862.

WHEATON SWORD

General Frank Wheaton received this sword from his native state of Rhode Island in 1865. The hilt features the Goddess of Victory holding a laurel wreath in her raised hand. The enamel medallion on the counterguard bears the initials "FW."

HANCOCK SWORD

Major General Winfield Scott Hancock was voted the winner of this Tiffany & Company sword at the Mississippi Valley Sanitary Fair in June 1864. The hilt depicts Liberty; laurel leaves and the Goddess of Victory adorn the knuckle guard.

HONORING BLACK TROOPS

FOURTEEN OF THE EIGHTEEN AFRICAN AMERICANS who received the Medal of Honor for valorous actions during the Civil War earned that award in one battle—a costly assault on Richmond's defenses mounted at New Market Heights in late September 1864 by Major General Benjamin F. Butler, commander of the Army of the James. Another two hundred or so black soldiers who fought there received an unofficial award for bravery that he issued in 1865: the Army of the James Medal, also known as the Butler Medal (inset). These men were surviving members of two regiments, the 4th Regiment and 6th Regiment, U.S. Colored Troops, who led the attack and suffered grievous casualties of more than 50 percent.

Throughout the Civil War, many white soldiers and commanders expressed skepticism about the ability of black soldiers to fight. General Butler—the notorious former commandant of Union-occupied New Orleans who was also a strong proponent of emancipation—stated in his memoirs that he placed those Colored Troops up front at New Market Heights to test their determination to fight. He was so impressed by their courage under fire, he wrote afterward, that "I felt in my innermost heart that the capacity of the negro race for soldiers had then and there been fully settled forever." The Latin inscription on the medal he presented to the recipients reads: "Freedom will be theirs by the sword." ✛ MGM

BUTLER MEDAL *Benjamin Butler issued such Butler Medals at his own expense and wrote afterward that "I have been fully rewarded by seeing the beaming eye of many a colored comrade as he drew his medal from the innermost recesses of its concealment to show me."*

SOJOURNER TRUTH

BY THE TIME THE CIVIL WAR ENDED, SOJOURNER Truth (ca. 1797–1883) was well known not just as an inspirational figure who had emerged from slavery to become a preacher, abolitionist, and advocate for women's rights. She was also recognized as an icon, who had a remarkable camera presence and sold portraits of herself like the one shown opposite to admirers. The powerful image she crafted for herself was genuine. She had experienced the evils of slavery not in the South but in New York, where her first master died when she was around nine and she was sold to another owner along with a flock of sheep. Unwilling to wait for freedom under New York's gradual emancipation process, she fled bondage in 1826 and later took the name Sojourner Truth and began speaking out against injustice and inequality.

Portraits of Sojourner Truth convey her forthright personality and contrast with other photographs of black women born into slavery, which are relatively rare and seldom show them as individuals. More often they are pictured at the periphery of a white family, in servant's attire, or as nursemaids holding a white child under their care. Sojourner Truth appears on her own, subordinate to no one. The photograph here displays not only her individuality but also her proud connections to family, cause, and country. She holds in her lap a daguerreotype said to portray her grandson, James Caldwell, who served in the all-black 54th Massachusetts Infantry. She thus represents herself as a mother and grandmother as well as a patriot of that evolving land of liberty for which Caldwell fought.

Sojourner Truth had printed under her photographs the words, "I sell the shadow to support the substance." But those images did more than help support her. They captured her in substance and brought her a measure of immortality. ✛ JDS

TRUE LIKENESS *This portrait of Sojourner Truth, taken between 1863 and 1870 and printed as a carte-de-visite, is held by the National Museum of African American History and Culture. She sold such images of herself during public appearances as well as by mail.*

143

A VISIT FROM THE OLD MISTRESS

COMPLETED IN 1879, WINSLOW HOMER'S PAINTING *A Visit from the Old Mistress* (right) evokes the unresolved tension between the races after the war ended. Inside a cabin, three black women, one holding a child, form a frieze arrayed in opposition to the rigid figure of their former mistress. Her garb suggests she is a widow, and the stern polarity of her black dress trimmed in white suggests her equally rigid mindset as she confronts her former slaves. The central figure facing her locks eyes with the old mistress. Equal in height and resolve, the two women appear as wary adversaries.

> *It seemed humiliating ... to bargain and haggle with our own former servants about wages.*
> **ELIZA FRANCES ANDREWS**

Homer leaves the reason for this visit ambiguous, as murky as the sepia tones of the cabin interior. But the old mistress may be facing a common postwar adjustment for former slaveholders—negotiating for the labor of those they once owned. Her irritated look echoes the reaction of Eliza Frances Andrews, who was raised in a Georgia household maintained by slave labor and wrote as the war ended, "It seemed humiliating to be compelled to bargain and haggle with our own former servants about wages." Such reactions suggest how indifferent some former slave owners were to the past humiliations and lingering grievances of their so-called "servants." In this powerful painting Homer makes visible racial tensions that the South's old masters and mistresses could no longer suppress. ✛ EJH

SLAVERY'S AFTERMATH *After visiting Virginia in 1876, Winslow Homer produced this painting, one of several that explored race relations in the postwar South.*

144

THE VOYAGE OF ROBERT SMALLS

BORN INTO SLAVERY IN BEAUFORT, SOUTH Carolina, Robert Smalls (1839–1915) won freedom and fame during the Civil War and went on to represent his district in the U.S. House of Representatives, where he served five terms. His remarkable journey to prominence began when he was twelve and his mother persuaded their master to hire him out to work in Charleston. He became a stevedore and eventually a skilled boat pilot, plying the waters from South Carolina to Florida. While in Charleston, he met and married Hannah Jones.

Soon after the Civil War began, Smalls and other enslaved men working aboard the steamboat *Planter* were pressed into service when the owner leased the vessel to the Confederate Army. One of the fastest ships in Charleston harbor, the *Planter* could turn sharply and quickly and had a carrying capacity of 1,400 bales of cotton or 1,000 men. The vessel and its crew served mainly to transport armaments and supplies to Confederate fortifications in the harbor.

On the night of May 12, 1862, after two weeks of grueling supply duty, the *Planter*'s officers left the ship to rest ashore—a violation of their duties. That gave Smalls, his wife and three children, and nine others who were intent on escaping slavery the opportunity they were awaiting. Around 3:00 a.m. on May 13, they embarked in the *Planter* with Smalls at the helm, dressed in a captain's uniform and straw hat. A deeply devout man, he offered a prayer on their behalf: "Oh Lord, we entrust ourselves to Thee. As Thou didst deliver the Israelites from bondage in Egypt, be with us today and deliver us to our promised land of freedom."

Flying the South Carolina state flag and the Confederate battle flag, the *Planter* slipped safely past the guns of Fort Sumter and other Confederate fortifications, but greater danger lay ahead. Officers aboard Union ships blockading the harbor did not know that the *Planter* was manned by runaway slaves. The U.S.S. *Onward* was about to fire on them when they grabbed a white bed sheet that Hannah had wisely brought along, ran it up the flagpole, and delivered their ship into Union hands.

Hailed as a hero, Smalls served as a pilot in the U.S. Navy before returning to Beaufort at war's end. In 1868 he was chosen as a delegate to the South Carolina State Constitutional Convention. The new state constitution adopted by that convention did more than affirm the voting rights of black men. It gave all men, whether poor or wealthy, equal political rights and representation and called for free public education. Federal efforts to uphold civil rights in the South ceased in 1877, bringing an end to Reconstruction, but Smalls and his supporters continued to campaign for equity and justice for all citizens. He served in the U.S. Congress until 1887 and remained prominent as Beaufort's customs collector even after the adoption in 1895 of a new state constitution that effectively disenfranchised African Americans—a document he denounced and refused to sign. ⊹ EN

POLITICIAN ON THE RISE *Robert Smalls is pictured here in a signed photograph taken around 1868, the year in which he helped draw up a new constitution for South Carolina and won election to the state legislature.*

ACKNOWLEDGED LEADER

An inspirational figure to many, Robert Smalls appears in the lower left corner of this hand-colored 1881 lithograph labeled "Heroes of the Colored Race." Featured at center is Frederick Douglass, flanked by Hiram R. Revels of Mississippi, the first African American elected to the U.S. Senate, at right and another U.S. senator from that state, Blanche K. Bruce, at left.

SYMBOL OF WEALTH

The Victorian-era sofa (BELOW), with wing scroll arms, a serpentine tufted back, and decorative veneer, graced the Prince Street home of Robert Smalls in Beaufort, South Carolina. He purchased the house, where he was raised in slavery, in 1863.

REMEMBERING SLAVERY

AROUND 1880 NORTHERN PHOTOGRAPHER, J. H. AYLSWORTH, SEEKING bucolic scenes of the South staged the picture at right. He could have portrayed the women and children hunched over, as when picking cotton. Instead, he showed them standing placidly in the field, with several women holding cotton stems like bouquets. Some of them were probably old enough to remember slavery and forced labor at tasks not unlike the work they did now. Most of those enslaved in the South performed hard agricultural chores such as raising cotton, sugarcane, rice, and wheat. On small farms, many worked both as house servants and as field hands and had little time to care for their families. As one woman recalled, "Just work, an' work, an' work. I never know nothin' but work." Later, as free laborers on postwar plantations, African Americans received wages or a share of the crop, but that remuneration often failed to meet their needs and many became indebted to their employers. Their basic conditions—backbreaking labor and unequal treatment—had changed little since slavery.

The clothing worn by these women and children was better than that described by some who knew slavery, like Frederick Douglass who wrote that on Maryland plantations youngsters "almost naked, might be seen at all seasons of the year." Slaves did have clothing that they valued, however, as evidenced by the skirt shown at left, a rare surviving article of slave clothing preserved by a freed woman in Macon, Georgia. The fact that family members saved a garment for generations speaks to the power of memory and the desire to preserve one's past, however difficult it may have been. The former owner explained what the skirt meant to her family, whose ancestors were enslaved. "My grandmother would always get moved to anger if any of the children or adults would go anywhere near this old treasure chest," she recalled. On her deathbed, the woman's grandmother revealed to her that the treasure chest held clothing "worn by slaves and she wanted me to care for it and she wanted me to assure her that I would treasure it and respect its authenticity always." ✛ MGM

TIMEWORN RELIC *Scientific testing confirmed that this skirt, preserved as a reminder of slavery, was consistent with materials and methods used to produce clothing before 1865.*

146

THE MOSES OF HER PEOPLE

BY THE TIME THE CIVIL WAR ENDED AND SLAVERY was abolished, Harriet Tubman (ca.1822–1913) had earned a reputation as a modern-day Moses, who freed herself from bondage and led many others to freedom. In a letter to her, Frederick Douglass stated that with the exception of John Brown, "I know of no one who has willingly encountered more perils and hardship to serve our enslaved people than you have."

Born on Maryland's Eastern Shore, she was given the name Araminta Ross by her enslaved parents and took her mother's name, Harriet, around the time she wed John Tubman, a free black man. That marriage, which later ended, did not free her from slavery. In 1849, fearing that she and others in her family might be sold to another owner, she escaped to Philadelphia.

Tubman had suffered a serious head injury in her teens at the hands of an overseer and experienced occasional seizures for the rest of her life. Despite that infirmity, she became a "conductor" on a branch of the Underground Railroad and returned repeatedly to Maryland in the 1850s to liberate many of her relatives and scores of others. During the Civil War, Tubman served the Union as a spy and scout and helped train women who had fled slavery to work for the army. In 1863 she guided black troops on a raid that freed hundreds of slaves from plantations along the Combahee River in South Carolina. Tubman received almost no pay from the Union, but her service enhanced her reputation. In 1869 she wed Nelson Davis, a black Union veteran, who according to family lore was so impressed by stories of her wartime exploits that he traveled to her home in New York, determined to make her his wife.

Proceeds from a popular account of her life, *Harriet Tubman: The Moses of Her People*, (1886) helped to relieve her financial burdens. The book may have brought her to the attention of Britain's Queen Victoria, who sent her an elegant silk shawl (below). When the shawl was later donated to the Smithsonian, conservators found that the fabric still retained the impression of Harriet Tubman's shoulders. ✛ JDS

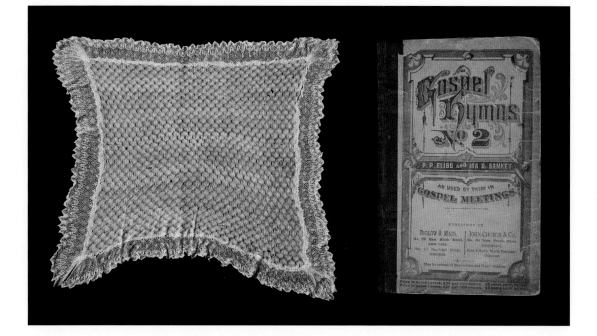

CHERISHED KEEPSAKES
Harriet Tubman, pictured in 1885 at her home in Auburn, New York, treasured the shawl she received from Queen Victoria around 1897 (FAR LEFT) and wore it often. Tubman's hymnal (LEFT) contains pages marked with an X to indicate her favorite hymns. Although she could not read, she was well versed in the Bible and kept the hymnal close by, sharing the songs with her companions.

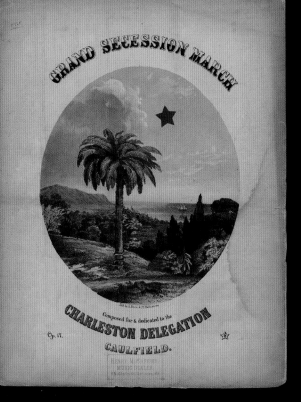

GRAND SECESSION MARCH

Lith by A. Hoen & Co. Baltimore.

Composed for & dedicated to the

CHARLESTON DELEGATION

CAULFIELD.

Op. 17.

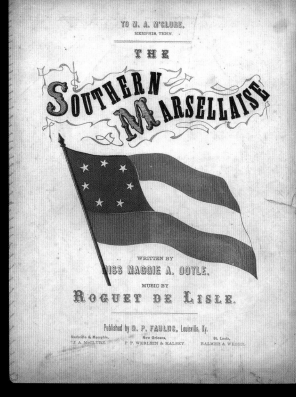

TO D. A. M'CLURE,
MEMPHIS, TENN.

THE

SOUTHERN MARSELLAISE

WRITTEN BY

MISS MAGGIE A. DOYLE.

MUSIC BY

ROGUET DE LISLE.

Published by D. P. FAULDS, Louisville, Ky.

Nashville & Memphis,   New Orleans,   St. Louis,
J. A. McCLURE.   P. P. WERLEIN & HALSEY.   BALMER & WEBER.

THE FLOWERS COLLECTION

WHO WILL CARE FOR MOTHER NOW

Ballad

Music by C.F. Thompson.

Poetry by C.C. Sawyer, Author of

When This Cruel War is Over

Richmond Va. Litho'd & Published by Geo. Dunn & Comp? P.O. Box 391. Columbia S.C. Julian A. Selby.

ENTERED ACCORDING TO ACT OF CONGRESS IN THE YEAR 1863, by GEORGE DUNN IN THE CLERK'S OFFICE OF THE DISTRICT COURT OF THE
CONFEDERATE STATES OF AMERICA FOR THE EASTERN DISTRICT OF VIRGINIA.

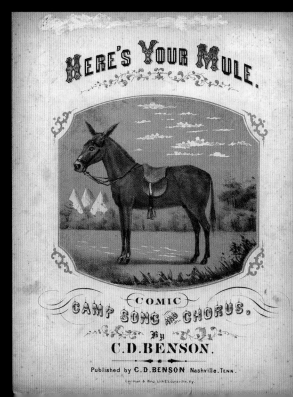

HERE'S YOUR MULE.

COMIC

CAMP SONG AND CHORUS,

BY

C. D. BENSON.

Published by C. D. BENSON Nashville, Tenn.

German & Bro. Lith. St. Louisville, Ky.

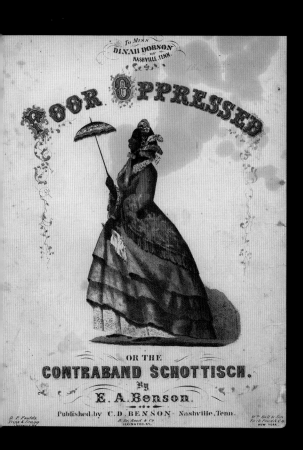

SONGS OF THE SOUTH

THE SHEET MUSIC COVERS SHOWN HERE PROVIDE insights into the values and mindset of Southerners during and after the Civil War. Among the first tunes celebrating the Confederate cause was "Grand Secession March," composed by Thomas J. Caulfield, a music professor at Georgetown College, to honor South Carolina's secession in December 1860. This copy bears the stamp of a music dealer in Maryland—a state of questionable loyalty when the piece was published. Other songs likened secession to a revolt against tyranny as in the American or French Revolutions. Based on the French revolutionary anthem, "The Southern Marseillaise" exhorted Confederates to defend their cause and "repulse the foe."

Some Civil War songs of Northern origin proved popular in the South because they expressed emotions shared by people on both sides. In one such song, "Who Will Care for Mother Now," a dying soldier's last thoughts are for his mother: "To my fate I meekly bow; / If you'll only tell me truly, / Who will care for Mother now?" A favorite among Confederate soldiers was the comic song "Here's Your Mule," based on a practical joke played on a farmer selling food to soldiers, who hid the farmer's mule in a tent and called out "Here's your mule!" from various places as he searched frantically for it.

Among the few Southern songs addressing slavery and emancipation was "Poor Oppressed, or the Contraband Schottisch." The sheet music cover for this 1862 ballroom tune ridicules the idea of racial equality by depicting an escaped slave dressed in the finery of a white woman. Postwar efforts by Klansmen to restore white supremacy in the South were touted by the song "Ku Klux Klan, or Bloody Moon Waltz," which was published in several cities in 1868 and invited people to dance to a tune that celebrated acts of terror. ✛ CAO

SOUTHERN COVERS *Despite wartime shortages of paper and ink, Southern firms printed sheet music with fancy covers like these from the archives of the National Museum of American History.*

148

WARS IN THE WEST

BETWEEN THE LAST DAYS OF THE CIVIL WAR IN 1865 AND 1876, THE number of soldiers serving the United States fell from more than 1,000,000 to just 27,000. Army units enforced Reconstruction in the South and fought Native Americans who resisted confinement to reservations in the West. Leading that fight was an officer renowned for his punishing campaigns against Confederates, William Tecumseh Sherman, who became the army's commanding general in 1869. Sherman's strategy was to attack Indians in their winter camps and destroy their food supplies, forcing the survivors onto reservations. "The more we can kill this year," he wrote in late 1868, "the less will have to be killed the next war. For the more I see of these Indians the more convinced am I that they have all to be killed, or be maintained as a species of paupers."

Sherman's forces were supposed to uphold treaties with tribes like that negotiated in 1868 at Fort Laramie (right), which established the Great Sioux Reservation in and around the Black Hills. But there was no stopping settlers from intruding on tribal lands. When prospectors overran the Black Hills, Sioux led by Sitting Bull refused to be confined there. Colonel George Armstrong Custer went after them and died with 268 of his troopers in June 1876 when Sioux and Cheyenne warriors overwhelmed them at the Little Bighorn. That defeat shocked the nation, but it did not reverse the tide.

By 1880 the Plains tribes had been largely subdued. Over the next decade, resistance among tribes of the Southwest was suppressed. In December 1890, after Sitting Bull was killed while resisting arrest at the Standing Rock Agency in South Dakota, his followers fled and joined other disaffected Sioux. U.S. troops pursued them and slaughtered more than 150 people at Wounded Knee. The massacre marked the effective end of the Indian Wars and concluded a sad chapter in the army's history. ✢ TC

FRAGILE ACCORD *Tribal leaders meet with General Sherman (SEATED THIRD FROM LEFT) and other officials at Fort Laramie. The collapse of the treaty negotiated there led to death of Colonel Custer, whose widow donated to the Smithsonian the buckskin jacket he wore (INSET).*

149

REUNIONS AND REMEMBERANCE

THE CIVIL WAR WAS THE EPIC EVENT IN THE LIVES of hundreds of thousands of military veterans. Their shared experiences in camps, on marches, and in battle bound them in brotherhood long after the war ended. Organizations such as the United Confederate Veterans (UCV) and the Union's Grand Army of the Republic (GAR) aided veterans and their kin and reunited them at gatherings where they saluted the living and honored the dead. Over time the collective memories of Union and Confederate veterans became, in the words of author Robert Penn Warren, "our only 'felt' history—history lived in the national imagination."

Americans have been collecting that history ever since Ulysses S. Grant and Robert E. Lee sat down together at Appomattox on chairs that are preserved now as emblems of peace and goodwill. Such artifacts substantiate the voluminous written records of the conflict and help bring the past to life. No account or reenactment of the Battle of Gettysburg can reproduce the mortal danger faced by Major General Winfield Scott Hancock on July 3, 1863, when he rode forward to rally Union troops as they withstood Pickett's Charge and was shot through the thigh. Hancock returned to Gettysburg in 1885 and was presented with a box of relics retrieved on the battlefield (opposite). Its rusted, fragmented contents, including iron shrapnel and lead bullets, serve as vivid reminders of the courage it took for ordinary men to face lethal hail without shirking duty.

Those who survived the war had to reckon with painful memories of those who did not, which could weigh heavily on veteran commanders in a losing cause. The photograph at left was taken in April 1870 in Savannah, Georgia, where two former Confederate generals and classmates at West Point, Robert E. Lee (near left) and Joseph E. Johnston (facing Lee), met for the first time since the war ended. Both sixty-three, they had retired their uniforms for civilian dress and duties. The noticeable shine on Lee's shoes, in contrast to Johnston's, was characteristic of that model officer, who had graduated forty-one years earlier from the U.S. Military Academy without a single demerit. ✣ JGB

Gins. Lee and Joe Johnson

CONFEDERATE ICONS *In April 1865, five years before this memorable picture was taken, Robert E. Lee and Joseph Johnston surrendered the South's last two effective armies. Photographer David J. Ryan of Savannah made this and a similar second image of Lee and Johnston, probably in his downtown studio. Copies were sold to aid the Ladies' Memorial Association of Savannah.*

GAR MEMORABILIA *Caps and badges such as those at right were worn at gatherings by members of the Grand Army of the Republic, a Union veterans' organization founded in 1866. This badge belonged to Ulysses S. Grant.*

BATTLEFIELD RELICS *Winfield Scott Hancock received this box of relics on his last visit to Gettysburg in November 1885, marking the twenty-second anniversary of President Lincoln's famous address.*

150

DESIGNING THE LINCOLN PENNY

THE FAMOUS LINCOLN PENNY, INTRODUCED TO commemorate the centennial of Abraham Lincoln's birth in 1909, was based on a medal produced three years earlier by sculptor and designer Victor David Brenner (1871–1924). Brenner's career started in Lithuania, where family members were engravers and seal cutters. He emigrated, studying art and design at the Académie Julian in Paris and at New York City's Cooper Union. He presented the Lincoln medal (inset) among "several specimens" of his work with a letter addressed on December 6, 1906, to Sarah Cooper Hewitt, a granddaughter of Peter Cooper and co-founder with her sister Eleanor of the Cooper Union Museum for the Arts of Decoration (now the Smithsonian Institution's Cooper-Hewitt National Design Museum). The Cooper Union Museum promptly acquired Brenner's medal, which includes the year of Lincoln's birth, 1809, on one side of the president's profile and 1909 on the other side, indicating that the artist was well aware in 1906 of the impending centennial.

How did Brenner achieve such a faithful likeness of Lincoln, who died four decades before this medal was made? He based his portrayal on a photograph of Lincoln (opposite), taken at Mathew Brady's Washington, D.C., studio in February 1864 and held now by the National Portrait Gallery. Showing Lincoln in profile, that picture of him has a timeless, statuesque quality. Produced by Brady, a master of his craft born in New York to Irish immigrants, it was transformed by Brenner, a gifted first-generation American, into the most renowned image of Lincoln ever made.

Brenner's medal became the prototype for the Lincoln penny at the urging of President Theodore Roosevelt, who posed for a medal Brenner created in 1908. Roosevelt was a great admirer of Lincoln, having witnessed as a boy in 1865 the slain president's funeral procession in New York City. His decision to honor Lincoln by placing his image on the penny in 1909 broke with the precedent of portraying only symbolic figures such as Lady Liberty or an idealized American Indian on U.S. coins. Some people felt that the existing Indian-head penny, which had been in use since 1859, should not be replaced by one glorifying a specific leader, however esteemed, but Roosevelt had his way.

Brenner's image of Lincoln was just what Roosevelt wanted on the head of the new penny. A few changes in the design were called for, however. In addition to featuring only one date, the year in which the coin was issued, it had to meet a requirement set forth in the Mint Act of 1792, which stated that on one side of every U.S. coin, "there shall be an impression emblematic of liberty." Brenner complied by adding the word "Liberty" to the left of Lincoln's image on his final design for the coin, but the portrait of Lincoln in itself could be considered enough to fulfill that requirement. By the time the centennial of his birth arrived on February 12, 1909, and the first Lincoln pennies were minted, his reputation was firmly established as the president who restored the Union, abolished slavery, and made possible what he foresaw in his Gettysburg Address— a "new birth of freedom." For those like Victor Brenner who came to America seeking a better life, Lincoln embodied liberty and opportunity, and Brenner's iconic image of him on a common coin of little intrinsic value became one of the nation's enduring treasures. ✢ SDC

AMERICAN ICON *Mathew Brady's 1864 portrait of Abraham Lincoln inspired Victor David Brenner's 1906 medal (INSET), the precursor to his 1909 Lincoln penny. Within six months of the Lincoln centennial that February, twenty-two million of those pennies had been coined.*

OBJECT LIST

Museum Acronym Key

ACM — Anacostia Community Museum
CHNDM — Cooper-Hewitt National Design Museum
HMSG — Hirshhorn Museum and Sculpture Garden
NASM — National Air and Space Museum
NMAH — National Museum of American History
NMAI — National Museum of the American Indian
NMAAHC — National Museum of African American History and Culture
NMNH — National Museum of Natural History
NPG — National Portrait Gallery
NPM — National Postal Museum
SAAM — Smithsonian American Art Museum
SIA — Smithsonian Institution Archives
SL — Smithsonian Libraries

Division Acronym Key

AC — Archives Center
AFH — Armed Forces History
CA — Culture and Arts
GA — Graphic Arts
HCL — Home and Community Life
MS — Medicine and Science
NM — Numismatics
PH — Political History
PHC — Photographic History Collection
WI — Work and Industry

Directionals Key

(b) bottom
(bc) bottom center
(bl) bottom left
(br) bottom right
(c) center

(cl) center left
(cr) center right
(l) left
(r) right
(t) top

(tc) top center
(tl) top left
(tr) top right

1: NMAH, AFH, 308845/78967M. 2: Photographer unknown, two Union soldiers posing with flag, c. 1863–1865, ambrotype. NMAH, PHC, 322775/75.17.922. 3: NMAH, CA, 274169/69758. 5: Mathew Brady, *Washington, D.C.*, c. 1863, photographic print. SIA, SIA2011-1448. 6 (l): NMAH, PH, gift of the Thirty-three Subscribers, 20084/4412. 6 (c): NMAH, AFH, 227582/65427M. 6 (r): Mathew Brady Studio, copy after William D. McPherson, copy after Mr. Oliver, *Gordon*, 1863, albumen silver print. NPG, NPG.2002.89. 7 (l): NMAH, AFH, 64127/RSN80759W13. 7 (c): Photograph by David Knox, print by Alexander Gardner, *Mortar Dictator, Front of Petersburg*, 1864, albumen print. NMAH, PHC, 1986.0711.0283.25. 7 (r): NMAH, AFH, 223708/60850M. 9: William Judkins Thomson, *Abraham Lincoln*, October 11, 1858, half-plate ambrotype. NPG, NPG.82.52. 10: Photographer unknown, historic record photograph of Lincoln office suit and hat, c. 1870s–1920s. NMAH, PH, negative # 29641. 11 (l): NMAAHC, 2009.32.1. 11 (c): NMAAHC, 2009.32.3. 11 (r): NMAAHC, 2009.32.2. 12: Thomas Painter Collins, man posing as a Confederate soldier in Zouave uniform, c. 1861–63, ambrotype. NMAH, PHC, 189067/4697. 13: NMAH, AFH, 20063/4409(A). 14: NMAH, HCL, 157340/T.8420. 15 (l): NMAH, AFH, 1980.0399.0288. 15 (r): NMAH, AFH, 1980.0399.0287. 16: Andrew J. Russell, *Smithsonian Institution Building, North Façade*, c. 1860, photographic print. SIA, MAH-9748a. 17: Photographer unknown, *Jefferson Davis*, Regent, c. 1855, photographic print. SIA, SA-464. 18: Jesse H. Whitehurst, portrait of Joseph Henry, c. 1850s, daguerreotype. NMAH, PHC, 55663/1711. 18–19: Alexander Gardner, *Smithsonian Institution Building Fire*, January 24, 1865, photographic print with hand-painting, SIA, MAH-37082. 20: NMAH, HCL, 1987.0005/68.150. 21: CHNDM, bequest of Gertrude M. Oppenheimer, 1981-28-77. 22: NMAH, PH, transfer from the U.S. Patent Office, 13152/16155. 23: NMAH, PH, gift of Society for the Oldest Inhabitants of Washington, D.C., 277275.35. 24: ACM, gift of Bert and Caroly Vorchheimer, 1994.0001.0001. 25: NMAH, HCL, T08791.000. 26: Photographer unknown, *Ulysses S. Grant*, undated tintype after an 1843 daguerreotype. NPG, gift of Mr. and Mrs. Ralph Connor, S/NPG.79.4. 27: Attributed to H. B. Hull, *Stonewall Jackson*, 1855, daguerreotype. NPG, NPG.77.57. 28 (l): Photographer unknown, *Horace Greeley*, c. 1850, daguerreotype. NPG, NPG.77.9. 28 (r): Marcus Aurelius Root, *Lucretia Coffin Mott*, 1851, daguerreotype. NPG, NPG.2009.32. 29 (l): Attributed to Samuel Root or Marcus Aurelius Root, *P.T. Barnum and General Tom Thumb*, c. 1850, daguerreotype. NPG, NPG.93.154. 29 (r): Mathew Brady, *George Henry Thomas*, 1853, daguerreotype. NPG, NPG.77.61. 30 (l): Photographer unknown, *Dorothea Lynde Dix*, c. 1849, daguerreotype. NPG, NPG.77.261. 30 (r): Joseph White, *Samuel Cooper*, c. 1856, daguerreotype. NPG, NPG.98.92. 31 (l): Photographer unknown, *Peter Cooper and Family*, c. 1850, daguerreotype. NPG, NPG.96.86. 31 (r): William R. Phipps, *John Cabell Breckinridge*, c. 1855, daguerreotype. NPG, NPG.2005.110. 32 (l): Benjamin D. Maxham, *Henry David Thoreau*, 1856, daguerreotype. NPG, gift of anonymous donor, NPG.72.119. 32 (r): Mathew Brady, *Mathew Brady, Juliet Brady, and Mrs. Haggerty*, c. 1851, daguerreotype. NPG, NPG.85.78. 33: Lieutenant Henry Samuel Hawker R.N., *The Portuguese slaver Diligenté captured by H.M. Sloop Pearl with 600 slaves on board*, 1838, watercolor on paper. NMAAHC, 2010.21.2. 34–35: NMAH, HCL, 2007.0093.01. 36(t): NMAAHC, gift of the Liljenquist Family Collection, 2011.51.18. 36(b): NMAAHC, 2008.10.3. 37 (t): Taylor & Huntington, *Magic Lantern Slide of Alexandria, Virginia slave pen*, 1861, albumen, sodium chloride, silver nitrate, and glass. NMAAHC, 2012.17.1. 37 (bl): NMAAHC, 2009.9.8. 37 (br): Henry Louis Stephens, *The Sale*, c. 1863, lithographic ink on cardboard. NMAAHC, 2008.9.53. 38: NMAH, HCL, 1996.0344.01. 39 (tl): NMAAHC, gift of the Liljenquist Family Collection, 2011.51.10. 39 (tr): NMAAHC, 2010.27.1. 39 (cl): NMAAHC, 2010.27.2. 39 (cr): NMAAHC, 2010.27.3. 39 (bl): NMAAHC, 2008.4. 39 (br): NMAH, HCL, 1990.0410.02. 40: ACM, Henson Family papers, gift of Dr. Myrtle Henry, MS 06-030. 43: Photographer unknown, *Frederick Douglass*, 1856, quarter-plate ambrotype. NPG, NPG.74.75. 44: NMAH, AFH, 51210/258924. 45: Augustus Washington, *John Brown*, c. 1846–47, daguerreotype. NPG, purchased with major acquisitions funds and with funds donated by Betty Adler Schermer in honor of her great-grandfather, August M. Bondi, NPG.96.123. 46 (t): NMAH, AFH, 1982.0025.01. 46 (c): NMAH, AFH, 35097/7739. 46 (b): NMAH, AFH, 1982.0723.01. 46 (bl): James Wallace Black, *John Brown in 1858*, 1859, salted-paper print, copy after daguerreotype, c. 1858 by Martin M. Lawrence. NPG, NPG.74.76. 47: Letter from John Brown to George L. Stearns, August 10, 1857, ink on paper. NPG, AD/NPG.74.1. 48: NMAAHC, gift of the Liljenquist Family Collection, 2011.51.17. 49: NMAAHC, 2012.46.5. 50: SL, The Dibner Library of the History of Science and Technology, PS2954 .U5 1852. 51: Alanson Fisher, *Harriett Beecher Stowe*, 1853, oil on canvas. NPG, NPG 68.1. 52–53: NMAAHC, 2011.23.1. 54: Artist unknown, *Stephen Arnold Douglas*, c. 1858, polychromed wood. NPG, gift of Richard E. Guggenheim, NPG.71.59. 55 (l): Max Platz, copy after Alexander Hesler, *Abraham Lincoln*, after 1857, albumen silver print. NPG, S/NPG.78.163. 55 (r): John Carbutt, *Stephen Douglas*, c. 1861, albumen silver print. NPG, NPG.83.146. 56: NMAH, PH, gift of the Thirty-three Subscribers, 20084/4414. 57–59: NMAH, PH, gift of the Thirty-three Subscribers, 20084/4412. 60: NMAH, PH, gift of Ralph E. Becker, 227739.1860.X01. 61: NMAH, PH, gift of George L. and Mary E. Compton, 1980.0482.12. 62 (t): NMAH, PH, negative #73796. 62 (bl): NMAH, PH, gift of Mrs. Robert A. Hubbard, 238747.01. 62 (br): NMAH, NM, 1987.0697.0399. 63 (l): NMAH, PH, gift of Anthony E. Starevic, 233297.01. 63 (c): NMAH, PH, gift of Ralph E. Becker, 227739.1860.T08. 63 (r): NMAH, PH, gift of Ralph E. Becker, 227739.1860.T05. 64: NMAH, AFH, 69413/32960. 65: Adalbert J. Volck, *Passage through Baltimore*, 1863, etching on paper. NPG, NPG.79.95.B. 66: Thomas Nast, *New York Illustrated News*, March 23, 1861. NMAH, gift of Ralph E. Becker, PL*227739.1861.A69. 66–67: Alexander Gardner, *Lincoln's First Inauguration*, 1861, albumen print. NMAH, PH, bequest of Gen. Montgomery C. Meigs, 1996.0090.135. 68: Artist unknown, *Edmund Ruffin*, c. 1861, salted-paper print with black ink wash and white watercolor. NPG, NPG.99.157. 69: "The House-tops in Charleston during the Bombardment of Sumter," *Harper's Weekly*, May 4, 1861, lithograph. SL, AA/PG, AP1.H293. 70–71: NMAH, PH, gift of Lincoln Isham, 219098.01. 72 (t): NMAH, AFH, 208701/58182M. 72 (b): NMAH, AFH, 165001/42724. 73: NMAH, AFH, 219818/59858M. 74: Mathew Brady Studio, *Winfield Scott*, c. 1860–1861, salted-paper print. NPG, NPG.78.245. 75: Photographer unknown, *Robert E. Lee*, undated, albumen silver print. NPG, gift of Charles A. L. Totten, NPG.2012.6.5. 76: NMAH, AFH, 134018/39361. 77 (t): Photographer unknown, *George Armstrong Custer*, c. 1859, quarter-plate ambrotype. NPG, NPG.81.138. 77 (b): Mathew Brady, *John Pelham*, 1858, half-plate ambrotype. NPG, NPG.2010.68. 78: NMAH, AFH, 1997.3044.268. 79 (tl): NMAH, AFH, 223708/61151M. 79 (tr):

NMAH, AFH, 96111/35633(1). **79 (bl):** NMAH, AFH, 223708/61065M. **79 (br):** NMAH, AFH, 223708/61063M. **80 (l):** Photographer unknown, *Elizabeth Keckley*, c. 1890, photographic print. ACM, ACMA, courtesy of Catherine Grey Hurley, BLW-037. **80 (r):** NMAH, PH, gift of Captain George Van Deurs, 181810/46663. **81:** NMAH, PH, bequest of Mrs. Julian James, 70138/33280. **82 (tr):** John Wood Dodge, *Varina Howell Davis*, 1849, watercolor on ivory. NPG, NPG.80.113. **82 (cl):** NMAH, PH, gift of Mrs. John W. Stewart, 1977.0237.03. **82 (cc):** NMAH, PH, gift of Mrs. John W. Stewart, 1977.0237.04. **82 (cr):** NMAH, PH, 1977.0237.09. **82 (bl):** NMAH, PH, gift of Mrs. John W. Stewart, 1977.0237.05. **82 (br):** NMAH, PH, gift of Mrs. John W. Stewart, 1977.0237.01. **83 (tl):** NMAH, PH, gift of Lincoln Isham, 278039.01. **83 (tc):** NMAH, PH, gift of Lincoln Isham, 225754.01. **83 (tr):** Mathew Brady Studio, *Mary Todd Lincoln*, 1861, albumen silver print. NPG, NPG.2005.111. **83 (bl):** NMAH, PH, gift of Lincoln Isham, 278039.02. **83 (br):** NMAH, PH, gift of Lincoln Isham, 216335.06 -.13. **84:** NMAH, NM, 305034.0005. **85:** NMAH, AFH, 68826/32398. **86:** Photographer unknown, portrait of young Union soldier in fatigue blouse, c. 1861–65, tintype. NMAH, AFH, 1980.0399.0378. **87:** NMAH, AFH, 308845/78969M. **88–89:** John Henry Buford, *Yankee Volunteers Marching into Dixie*, 1862, chromolithograph. NMAH, HCL, 228146/60.3308. **90–91:** Charles Magnus and Company, *Union Military Chart*, 1861, engraving. NMAH, HCL, 228146/60.3310. **91 (t):** E.B. and E.C. Kellogg, *Eagle's Nest*, 1861, lithograph. NMAH, HCL, 228146/60.2550. **91 (b):** E.B. and E.C. Kellogg, *Battle of Bull's Run, Va. July 21st 1861*, n.d. NMAH, HCL, 228146/60.3314. **92:** Photograph by William R. Pywell, print by Alexander Gardner, *Marshall House, Alexandria, VA*, 1862, albumen print. NMAH, PHC, 1986.0711.0334.01. **93:** Thomas S. Sinclair, *Col. Ellsworth Funeral March*, 1861, color lithograph on paper. NPG, gift of James and Bridget Barber, NPG.2008.112. **93 (c):** NMAH, AFH, 22306/202729. **93 (r):** NMAH, AFH, 22306/5611. **94 (l):** Mathew Brady Studio, *Francis E. Brownell*, 1861, glass-plate collodion negative. NPG, Frederick Hill Meserve Collection, Meserve.236:9. **95:** NMAH, AFH, 64127/RSN80846W05. **96 (tl):** NMAH, AFH, 64127/RSN80846W02. **96 (tc):** NMAH, AFH, 64127/RSN80784W09. **96 (tr):** NMAH, AFH, 64127/RSN80784W16. **96 (cr):** NMAH, AFH, 64127/RSN80784W15. **96 (bl):** NMAH, AFH, 1997.3044.286. **96 (br):** NMAH, AFH, 64127/RSN80845W45. **97 (l):** Winslow Homer, *Zouave*, 1864, black and white chalk on blue-green paper. CHNDM, gift of Charles Savage Homer Jr., 1912-12-109. **97 (tr):** NMAH, AFH, 64127/RSN80846W14. **97 (br):** NMAH, AFH, 64127/RSN80846W09. **98 (l):** NMAH, AFH, accession 64127 (jacket), 64127/RSN80846W40 (skirt). **98 (r):** NMAH, AFH, 64127/RSN80846W38. **99:** Photographer unknown, *Three Boys in Zouave Costume* (detail), c. 1863, albumen silver print with applied color. SAAM, museum purchase through the Smithsonian Institution Collections Acquisition Program, 2000.47.32. **100–101:** NMAH, PHC, 1995.20.07.01 (lens), 158846/4211E (global wide-angle lens), 164051/4268C (field view camera), 302036/71.031.38 (drying rack). **102:** Photographer unknown, union case with four photographs, c. 1860s, tintypes and ambrotype. NMAH, PHC, 322775/75.17.107. **103:** H. Frank Beidel, portrait of a family, c. 1860s, carte-de-visite. NMAH, PHC, 1985.0736.41.07. **104–5:** Various photographers, "United States" carte-de-visite album, c. 1861–65. NMAH, PHC, 302789/71.62. **106:** Photograph by William R. Pywell, print by Alexander Gardner, *Ruins of Stone Bridge, Bull Run, VA*, 1862, albumen print. NMAH, PHC, 1986.0711.0334.07. **107:** Mathew Brady, *Brady—the Photographer returned from Bull Run*, 1861, albumen print cabinet card. NMAH, PHC, 2002.0131.01. **108–9:** Mathew Brady or Mathew Brady Studio, untitled, 1862, copy photograph. NASM, NASM Archives, Thaddeus Lowe Collection, NASM Acc. XXXX-0132, NASM 2009-8683. **110 (tl):** NASM, NASM Archives, Thaddeus Lowe Collection, NASM Acc. XXXX-0132, NASM 99-40777. **110 (bl):** NASM, gift of heirs of T.S.C. Lowe, A19310040000. **110 (br):** NASM, gift of heirs of T.S.C. Lowe, A19310041000. **110–11:** Arthur Lumley, untitled, c. 1862, copy photograph of engraving. NASM, NASM Archives, NASM 2009-7378. **111 (b):** Photographer unknown, *Thaddeus S. C. Lowe*, 1862, tintype on sheet iron. NPG, NPG.97.121. **112:** Alexander Gardner, *What Do I Want, John Henry?—Scene Near Warrenton, VA*, 1862, albumen print. NMAH, PHC, 1986.0711.0334.27. **112–13:** Winslow Homer, *Army Boots*, 1865, oil on canvas. HMSG, gift of the Joseph H. Hirshhorn Foundation, 66.2491. **114 (l):** NPM, 2005.2004.1771. **114 (c):** NPM, 2010.2020.3. **114 (r):** NPM, 2005.2004.1776. **115 (t):** NPM, 2003.2004.26. **115 (b):** NPM, 1993.2002.30. **116:** NPM, 2011.2006.1. **117:** Mathew Brady, *Clara Barton*, c. 1865, albumen silver print. NPG, acquired through the generosity of Elizabeth A. Hylton, NPG.2013.2. **118 (l):** Winslow Homer, *The Army of the Potomac—A Sharpshooter on Picket Duty* (detail), 1862, wood engraving on paper. SAAM, gift of International Business Machines Corporation, 1966.48.81. **118 (r):** NMAH, AFH, 24158/5826. **119 (l):** NMAH, AFH, 64127/24939.103. **119 (r):** NMAH, AFH, 64127/24939. **120:** NMAH, AFH, 62012/18769. **121:** Barr & Young, *Ulysses Simpson Grant*, c. 1862, albumen silver print. NPG, NPG.79.246.1. **122:** NMAH, AFH, RSN81656W34. **122–23:** Christian Schussele, *Men of Progress*, 1862, oil on canvas. NPG, transfer from the National Gallery of Art: gift of the A.W. Mellon Educational and Charitable Trust, 1942, NPG.65.60. **124–25:** Bierstadt Brothers, *Patent Office, Washington D.C.*, c. 1865, photograph on cardboard. NPG, NPG.POB95. **126 (tl):** NMAH, MS, 1978.0273.07. **126 (tr):** NMAH, WI, 48856/251265. **126 (b):** NMAH, HCL, T011411.149. **127 (t):** NMAH, PH, transfer from the U.S. Patent Office, 48865/31940. **127 (c):** NMAH, HCL, T06050. **127 (b):** NMAH, AFH, 49064/252590. **128:** NMAH, WI, 222961/315875. **129 (t):** Andrew J. Russell, *Herman Haupt in a pontoon boat*, original photograph in *Photographs Illustrative of Operations in Construction and Transportation*, Boston: Wright & Potter, printers ..., 1863. SL, The Dibner Library of the History of Science and Technology, E491 .H37. **129 (b):** Andrew J. Russell, *The Potomac Creek Bridge*, original photograph in *Photographs Illustrative of Operations in Construction and Transportation*, Boston: Wright & Potter, printers ..., 1863. SL, The Dibner Library of the History of Science and Technology, E491 .H37. **130:** NMAH, AFH, 69281/32605. **131 (l):** Photographer unknown, First Lieutenant Pleasant Porter of the Creek Mounted Volunteers, CSA, c. 1863, copy negative no. 45289 made in 1958 from copy print lent by Ralph Goodwin, Harvard University, and obtained by him through courtesy of Mrs. William Adair Porter, Leonard, OK. NMNH, National Anthropological Archives. **131 (r):** E. C. Kropp Co., *Joe Tasson (Sac and Fox)*, c. after 1905, half-tone postcard. NMAI, P22628. **132:** Robert W. Addis, *George B. and Ellen Marcy McClellan*, 1862, albumen silver print. NPG, gift of Francis James Dallett, NPG.88.8. **133 (tl):** NMAH, AFH, 61384/17433. **133 (tr):** NMAH, AFH, 61384/17501. **133 (b):** NMAH, AFH, 68019/32016B. **134–35:** Photograph by D. B. Woodbury, print by Alexander Gardner, *Military Bridge across the Chickahominy, VA*, 1862, albumen print. NMAH, PHC, 1986.0711.0334.17. **135 (l):** NMAH, MS, 1980.0399.0079. **135 (c):** NMAH, MS, M-09419. **135 (r):** NMAH, MS, 1980.0399/RSN82561W45. **136:** NMAH, AFH, 1979.0916.02. **137:** NMAH, AFH, 206541/58175M (coffee sack), 52412/12071 (tin coffee can), 1980.0399.0149 (tin cup), 206541/58176M (sugar bag), exhibit prop (tobacco twist), 60666/17090 (soldier's sewing kit). **138 (l):** NMAH, AFH, 64127/25125.091. **138 (tr):** NMAH, AFH, 64127/22828. **138 (br):** NMAH, AFH, 64127/22828. **139 (tr):** NMAH, AFH, 64127/25124.021. **139 (cl):** NMAH, AFH, 2004.0181.01. **139 (bl):** Photographer unknown, portrait of Thomas Anthony, c.1861–65, ambrotype. NMAH, PHC, 1974.19.18. **139 (br):** NMAH, AFH, 64127/22817. **140 (l):** NMAH, AFH, 1997.3044.294. **140 (tr):** NMAH, AFH, 1980.0399.1042. **140 (cr):** NMAH, AFH, 97652/35635R.1. **140–41:** NMAH, AFH, 225158/60201M. **141 (tl):** NMAH, AFH, 35091/202755. **141 (tr):** NMAH, AFH, 1997.3044.21. **141 (cr):** NMAH, AFH, RSN81590W01. **141 (bl):** NMAH, AFH, 1980.0399.0972. **141 (br):** NMAH, AFH, 224978/60235M. **142 (l):** NMAH, AFH, 1980.0399.1207. **142 (tr):** NMAH, AFH, 63704/42580. **142 (br):** NMAH, AFH, 310596/77555M. **143 (tl):** NMAH, AFH, 1980.0399.0921. **143 (cl):** NMAH, AFH, 222708/60667M. **143 (cr):** NMAH, AFH, 220760/67634M. **143 (bl):** NMAH, AFH, RSN81766W31, RSN81766W07, RSN81766W40, RSN81766W11 (from top left to right), RSN81766W24, RSN81766W32, RSN81746W95, RSN81746T00 (from bottom left to right). **144 (tl):** NMAH, AFH, 21203/4717. **144 (tr):** NMAH, AFH, 17942/1886(B). **144 (cl):** NMAH, AFH, 1980.0399.1600. **144–45:** NMAH, AFH, 69413/32777. **145 (tl):** NMAH, AFH, 1980.0399.1037. **144 (r):** NMAH, AFH, 1980.0399.0138. **144 (bl):** NMAH, AFH, 1980.0399.0992. **146:** NMAH, AFH, 246404/67880M. **147 (tl):** NMAH, AFH, 223708/60669M. **147 (tr):** NMAH, AFH, 223708/60670M. **147 (cl):** NMAH, AFH, 223708/60623M. **147 (cr):** NMAH, AFH, 223708/60850M. **147 (bl):** NMAH, AFH, 223708/60706M. **147 (br):** NMAH, AFH, 58300/15399. **148:** NMAH, AFH, 1977.0294/76.32. **149 (l):** NMAH, AFH, 64127/22818. **149 (tr):** NMAH, AFH, 64127/25156.101. **149 (br):** NMAH, CA, 232422/66624. **150:** Photographer unknown, portrait of a Union drummer boy, c. 1861–65, tintype. NMAH, AFH, 2009.0192.01. **151:** NMAH, CA, 274169/69758. **152:** Edward Jacobs, *David Glasgow Farragut*, c. 1862, albumen silver print. NPG, NPG.78.65. **153 (l):** NMAH, AFH, 51104/11781. **153 (tr):** NMAH, AFH, 64127/25156.101. **153 (br):** NMAH, AFH, 61288/17388A. **154:** Edward Augustus Brackett, *Benjamin Franklin Butler*, 1863, white marble. NPG, gift of the Children of Oakes and Blanche Ames, NPG.73.1. **155:** Mathew Brady Studio, *Benjamin Franklin Butler*, c. 1864, albumen silver print. NPG, NPG.84.151. **156:** NMAH, NM, 91728/35531. **157:** NMAH, NM, 91728/35527. **158 (l):** C. R. Rees, view of Libby Prison, 1863, carte-de-visite. NMAH, AFH, 2006.0247.24. **158 (r):** NMAH, AFH, 195333/55596 (cracker), 296035/75528M (knife and fork), 296035/75529M (tin plate). **159:** NMAH, AFH, 99695/33675. **160–61:** Otto Botticher, *Union Prisoners at Salisbury, N.C.*, c. 1862, hand-colored lithograph. NMAH, 60.3741. **162:** NMAH, AFH, 64127/25124.008. **163:** Photographer unknown, portrait of U.S. Army artillery officer, c. 1860s, tintype. NMAH, PHC, 322775/75.17.187. **164 (t):** NMAH, AFH, 1980.0399.1166. **164 (c):** NMAH, AFH, 64127/RSN80784W06. **164 (b):** NMAH, AFH, 163704/42579. **165 (t):** NMAH, AFH, 200641/56531. **165 (c):** NMAH, AFH, 61384/17435. **165 (b):** NMAH, AFH, 1980.0399.1158. **166 (t):** NMAH, AFH, 64127/RSN80782W00. **166 (c):** NMAH, AFH, 220670/67635M. **166 (b):** NMAH, AFH, 227582/65427M. **167 (t):** NMAH, AFH, 163704/42579B. **167 (c):** NMAH, AFH, 172699/44416M. **167 (b):** NMAH, AFH, TEMP.MHCP4.0130. **168:** A. J. Russell, *Worker repairing telegraph line* (detail), 1863, albumen print. NMAH, AFH, reference photo. **169 (l):** NMAH, WI, 175456/313140. **169 (r):** NMAH, WI, 41421/220375. **170 (t):** NMAH, WI, 25413/181120. **170 (b):** Photograph by T. H. O'Sullivan, print by Alexander Gardner, *U.S. Military Telegraph Construction Corps*, 1864, albumen print. NMAH, PHC, 1986.0711.0283.12. **171:** NMAH, PH, transfer from the Library of Congress, 244699.02. **172–73:** Alexander Gardner, *Abraham Lincoln and George McClellan*, 1862, albumen silver print. NPG, NPG.80.106. **174–75:** NPM, gift of June Walters Leonard, 1991.0291.5.1. 175 (b): NPM, gift of Arthur W. Walters, 0.256400.3. 176 (t): NPM, Collections Acquisition Fund Purchase, 2009.2031.1. 176 (b): NPM, Collections Acquisition Fund Purchase, 2010.2017.1. 177 (t): NPM, bequest of Bessie L. Cullen, 0.286977.10.1. 177 (b): NPM, gift of Mortimer L. Neinken, 0.315252.1. 178–79: Homer Dodge Martin, *The Iron Mine, Port Henry, New York*, c. 1862, oil on canvas. SAAM, gift of William T. Evans, 1910.9.11. 180: NMAH, AFH, 45871/237846. 180–81: Photograph by T. H. O'Sullivan, print by Alexander Gardner, *Fredericksburg, VA*, 1862, albumen print. NMAH, PHC, 1986.0711.0334.30. 182: NMAH, CA, 1982.0203.2739. 183 (t): NMAH, CA, 2007.0186.01. 183 (b): NMAH, CA, 1982.0203.2740. 184: NMAAHC, 2012.40. 185: Eastman Johnson, *The Lord Is My Shepherd* (detail), 1863, oil on wood. SAAM, gift of Mrs. Francis P. Garvan, 1979.5.13. 186: NMAAHC, 2012.133. 187: P. S. Duval & Son Lith., *Come and Join Us Brothers*, c. 1863–65, chromolithograph. NMAH, HCL, 228146/60.3320. 188: Photographer unknown, *Tintype of an African American soldier*, c. 1861–65, silver on iron photographic plates. NMAAHC, gift from the Liljenquist Family Collection, 2011.51.12. 189: Photographer unknown, *Ambrotype of Qualls Tibbs, 5th Sergeant, 27th U.S. Colored Infantry Regiment*, c. 1864–65, silver nitrate on glass photographic plate. NMAAHC, 2011.4.2. 190: NMAH, NM, 1985.0441.0609. 191 (tl): NMAH, NM, Accession 207949. 191 (tr): NMAH, NM, 2001.0009.0696 (Washington), 1979.112.0462 (Franklin), 1979.112.0463 (Jefferson). 191 (b): NMAH, NM, Accession 207949. 192 (t): NMAH, NM, 72.188.75 (tl), Accession 1979.0779 (tc), 2001.0009.0343 (tr), 71.167.45 (bl), 72.118.76 (bc), 2013.0023.006 (br). 192 (c): NMAH, NM, 2013.0023.003. 192 (b): NMAH, NM, Accession 170666. 193 (t): NMAH, NM, 1992.0281.1723. 193 (c): NMAH, NM, 170666.6. 193 (b): NMAH, NM, BM 01449C. 194: Leopold Grozelier, *Salmon P. Chase*, 1855, lithograph on paper. NPG, NPG.77.73. 195: NMAH, NM, 1978.0941.0747. 196–97: David and Daniel Bendann, *Mosby and His Rangers*, c. 1865, albumen silver print. NPG, NPG.83.213. 198 (t): NMAH, AFH, 58977/15726. 198 (bl): NMAH, AFH, 11762.1. 198 (bc): NMAH, AFH, 20063/4409B. 198 (br): NMAH, AFH, 51962/11971. 199: NPM, gift of David Kohn, 0.228950.2. 200: NMAAHC, 2010.21.1.2. 201: Mathew Brady Studio, copy after William D. McPherson, copy after Mr. Oliver, *Gordon*, 1863, albumen silver print. NPG, NPG.2002.89. 203: A. Hurdle, *Stonewall Jackson*, published in *Southern Illustrated News*, August 29, 1863, wood engraving on paper. NPG, NPG.84.351. 204: George S. Cook, *Jeb Stuart*, 1863, salted-paper print. NPG, NPG.81.31. 205: NMAH, AFH, 245168.106. 206: O. D. Finch, *Bivouac of the 45th Illinois near the Shirley House, Vicksburg, Mississippi* (detail), 1863, salted-paper print. SAAM, museum purchase from the Charles Isaacs Collection made possible in part by the Luisita L. and Franz H. Denghausen Endowment, 1994.91.49. 207: NMAH, AFH, 18528.0004/3000. 208: NMAH, AFH, 46623/10625. 209: NMAH, AFH, 1982.0379.01. 210–11: From a sketch by A. Lumley, *New York Illustrated News*, "Camp of the 1st District Volunteers (Colored) on Mason's Island, Opposite Georgetown, D.C.," 1863, engraved wood block. NMAH, GA, 305359/23718.02. 212: George S. Cook, copy after Julian Vannerson, *Ambrose P. Hill*, c. 1867, glossy collodion print. NPG, NPG.2001.39. 213: NMAH, AFH, 53564/12761. 214: NMAH, AFH, 1996.0340.01. 215: NMAH, AFH, 55740/14438. 216–17: Timothy H. O'Sullivan, *Incidents of the War: A Harvest of Death* (detail), 1863, albumen silver print. SAAM, museum purchase through the Julia D. Strong Endowment, 2007.4.1. 218: Photographer unknown, portrait of woman with infant on lap, c. 1860–63, ambrotype. NMAH, AFH, 1997.3044.233. 220 (l): NMAH, MS, 219146/M-07265. 220 (r): NMAH, MS, 292537/M-13865. 221: NMAH, MS, 116996/M-03130. 222: NMAH, MS, 112986/M-02999. 223 (l): NMAH, MS, 112986/M-02999. 223 (r): NMAH, MS, Accession 112986. 224: NMAAHC, gift from the Liljenquist Family Collection, 2011.51.7. 225 (t): "Hanging a Negro in Clarkson Street," *Harper's Weekly*, August 1, 1863, lithograph. SL, AA/PG, AP1.H293. 225 (b): NMAH, PH, transfer from the U.S. War Department, 64127/25222. 226: J. D. Edwards, *Braxton Bragg*, c. 1861, albumen silver print. NPG, NPG.77.192. 227: Mathew Brady Studio, *Pauline Cushman*, c. 1864, glass-plate collodion negative. NPG, Frederick Hill Meserve Collection, Meserve.416:15. 228: Edward and Henry T. Anthony & Company, *George Henry Thomas*, c. 1864, albumen silver print. NPG, NPG.79.246.22. 229: NMAH, AFH, 64127/25309. 230–31: NMAH, AFH, 1988.0716.01. 232: Mathew Brady Studio, *Montgomery Cunningham Meigs*, c. 1861, albumen silver print. NPG, NPG.79.246.80. 233 (l): Photographer unknown, *Cavalry Sergeant*, 1866, hand-colored albumen print. NMAH, AFH, Accession 64127. 233 (r): NMAH, AFH, 64127/RSN80759W13. 234 (l): Photographer unknown, *Light Artillery Sergeant Major*, 1866, hand-colored albumen print. NMAH, AFH, Accession 64127. 234 (r): NMAH, AFH, 64127/25125.106. 235 (l): Photographer unknown, *Cavalry Musician*, 1866, hand-colored albumen print. NMAH, AFH, Accession 64127. 235 (r): NMAH, AFH, 64127/22799. 236 (l): Photographer unknown, *Hospital Steward*, 1866, hand-colored albumen print. NMAH, AFH, Accession 64127. 236 (r): NMAH, AFH, 64127/RSN80767W18. 237 (t): NMAH, AFH, 50774/256991. 237 (b): NMAH, AFH, 69413/32782. 238–39 (t): NMAH, AFH, 54205/272955. 238–39 (tc): NMAH, AFH, 41356/222304. 238–39 (bc): NMAH, AFH, 164794/43490. 238–39 (b): NMAH, AFH, 297603.3. 239 (t): NMAH, AFH, 41356/222304. 239 (b): NMAH, AFH, 297603.3. 240–41 (t): NMAH, AFH, 69413/32707. 240–41 (tc): NMAH, AFH, 41356/222372. 240–41 (bc): NMAH, AFH,

37586/209405. 240–41 (b): NMAH, AFH, 69413/32701B. 241 (t): NMAH, AFH, 41356/222372. 241 (b): NMAH, AFH, 69413/32701B. 242–43: Photograph by T. H. O'Sullivan, print by Alexander Gardner, *Camp Architecture, Brandy Station, Va*, 1864, albumen print. NMAH, PHC, 1986.0711.0283.07. 244: NMAH, PH, 2007.0164.01. 245 (tl): George Kendall Warren, *Ralph Waldo Emerson*, c. 1870, albumen silver print. NPG, NPG.79.21. 245 (tc): Emanuel Gottlieb Leutze, *Nathaniel Hawthorne*, 1862, oil on canvas. NPG, transfer from the National Gallery of Art: gift of the A. W. Mellon Educational and Charitable Trust, 1942, NPG.65.55. 245 (tr): Photographer unknown, *Harriet Beecher Stowe*, c. 1865, albumen silver print. NPG, NPG.2006.57. 245 (cl): Begun by John Elliott, finished by William Henry Cotton, *Julia Ward Howe*, begun c. 1910, finished c. 1925, oil on canvas. NPG, transfer from the Smithsonian American Art Museum: gift of Maud Howe Elliott to the Smithsonian Institution, 1933, NPG.65.31. 245 (cc): James Notman, *Oliver Wendell Holmes Sr.*, c. 1880, albumen silver print. NPG, NPG.67.32. 245 (cr): John Jabez Edwin Mayall, *George Bancroft*, c. 1847, daguerreotype (hand-colored). NPG, partial gift of Dr. and Mrs. Lester Tuchman and Gallery purchase, NPG.79.214. 245 (bl): Charles DeForest Fredricks, *Edward Everett*, c. 1861, albumen silver print. NPG, gift of Mrs. F. B. Wilde, NPG.83.284.43. 245 (bc): Julia Margaret Cameron, *Henry Wadsworth Longfellow*, 1868, albumen silver print. NPG, NPG.82.61. 245 (br): George Kendall Warren, *Edgar Allan Poe*, c. 1874, after c. 1849 daguerreotype, albumen silver print. NPG, NPG.2000.13. 246: "The Rebel General Robert Edmund Lee," *Harper's Weekly*, July 2, 1861, lithograph. SL, AA/PG, AP1.H293. 247 (t): Mathew Brady, *Ulysses S. Grant*, 1864, albumen silver print. NPG, NPG.77.56. 247 (bl): NMAH, AFH, 308316/77336M. 247 (br): NMAH, AFH, 1985.0713.01. 248: Thomas A. Gray and Thomas Faris, *Winslow Homer*, 1863, albumen silver print. NPG, NPG.2001.50. 248–49: Winslow Homer, *Wounded Soldier Being Given a Drink from a Canteen*, 1864, charcoal and white chalk on blue paper (faded). CHNDM, gift of Charles Savage Homer Jr., 1912-12-100. 250 (l): Winslow Homer, *Four Studies of Soldiers' Heads*, c. 1863, black chalk on beige paper (darkened). CHNDM, gift of Charles Savage Homer Jr., 1912-12-102. 250 (c): Winslow Homer, *Young Soldier*, 1864, brush and oil paint, gouache, graphite on canvas. CHNDM, gift of Charles Savage Homer Jr., 1912-12-110. 250–51: Winslow Homer, *Drummer Seen from the Back*, c. 1864, charcoal and white chalk on blue paper, CHNDM, gift of Charles Savage Homer Jr., 1912-12-108. 251 (l): Winslow Homer, *Cavalry Soldier with a Sword on Horseback*, 1863, black chalk on beige paper (darkened). CHNDM, gift of Charles Savage Homer Jr., 1912-12-107. 251 (r): Winslow Homer, *Cavalry Soldier Loading a Rifle*, 1863-64, black and white chalk on gray-green paper. CHNDM, gift of Charles Savage Homer Jr., 1912-12-99. 252–53: NMAH, AFH, 20209/4435. 253: Timothy O'Sullivan, *Burying the Dead, Fredericksburg, Virginia*, 1864, stereograph. NMAH, PHC, 1988.3071.0069. 254: NMAH, AFH, 59388/15935. 255 (t): NMAH, AFH, 59388/15953. 255 (c): George Barnard, portrait of William Tecumseh Sherman, 1864, stereograph. NMAH, PHC, 1988.3071.0077. 255 (b): NMAH, AFH, 59388/15926. 256–57: William Boell and William D. Broom, *Bird's-eye View of Andersonville Prison Ga.*, 1866, lithograph. NMAH, HCL, 228146/60.2577. 258–59: Photograph by David Knox, print by Alexander Gardner, *Mortar Dictator, Front of Petersburg*, 1864, albumen print. NMAH, PHC, 1986.0711.0283.25. 260 (t): NMAH, AFH, 64127/25267E. 260 (c): NMAH, AFH, 64127/25276D. 260 (b): NMAH, AFH, 64127/25264G. 261 (tl): NMAH, AFH, 64127/25239D. 261 (tr): NMAH, AFH, 64127/25243L. 261 (cl): NMAH, AFH, 64127/25228X. 261 (cr): NMAH, AFH, 64127/25263D. 261 (bl): NMAH, AFH, 64127/25236A. 261 (br): NMAH, AFH, 64127/25239A. 262 (tl): NMAH, AFH, 64127/25232W. 262 (tr): NMAH, AFH, 64127/25263E. 262 (cl): NMAH, AFH, 64127/25236D. 262 (cr): NMAH, AFH, 64127/25236A. 262 (bl): NMAH, AFH, 64127/25232Y. 262 (br): NMAH, AFH, 64127/25239B. 263: Robert Cornelius, *Solomon Andrews*, c. 1842, daguerreotype. NPG, NPG.2002.374. 264 (t): William C. Powers, untitled drawing (drive train), c. 1862, pencil on paper. NASM, NASM Archives, Powers Bomber, NASM Acc. XXXX-0562, NASM A-34449-B. 264 (b): Unknown artist, *The Aereon*, c. 1863, copy photograph of engraving. NASM, NASM Archives, NASM 9A05358. 264–65: Edward Wellman Serrell, untitled drawing (detail of "Valomotive" flying machine design), c. 1861–65, pencil on paper. NASM, NASM Archives, Edward Wellman Serrell "Valomotive" Papers, NASM Acc. 2011-0040, NASM 9A09818. 266: Photographer unknown, portrait of U.S. Navy Seaman Arnold Reichart, c. 1861–65, carte-de-visite. NMAH, AFH, reference photo. 267 (l): NMAH, AFH, 1993.0433.01. 267 (tr): NMAH, AFH, 25148/5854. 267 (br): NMAH, AFH, 1984.0342.01. 268–69 (t): NMAH, AFH, 1980.0399.0204. 268–69 (tc): NMAH, AFH, 58284/287124. 268–69 (bc): NMAH, AFH, 45729/10540. 268–69 (b): NMAH, AFH, 50774/256986. 268 (b): NMAH, AFH, 41356/222451. 269 (b): NMAH, AFH, 41356/222410. 270: NMAH, AFH, 235044/58709N. 271 (l): Photographer unknown, *Captain John Feilner*, c. 1864, albumen silver print. NPG, Graphics File. 271 (c): Photographer unknown, *Mrs. John Feilner*, c. 1864, albumen silver print. NPG, Graphics File. 271 (r): NMAI, 19/3667. 272 (bl): NMNH, Division of Birds, USNM 34206. 272–73 (t): NMNH, Division of Birds, USNM 16263. 272–73 (c): NMNH, Department of Anthropology, Catalogue No. E2323 (bow), Catalogue No. E2324 (arrows). 272–73 (b): NMNH, Division of Birds, USNM 34165. 273 (c): NMNH, Division of Birds, USNM 34177. 273 (tr): NMNH, Division of Birds, USNM 16073. 274 (tl):

Photographer unknown, *Solomon G. Brown*, 1891, photographic print. SIA, SIA2007-0039. **274 (b):** SIA, SIA2011-0975. **275:** NMAH, AFH, 112646/36931. **276 (t):** NMAH, AFH, 112646/36927. **276 (c):** NMAH, AFH, 41356/222364. **276 (b):** Photographer unknown, *David McMurtrie Gregg*, c. 1864, albumen silver print. NPG, NPG.81.26. **277 (t):** Photograph by David Knox, print by Alexander Gardner, *Army Forge Scene, Front of Petersburg*, 1864, albumen print. NMAH, PHC, 1986.0711.0283.27. **277 (bl):** NMAH, AFH, 1980.0399.1598. **277 (br):** NMAH, AFH, 54537/273382A. **278:** Photographer unknown, portrait of U.S. Army infantry sergeant, c. 1861–65, tintype. NMAH, PHC, 322775/75.17.309. **279 (t):** NMAH, AFH, 1980.0399.0696. **279 (c):** NMAH, AFH, 278038/70814M. **279 (b):** NMAH, AFH, 41356/222418. **280 (t):** NMAH, AFH, 41356/222402. **280 (c):** NMAH, AFH, 37097/207718. **280 (b):** NMAH, AFH, 306420/77204M. **281 (t):** NMAH, AFH, 41356/222414. **281 (c):** NMAH, AFH, 61709/300848. **281 (b):** NMAH, AFH, 37533/209340. **282:** Thomas Buchanan Read, *Philip Henry Sheridan*, 1871, oil on canvas. NPG, transfer from the National Museum of American History: gift of Ulysses S. Grant III, 1939, NPG.68.51. **282–83:** NMAH, AFH, 69413/32870. **283:** Photographer unknown, photograph of Winchester and attendant, c. 1865–78, albumen print. NMAH, AFH, reference photo. **284 (l):** NMAH, NM, 1987.0697.0486. **284 (c):** NMAH, NM, 1987.0697.0487. **284 (r):** NMAH, NM, 1987.0697.0488. **285:** NMAH, PH, gift of Ralph E. Becker, 227739.1864.F07. **286–87:** Thomas Henry Atwell, *The Miscegenation Ball/Political Caricature*, 1864, lithograph. NMAH, HCL, 228146/60.3341. **288–89:** Frederic Edwin Church, *Aurora Borealis* (detail), 1865, oil on canvas. SAAM, gift of Eleanor Blodgett, 1911.4.1. **290:** Photograph by T. H. O'Sullivan, print by Alexander Gardner, *The Pulpit, Fort Fisher, N.C.*, 1865, albumen print. NMAH, PHC, 1986.0711.0283.29. **291:** Alexander Gardner, *David Dixon Porter*, 1865, albumen silver print. NPG, NPG.78.155. **292:** Mathew Brady Studio, *William Seward*, c. 1860, albumen silver print. NPG, NPG.79.246.146. **293:** NMAH, PH, gift of Ralph E. Becker, 227739.1864.F07. **294–95:** Photograph by T. H. O'Sullivan, print by Alexander Gardner, *Quarters of Men in Fort Sedgwick, Generally Known as Fort Hell*, 1865, albumen print. NMAH, PHC, 1986.0711.0283.33. **296:** Alexander Gardner, *Rebel Soldiers Killed in the Trenches of Fort Mahone, Called by the Soldiers "Fort Damnation,"* 1865, stereograph. NMAH, PHC, 1988.3071.0107. **297:** NMAH, PH, bequest of Elizabeth B. Custer, 124419/39765. **298 (t):** Photograph by T. H. O'Sullivan, print by Alexander Gardner, *McLean's House, Appomattox Court-House, Where Grant and Lee Signed the Capitulation*, 1865, albumen print. NMAH, PHC, 1986.0711.0283.49. **298 (bl):** NMAH, PH, bequest of Gen. Wilmon W. Blackmar, 45493/10517. **298 (bc):** NMAH, PH, bequest of Elizabeth B. Custer, 124419/39767. **298 (br):** NMAH, PH, gift of Bridget O'Farrell, 59140/15820. **299:** NMAH, PH, 2012.0214.04. **300:** NMAH, GA, 2009.0159.01. **301:** Mathew Brady, *Robert E. Lee*, 1865, albumen silver print. NPG, NPG.78.243. **302:** NMAH, PH, transfer from the U.S. War Department, 1984.0623.03-.04. **303:** Photographer unknown, portrait of an African American washerwoman, c. 1865, ambrotype. NMAH, PHC, 2005.0002.01. **304–5:** Ole Peter Hansen Balling, *Grant and His Generals*, 1865, oil on canvas. NPG, gift of Mrs. Harry Newton Blue in memory of her husband Harry Newton Blue (1893–1925), who served as an officer of the Regular U.S. Army 1917–25, NPG.66.37. **306–7:** Photograph by John Reekie, print by Alexander Gardner, *A Burial Party on the Battle-field of Cold Harbor*, 1865, albumen print. NMAH, PHC, 1986.0711.0283.44. **308:** William Bell, *Major H. S. Barnum, Recovery after a Penetrating Gunshot Wound of the Abdomen with Perforation of the Left Ilium*, from the *Photographic Catalogue of the Surgical Section*, 1865, albumen silver print. SAAM, museum purchase from the Charles Isaacs Collection made possible in part by the Luisita L. and Frank H. Denghausen Endowment, 1994.91.14. **309:** William Bell, *Lieutenant Goodwin, Deceased Ununited Gunshot Fracture of the Upper Third of the Right Femur, Seven Months after the Injury*, from the *Photographic Catalogue of the Surgical Section*, 1865, albumen silver print. SAAM, museum purchase from the Charles Isaacs Collection made possible in part by the Luisita L. and Frank H. Denghausen Endowment, 1994.91.13. **310:** Alexander Gardner, *Abraham Lincoln*, 1865, albumen silver print. NPG, NPG.81.M1. **311:** NMAH, PH, gift of Lincoln Isham, 219098.09. **312:** NMAH, PH, bequest of Virginia Adler Thompson, 242707.01. **313 (l):** NMAH, PH, gift of Grace S. Wright, 232215.1. **313 (r):** Charles DeForest Fredricks, *Laura Keene*, c. 1863, albumen silver print. NPG, NPG.80.220. **314:** Currier & Ives Lithography Company, *Death Bed of the Martyr President*, 1865, lithograph on paper. NPG, gift of Dr. Fred W. Hicks III, NPG.89.219. **315 (l):** Photographer unknown, *Mary A. Henry*, c. 1855, photographic print. SIA, 82-3258. **315 (r):** SIA, SIA2013-01997. **316:** NMAH, transfer from the U.S. War Department, 38912/9321. **317:** Alexander Gardner, *Abraham Lincoln, John McClernand, and Allan Pinkerton*, 1862 (printed c. 1890), albumen silver print. NPG, S/NPG.81.17. **318:** Artist unknown, *One Hundred Thousand Dollar Reward*, 1865, printed broadside with albumen silver prints. NPG, NPG.85.32. **319:** NMAH, NM, Accession 1998.0063. **320:** Alexander Gardner, *Lewis Thornton Powell*, 1865, albumen silver print. NPG, NPG.80.172. **321 (t):** NMAH, PH, transfer from the U.S. War Department, 42272/10239a. **321 (c):** NMAH, PH, transfer from the U.S. War Department, 42272/10238a. **321 (b):** NMAH, PH, transfer from the U.S. War Department, 42272/10240b. **322 (tl):** NMAH, PH, transfer from the U.S. War Department, 42272/10245f. **322 (tr):** NMAH, PH, transfer from the U.S. War Department, 42272/10245b. **322 (bl):** NMAH, PH, transfer from the U.S. War Department, 42272/10245e. **322 (br):** NMAH, PH, transfer from the U.S. War Department, 42272/10245a. **323 (tl):** NMAH, PH, transfer from the U.S. War Department, 42272/10245h. **323 (tr):** NMAH, PH, transfer from the U.S. War Department, 42272/10245c. **323 (bl):** NMAH, PH, transfer from the U.S. War Department, 42272/10245d. **323 (br):** NMAH, PH, transfer from the U.S. War Department, 42272/10245g. **324:** NMAH, PH, gift of Ralph E. Becker, 227739.1865.J5. **325 (t):** NMAH, PH, gift of Walter McCulloch, 90668/35351a. **325 (b):** NMAH, PH, reference photo. **326–27:** NMAH, PH, gift of Ralph E. Becker, 227739.1865.G33. **327 (l):** NMAH, PH, gift of the Lake County Historical Society, 242158.1. **327 (r):** NMAH, PH, gift of Helen Leale Harper, 2006.0251.01. **328 (l):** Mathew Brady Studio, *Mary Todd Lincoln*, c. 1863, albumen silver print. NPG, S/NPG.93.139. **328 (r):** NMAH, PH, gift of Lincoln Isham, 225754.02. **329 (l):** NMAH, PHC, 1982.0545.03 (stereoviewer). **329 (r):** John P. Soule, *Sally-port of Fort Moultrie*, 1865, stereograph published in *Scenes of the Great Rebellion* series. NMAH, PHC, 1988.3071.4939. **330 (t):** John P. Soule, *Int. of Ft. Sumpter, shewing Gabions and Bomb Proofs*, 1865, stereograph. NMAH, PHC, 1988.3071.4933. **330 (b):** James F. Gibson, *Headquarters Gen'l Porter, Farnhold's House and York River in the Distance*, 1862, stereograph. NMAH, PHC, 1988.3071.0095. **331 (t):** George N. Barnard, *Fort Sumner, near Fair Oaks, Va.*, 1862, stereograph. NMAH, PHC, 1988.3071.4939. **331 (b):** Brady & Co., *U.S.S. monitor CANONICUS taking coal from a schooner*, 1864, stereograph. NMAH, PHC, 1988.3071.0113. **332:** James Gardner, *Alexander Gardner*, 1863, albumen silver print. NPG, gift of Larry J. West, NPG.2007.62. **333:** Alexander Gardner, title page of *Gardner's Photographic Sketch Book of the War*, Vol. 2, 1866. NMAH, PHC, 1986.0711.0283. **334:** Alexander Gardner, *Home of a Rebel Sharpshooter, Gettysburg*, 1863, albumen print. NMAH, PHC, 1986.0711.0334.41. **335:** Alexander Gardner, *A Fancy Group, in Front of Petersburg*, 1864, albumen print. NMAH, PHC, 1986.0711.0283.26. **336 (l):** NMAH, AFH, 30411/6955. **336 (r):** NMAH, AFH, 89848/35263. **337:** NMAH, AFH, 89848/35263. **338 (l):** NMAH, AFH, 46071/10572. **338 (r):** NMAH, AFH, 56944/14946. **339 (l):** NMAH, AFH, 84827/34845A. **339 (r):** NMAH, AFH, 115588/37219. **340:** NMAAHC, gift of the Family of Irving and Estelle Liss, 2012.37. **341:** Photographer unknown, *Sojourner Truth*, c. 1866, albumen and silver nitrate on photographic paper. NMAAHC, 2012.46.11. **342–43:** Winslow Homer, *A Visit from the Old Mistress*, 1876, oil on canvas. SAAM, gift of William T. Evans, 1909.7.28. **344:** Wearn & Hix Studio, *Robert Smalls*, c. 1868, albumen silver print. NPG, NPG.2011.76. **345 (t):** Joseph Hoover, *Heroes of the Colored Race*, 1881, chromolithograph (hand-colored) on paper. NPG, NPG.2009.56. **345 (b):** NMAAHC, 2010.28.1. **346:** NMAAHC, 2011.52. **346–47:** J. H. Aylsworth, *Slave Women and Children in a Plantation Cotton Field*, c. 1860s, albumen and silver nitrate on photographic paper. NMAAHC, 2008.9.26 **348 (l):** NMAAHC, gift of Charles L. Blockson, 2009.50.39. **348 (r):** NMAAHC, gift of Charles L. Blockson, 2009.50.25. **349:** H. Seymour Squyer, *Harriet Tubman*, c. 1885, printing-out paper photograph. NPG, NPG.2006.86. **350 (tl):** NMAH, AC, Collection of Illustrated American Sheet Music, AC0300-0000947. **350 (tr):** NMAH, AC, BMI Archives Confederate Sheet Music Collection, AC1258-0000050. **350 (bl):** NMAH, AC, BMI Archives Confederate Sheet Music Collection, AC1258-0000032. **350 (br):** NMAH, AC, BMI Archives Confederate Sheet Music Collection, AC1258-0000010. **351 (t):** NMAH, AC, BMI Archives Confederate Sheet Music Collection, AC1258-0000001. **351 (b):** NMAH, AC, BMI Archives Confederate Sheet Music Collection, AC1258-0000012. **352:** NMAH, AFH, 54045/13044. **352–53:** Alexander Gardner, *General Sherman and Indian Commissioners in Conference with Native Americans at Fort Laramie*, May 1868, albumen silver print. NMAI, P01259. **354:** David J. Ryan, *Robert E. Lee and Joseph E. Johnston*, 1870, albumen silver print. NPG, NPG.78.273. **355 (tl):** NMAH, AFH, 1979.1267.001. **355 (tr):** NMAH, AFH, 18528/3113. **355 (b):** NMAH, AFH, 115588/37245. **356:** Mathew Brady Studio, *Abraham Lincoln*, undated, glass plate collodion negative. NPG, Frederick Hill Meserve Collection, Meserve.959:34. **357:** Victor David Brenner, *Abraham Lincoln Centennial Medal*, 1906, bronze. CHNDM, gift of Victor David Brenner, 1906-33-1.

INDEX

Written by Smithsonian Contributors as listed on page 4
Foreword by Jon Meacham
Introduction by Michelle Delaney
Note from the Secretary by G. Wayne Clough
Principal photography by Hugh Talman
Additional photography by Ernest Amoroso, Mildred Baldwin,
Mark Gulezian, Donald Hurlbert, Eric Long, Jaclyn Nash,
and Gene Young

Smithsonian Editorial Committee
Chair: Michelle Delaney
Project Leaders: Frank H. Goodyear III and Jennifer L. Jones
Members: James G. Barber, Tom Crouch, Rex M. Ellis, Paul
Gardullo, Eleanor Jones Harvey, Pamela M. Henson, William S.
Pretzer, Harry R. Rubenstein
Project Assistants: Sarah Campbell and Ryan Lintelman

Published by Smithsonian Books
Director: Carolyn Gleason
Production Editor: Christina Wiginton
Editorial Assistants: Leah Enser, Jane Gardner, Ashley Montague

Produced by Kagan & Associates, Inc.
Neil Kagan, President and Editor-in-Chief
Sharyn Kagan, Vice President and Director of Administration
Staff for Smithsonian Civil War
Editor: Neil Kagan
Text Editor: Stephen G. Hyslop
Design: Studio A
Art Director: Antonio Alcalá
Designer: Leslie Badani
Military Historian: Harris J. Andrews
Copy Editor: Lise Sajewski
Indexer: Nanette Cardon

This book may be purchased for educational, business, or sales
promotional use. For information, please write: Special Markets
Department, Smithsonian Books, P. O. Box 37012, MRC 513,
Washington, DC 20013

Library of Congress Cataloging-in-Publication Data
Smithsonian Civil War : Inside the National Collection / Edited by
Neil Kagan; Smithsonian Editorial Committee: James G. Barber,
Tom Crouch, Michelle Delaney, Rex M. Ellis, Paul Gardullo,
Frank H. Goodyear III, Eleanor Jones Harvey, Pamela M. Henson,
Jennifer L. Jones, William S. Pretzer, Harry R. Rubenstein ;
Foreword by Jon Meacham ; Introduction by Michelle Delaney ;
Principal photography by Hugh Talman.
pages cm
ISBN 978-1-58834-389-5
1. United States—History—Civil War, 1861–1865—Exhibitions.
I. Kagan, Neil.
E467.S65 2013
973.7074—dc23   2013017222

Manufactured in China through Oceanic Graphic Printing, not at
government expense

17 16 15 14 13   5 4 3 2 1

For permission to reproduce illustrations appearing in this
book, please correspond directly with the museums, as listed on
pages 358–361. Smithsonian Books does not retain reproduction
rights for these images individually, or maintain a file of addresses
for sources.

Endpapers: Pages from a Civil War-era photo album portray
Jefferson Davis and an array of Confederate generals (front), and
Ulysses S. Grant and other Union generals (back).
Page 1: A recruitment poster for the 119th Pennsylvania Infantry
invites volunteers to join up at 204 Walnut Street in Philadelphia.
The regiment that formed there later fought at Gettysburg.
Page 2: Two young Union soldiers sit for their portrait beside an
unofficial American flag.
Page 3: This U.S. snare drum with a stenciled spread eagle urged
men to battle during the war.

Ulysses. S. Grant, Gen. Lieutenant,
Comandant en chef der Ver. Staaten - Armee.

Gen. Major Sherman.

Gen. Major Sheridan.